A Guide to Documentary Editing

A Guide to Documentary Editing

Mary-Jo Kline

Prepared for the Association for Documentary Editing

THE JOHNS HOPKINS UNIVERSITY PRESS

BALTIMORE AND LONDON

This book has been brought to publication with the generous assistance
of the National Endowment for the Humanities.

Second printing, 1988

The Johns Hopkins University Press
701 West 40th Street
Baltimore, Maryland 21211
The Johns Hopkins Press Ltd., London

The paper used in this publication meets the minimum requirements of
the American National Standard for Information Sciences—Permanence
of Paper for Printed Library Materials, ANSI Z39.48-1984.

Library of Congress Cataloging-in-Publication Data

Kline, Mary-Jo.
  A guide to documentary editing.

  "Prepared for the Association for Documentary Editing."
  Includes bibliographies and index.
    1. Manuscripts—Editing.   2. Criticism, Textual.   3. Editing.   I.
Association for Documentary Editing.   II. Title.
Z113.3.K55   1986   808'.02   86-18507
ISBN 0-8018-3341-8 (alk. paper)

CONTENTS

FOREWORD

The organization of the Association for Documentary Editing in St. Louis on 10 November 1978 might well mark the coming of age of the editorial profession in the United States. Historical and literary editors came together to form an association for the discussion of common problems and needs. One of the most urgent of the needs was a guide to historical and literary editing which would combine the wisdom and experience accumulated since the beginning of the revolution in editorial methods in both history and literature in the early 1950s. Literary textual editors had given more thought to methodology than historical editors. For the latter, no authoritative manual or guide existed in any language when I pointed out, in my presidential address to the first annual meeting of the ADE in Princeton, New Jersey, on 9 November 1979: "Our most obvious need is an authoritative manual on documentary editing. The preparation of such a manual will involve many persons in various fields and require a long time for completion. But the task can be done."

As it turned out, I was, happily, a poor prophet. One of the first acts of my successor as president of the ADE, Lester J. Cappon, was to appoint a committee, headed by Richard K. Showman, editor of *The Nathanael Greene Papers*, to determine the practicability of the ADE's sponsorship of a manual for editors. This committee quickly decided that the project was both desirable and feasible; obtained seed money from the National Historical Publications and Records Commission and, soon afterward, a generous grant from the National Endowment for the Humanities to finance the project; and then appointed Mary-Jo Kline, editor of *The Political Correspondence and Public Papers of Aaron Burr*, as author of the manual.

With the NEH grant in hand, the project was well under way

by the summer of 1981. One result of Dr. Kline's research and reading, and most especially of her interviews with numerous editors, was the emergence of a strong consensus that the editing profession needed, not a *manual*, with a stern, single set of methods and standards, but a *guide* to historical and literary textual editing that would take into account alternative methods to deal with different—and sometimes widely different—bodies of documents. As Dr. Kline began to plan her book and write her chapters, she had the benefit of advice from an executive committee appointed by Mr. Showman, consisting of Paul Smith, David Nordloh, and David Chesnutt. In addition, the entire Committee on the Manual (Guide) read the penultimate draft of the book in early 1983.

Thus not only is this book sponsored by the Association for Documentary Editing but its author enjoyed the benefit of picking the best minds in the editing profession. It represents, in one sense, what can only be called a remarkable consensus among the most experienced historical and literary textual editors. However, I cannot emphasize too strongly the fact that this is Dr. Kline's own book. She took some advice and rejected other suggestions for changes. As all of us on the committee soon discovered, she has a tough and disciplined mind. She also has very strong opinions about certain things and has not hesitated forthrightly to express her own opinions about alternative methods. The result is, not a melding of good and bad methodologies, but a fair-minded laying out of the sometimes different ways of editing documents, and one that also sets firm parameters for going about the job. In short, the committee was singularly prescient in the choice of an author. She not only did a splendid job but did it expeditiously.

This book will be a boon to all editors, and it will surely constitute the basic textbook for courses in historical and literary editing. It should also be indispensable to all students and writers who deal with the grist of all research and writing in history and literature— the documents themselves.

Arthur S. Link,
Director and Editor, *The Papers of Woodrow Wilson*, and George Henry Davis '86 Professor of American History, Princeton University

PREFACE

Professor Link's foreword scarcely hints at the collaborative nature of this work. The extent of my debt to the scholars presently engaged in documentary editing arises in part from a phenomenon that became apparent only a few weeks after I had begun my work on this guide. As I complained to a friend, I found myself the victim of a conspiracy of silence some forty years past. "Documentary editors," I lamented, "have adopted as their professional motto 'Editing is more fun than *writing* about editing.' " Time and again I found that editors, among them my closest and most valued friends, had been too busy editing to publish the briefest essay describing their methods and their philosophies or even to jot down on paper "house rules" for their editions that could now be retrieved from an office file drawer.

In preparing this guide, I have combed editorial statements of method in hundreds of volumes and tested the patience of my colleagues with inquisitive letters, nagging telephone calls, and visits to their offices, asking again and again, "Why did you do that?" It is a testimonial to the good humor of American scholarly editors that most of the subjects of my interrogations still speak to me. Many of the men and women who helped me in this fashion are explicitly acknowledged in the pages that follow by attributions of their own statements. Others in the category of informal contributors include: John Blassingame, John Catanzariti, LeRoy Graf, Robert Hill, Donald Jackson, Sharon MacPherson, Richard B. Morris, Harold Moser, Gaspare Saladino, Harold and Patricia Syrett, and Eleanor Tilton. Representatives of university presses with wide experience in publishing documentary editions were especially generous in sharing their wisdom: Herbert Bailey and Gretchen Oberfranc of Princeton University Press, Gerard Mayers of Columbia

University Press, Ann Louise McLaughlin of Harvard University Press, and Elizabeth Steinberg of the University of Wisconsin Press.

The colleagues who deserve the greatest praise are the men and women who have reviewed one or more versions of this manuscript on behalf of the Association for Documentary Editing. The members of the association's Committee on the Manual (Guide) and of its council who merit such special commendation for their valor and painstaking proofreading are: John Morton Blum, Jo Ann Boydston, David Chesnutt, Don Cook, Charles Cullen, Thomas Jeffrey, John Kaminsky, Glenn LaFantasie, Arthur Link, Joel Myerson, David Nordloh, Barbara Oberg, Carol Orr, Nathan Reingold, Richard Showman, John Simon, Paul Smith, Raymond Smock, and G. Thomas Tanselle. Charlene Bickford oversaw the production and proofreading of the volume for the ADE and was assisted by Helen Veit and Allida Black. George Hoemann created the index, using CINDEX programs.

Henry Tom of the Johns Hopkins University Press encouraged the ADE and the author and supported the publication. The volume was ably copy-edited by Joanne Allen. Nancy West handled the production end efficiently.

Despite the association's review process, errors remain in the guide. These, of course, are my responsibility, not that of the ADE, its committees, or the volume's publisher.

Aside from these standard statements of my scholarly debts and authorial responsibility, documentary editing's policy of full disclosure demands that I warn the reader of four special idiosyncrasies of the guide:

1. The reader will find the book a sometimes disconcerting combination of theoretical discussions and practical descriptions of methodology. This merely reflects the realities of modern documentary editing: the scholar must divide his time between weighing the merits of sophisticated methods of textual treatment and finding adequate supplies of paper clips and typewriter ribbons.

2. For very practical reasons, the guide is designed to supplement the limited body of readily accessible published discussions of the problems of documentary editing. Thus the space allotted to certain topics reflects the amount of such published material to which the reader can turn and not the relative importance of these topics to the tasks of documentary editing. In areas where much has been written the book is little more than a guide to fuller printed treatments. When there is nothing to which I can refer the reader, I must supply information from scratch and at length.

3. I have chosen to employ the pronouns *he* and *him* with the antecedent noun *editor*. As the ADE has not adopted a convenient and gender-free term, I found it more graceful and efficient to eschew *he or she* and *him or her* at every turn. And I chose the masculine pronoun to avoid any charges of sexism against a female author.

4. I sometimes violate my mandate to prepare a "descriptive" rather than a "prescriptive" or "proscriptive" treatise on documentary editing. The book contains passages that describe certain methods and editorial decisions in less than laudatory terms. Unless such opinions are clearly attributed to others, they are my own. They should not, at all costs, be ascribed to the ADE.

Should readers be offended by my judgments, let them voice their objections—better still, let them publish them. I have prepared this book with a conscious view to ending the tradition of editors who choose not to write about editing. With this in mind, I have taken my motto for the guide from Sir Walter Greg: "My desire is rather to provoke discussion than to lay down the law."

When the history of scholarship in the twentieth century comes to be written, a very good case should be made for calling it the age of editing.

—Fredson Bowers, 1976

[Documentary] editing is, in my opinion, the most important scholarly work being done in the United States, and, if well done, it will be the most enduring.

—Arthur S. Link, 1979

CHAPTER I

Introduction

Great as the impact of modern American scholarly editing has been, practitioners of this craft have sometimes neglected to furnish the public with careful expositions of the principles and practices by which they have pursued their goals. This omission is most apparent in the methodology of *documentary*, or noncritical, editing that has emerged in this country and that can be distinguished from more traditional *textual*, or critical, editorial method. Even though these methods often overlap—with the text for one source in a series receiving noncritical treatment and that for another source receiving critical treatment—American scholars have neglected to define the occasions on which each approach should be used, much less to spell out the different methods appropriate to each.

The textual editor, who consciously applies critical judgment and scholarly experience in the process of producing new texts for his audience, is the heir of classical scholarship, in which scholars were forced to rely upon a variety of scribal copies instead of upon original and authentic documents. In order to divest these texts of corrupt words and phrases introduced over centuries of copying and recopying, classicists devised complex methods to achieve the *recension*, or recovery, of words, characters, and phrases of the lost archetype from which these copies had flowed. The invention of the printing press by no means halted such problems for scholars. Compositors corrupted the texts of the works that they set in type as surely and regularly as had the medieval scribes who distorted the writings of the authors of ancient Greece and Rome. To meet the challenge of this form of textual corruption, British scholars of medieval and early Renaissance drama devised new and ingenious methods, a process that culminated in Sir Walter Greg's exposition of the theory of copy-text.

Perhaps because the hazards and pitfalls of critical editing are so great, scholars in the field have left a comparatively rich methodological literature for the novice who will carry on their work, but this has not been the case in the field of noncritical, or documentary, editing, an area of special concern for American political, intellectual, and social history. Noncritical and critical editors are distinguished in part by the sources on which their scholarly texts are based. The noncritical editor usually prepares a modern printed edition from source materials that can themselves be described as documents—inscribed artifacts whose unique physical characteristics and original nature give them special evidentiary value. And the significance of such sources demands that their editors provide editorial texts that themselves will communicate as much of the sources' evidentiary value as possible. Generally, this demands a far more limited level of editorial intervention than would be seen were the same sources to be edited critically, for the documentary editor's goal is not to *supply* the words or phrases of a vanished archetype but rather to *preserve* the nuances of a source that has survived the ravages of time.

Until recently, America's documentary editors have shown a curious reluctance to spell out their aims and techniques. Novice editors, as well as the readers and reviewers of their editions, have been the poorer because so much of the knowledge and experience of documentary editors has not been described and analyzed in explicit terms. This scholarly idiosyncrasy is the more puzzling in light of the fact that the tradition of documentary publication in the United States is older than the nation itself.

I. EARLY AMERICAN DOCUMENTARY EDITING

From the beginning, Americans were almost painfully self-conscious about the historic role that their new republic would play, and both government and individual citizens showed this concern by publishing the records of the young government and of the men who had founded it. As early as 1774, Ebenezer Hazard planned a series of volumes of "American State Papers" that would "lay the Foundation of a good American history." By the time Hazard published his first volume of *Historical Collections* in 1792, the cause of documentary publication had been joined by the Massachusetts Historical Society, which issued the first volume of its collections of New England records in that same year.

The major phase of American documentary editing did not begin, however, until the second quarter of the nineteenth century, when

Jared Sparks of Harvard initiated his work. Sparks traveled widely to collect the manuscripts on which he based his *Diplomatic Correspondence of the American Revolution*, the *Writings of George Washington*, and the *Life and Correspondence of Gouverneur Morris*. In 1831 the federal government committed itself to the publication of its own records with the inauguration of the *American State Papers* series. In the decades that followed, the sons and grandsons of America's founding fathers joined in the work, and filiopietistic editing produced volumes of such varying quality as William Jay's *Life of John Jay* and Charles Francis Adams's far superior edition of the papers of his grandfather, John Adams.

At the close of the nineteenth century there was a new burst of editorial activity. Earlier in the century those who edited American correspondence and public papers considered themselves "men of letters," but as the division of academic disciplines developed, there was an increased sense of professional responsibility and standards. Some editions, like Henry Cabot Lodge's scissors-and-paste version of the *Works of Alexander Hamilton*, represented no improvement over earlier models. But others, like the editions prepared by the brothers Paul Leicester Ford and Worthington Chauncey Ford, showed considerable textual sophistication for the time.

As the twentieth century opened, the new professional historians were ready to make their voices felt in urging a systematic program of documentary publication. President Theodore Roosevelt, himself a historian and biographer, directed the creation of a committee to report on the problem. Worthington Ford chaired the committee, while J. Franklin Jameson, the great historian of the Carnegie Institution, acted as its secretary. The committee's report of 1908 urged the creation of a permanent federal commission on "national historical publications" as well as the revival of the *American State Papers* series. The American Historical Association urged adoption of the committee's recommendation, but nothing was done.

Piecemeal efforts were not wanting in those decades. In 1925 Congress authorized the collection of the official papers of the territories, and this led to the inception of a major publications project, *The Territorial Papers*. The Library of Congress continued to sponsor Worthington Ford's edition of the *Journals of the Continental Congress* and also began work on an edition of the *Writings of George Washington*. And at the Carnegie Institution, Jameson oversaw such major documentry series as *The Letters of Members of the Continental Congress* and *Documents Relative to the Slave Trade in America*.

In 1934 Congress created the National Historical Publications

Commission (NHPC) as part of the National Archives Act. For practical purposes, however, this commission remained a fiction, and in the next sixteen years its members met only six times. It was not until 1950 that a new Federal Records Act gave the commission specific duties regarding documentary publication and, even more important, a permanent staff with which to discharge those responsibilities.

II. "Historical" Editing

The transformation of the NHPC into an agency with real power and responsibility at this time was not happenstance. It merely recognized the optimism concerning new efforts to reform and revolutionize American documentary editing begun by individual scholars during World War II. Even forty years ago technological advances in microforms and photocopying offered an exciting prospect for the editors and publishers of documents. With these tools, photographic facsimiles of all the variant copies of a statesman's surviving letters, journals, and other writings could be assembled in one place for comparison and evaluation. For the first time, truly comprehensive and critical editions became a practical possibility.

During the war years, two scholars began projects that would produce the first fruits of modern "historical" editing. At Franklin and Marshall College, Lyman Butterfield undertook an edition of the correspondence of Benjamin Rush that drew on manuscript collections throughout the nation. At Princeton University, Julian P. Boyd won approval for a definitive edition of the papers of Thomas Jefferson. Butterfield joined Boyd's staff at Princeton, and under Boyd's direction the framework of a modern project in historical editing took shape. The availability of photocopies made possible a *variorum* edition, in which the locations of all extant copies of each document could be cited and variants among the versions could be noted. A systematic approach to the cataloging of manuscripts and photoreproductions allowed the editors to create an archive that encompassed Jefferson's correspondence, his literary works, and his state papers. With these sources at hand, the editors could select the most authoritative version of a Jefferson document for print publication. A system of critical symbols based on those employed by textual scholars for works of earlier eras was devised to reproduce in print certain details of the original manuscript such as authorial cancellations. For other details of the text, explanatory footnotes were provided.

The Boyd-Butterfield tradition of historical editing did not stop with supplying a reliable printed text for each document. These scholars felt an obligation to furnish their readers with explanatory footnotes that would allow them to understand the document in its historical context. These notes reflected scholarship as painstaking as any seen in major historical monographs of the time. And the combination of textual attention and explanatory annotation became the hallmarks of American historical editing with the publication of the first volume of the *Jefferson Papers* in 1950 and of the two-volume edition of Rush's correspondence the following year.

These ready-made examples of the promise and potential of documentary editing cleared the way for the moribund NHPC to begin its work. The commission initiated a survey among American historians to determine priorities for its program, and by the time that the final report on this survey was ready in 1954, the *Jefferson Papers* had been joined by three new "papers" projects: those preparing similar editions for Henry Clay, John C. Calhoun, and Benjamin Franklin. Later that year, the Adams Papers project began its work, and in 1955 and 1956 projects for editions of the papers of Alexander Hamilton and James Madison were initiated. Each project focused on a figure whose papers were given priority in the report issued by the NHPC in 1954, and they soon received more practical encouragement in the form of grants from the Ford and Rockefeller foundations and from the New York Times and the Time-Life Corporation.

In the 1950s the NHPC could offer guidance to editorial projects throughout the country and provide the services of its research facilities in Washington. After 1964 it could also offer money to these projects. The Ford Foundation granted $2 million to ensure the continuation of the five "priority" projects—the papers of Adams, Franklin, Hamilton, Jefferson, and Madison. And Congress made the NHPC a grants-making agency that not only administered the Ford Foundation monies but also could make grants of its own from federal appropriations.

By the early 1970s the NHPC had provided money or official endorsement to more than sixty editorial projects throughout the country. Its responsibilities were expanded to include the preservation of historical records, as well as the publication of documents, and in 1975 the agency's name was changed to the National Historical Publications and Records Commission (NHPRC). The NHPRC encouraged an increasing number of microform publication projects for historical figures and organizations whose significance did not seem to warrant the expense of comprehensive print publication of their records.

The selection of appropriate topics for projects soon reflected the needs of a wide spectrum of interests. It was a mark of the success of early documentary editions that scholars with concerns in modern American history and in areas outside such traditional ones as politics and government demanded equal attention to records serving their scholarly needs. By 1982 the NHPRC had given support or endorsement to 386 published volumes, whose subjects included not only individuals but institutions and organizations; women as well as men; and leaders of a variety of ethnic and racial groups whose significance lay in social and intellectual as well as political history.

III. "LITERARY" EDITING

American literary scholars joined historians in organized editorial pursuits, but their course was an independent one, and they created a somewhat different editorial tradition. While America's tradition of concern for editing papers with historical significance is an old one, the tradition of publishing authoritative texts of the works and correspondence of American literary figures is comparatively new. It was not until the twentieth century that America's role in the history of literature and world culture became recognized as an equally worthy topic of serious scholarly study. Such recognition was fully established by the late 1930s, but World War II delayed a coordinated effort to provide American literary and cultural historians with documentary records similar to those available to the political historian. In 1947 the Modern Language Association (MLA) named a Committee on Definitive Editions, which first sought funds for a coordinated program to publish authoritative texts of American literary works. This attempt failed, and it was not until the early 1960s that the crusade was revived. By that time American literary critics had already shown their talent and ingenuity in applying textual criticism to seminal American works. Fredson Bowers's edition of Walt Whitman's *Leaves of Grass* and Harrison Hayford and Merton Sealts's "genetic" text of Herman Melville's *Billy Budd* demonstrated both that the American scholarly community had the skills and talents necessary to provide authoritative texts and that the raw materials of American literary documents required such critical attention.

The MLA revived its crusade on behalf of reliable editions of American literary works in 1963 with the creation of an executive committee for a Center for Editions of American Authors (CEAA). By the time that the CEAA was created, five projects were already planned or under way to publish the writings of major American authors: Ralph Waldo Emerson, Mark Twain, Herman Melville, Walt Whitman, and Nathaniel Hawthorne. Not long afer the CEAA's committee was named, the federal government created the National Endowment for the Humanities (NEH), a grants-making agency receptive to the aims of the CEAA.

In the spring of 1966 the NEH made its first grants to the CEAA. Once these funds were available, the CEAA published the list of American writers whose editions would receive the first attention. The existing Emerson, Twain, Melville, Whitman, and Hawthorne projects were to be joined by new projects for the works of Washington Irving, Henry David Thoreau, William Dean Howells, and Stephen Crane.

Over the next decade the CEAA acted as a conduit for funds from the NEH to editorial projects that met the CEAA's standards. To make those standards explicit, the CEAA published the first edition of its *Statement of Editorial Principles* (1967), which set down guidelines for editors seeking the CEAA's endorsement. At the time that the CEAA issued its *Statement*, it also instituted an emblem, or "seal," to be awarded to volumes that met its standards of editorial accuracy.

For an author's *works*—writings written with the intention of publication—standards for the seal were clear. The CEAA demanded that such editions provide an edited *clear text*, that is, a reading text uncluttered with textual or informational footnotes of any kind. Approved volumes were to provide readers with a historical introduction tracing the work's creation and publication, as well as an essay on the modern editors' treatment of the author's text. The editors were to justify their choice of a *copy-text*, that version of the published work that served as the framework for an eclectic, critical edition presenting the editors' analytical judgment of the author's intentions. An appendix in each volume offered the *textual apparatus*, which included textual notes, lists of editorial corrections, or *emendations*, of the text, a *historical collation* of the copy-text with other editions of a printed work, and lists of line-end hyphenations of possible compounds as they had appeared in the copy-text as well as those line-end hyphenations to be retained when quoting from the critical text.

CEAA editions of an author's writings were to include not only those works composed with an eye to publication but also *private* materials, such as letters and diaries or journals that fell into the realm of documentary editing. These private writings usually survived only in manuscript form, and the conventions of textual editing for works intended for publication could not be transferred automatically. Thus the CEAA's requirements for approved editions of correspondence and journals were less specific than for works. For instance, the editors of letters and diaries were not confined to clear-text versions of these manuscripts, although they were expected to furnish complete textual apparatuses for any editorial emendations that they might make.

These policies were continued under the CEAA's successor, the Committee on Scholarly Editions (CSE), created by the MLA in 1976. Although the CSE no longer acted as a channel for funds to editorial projects, it continued the CEAA's role of issuing a seal to approved editions and of acting as a clearing house for information among editors. What is more significant, the CSE, as its name implied, hoped to spread the principles of textual scholarship beyond American literary figures, and its seal was awarded to volumes of the writings of the philosopher John Dewey and the psychologist William James and editions of British authors. In the decade 1966–76 the CEAA gave its seal to more than 140 volumes; by the close of 1982 the CSE had awarded its seal to 66 volumes.

IV. THE EVOLUTION OF DISTINCTIVE METHODOLOGIES

Thus, by the middle of the 1970s, two editorial establishments had developed in the United States, each focusing its attention on important American figures, each drawing on traditions of textual criticism and on modern technology. For the sake of convenience, they came to be known as *historical* and *literary* editing, a division that many scholars believed was unrealistic and unfortunate. Each editorial specialty had its own form of professional bureaucracy and oversight. Although the NHPRC, the NEH, the CEAA, and the CSE all tried to avoid the charge of dictating to the editors who looked to them for funds and guidance, there were distinct patterns that marked an edition as historical or literary in its approach.

Historical editors tended to organize projects for the publication of the *papers* of an individual or group. Photocopies or originals of all the surviving records that could be defined in such a category were to be collected by a project. Even if a project planned only a select print edition of these papers, increasingly NHPRC insisted that the editors make the entire collection available to the scholarly public, usually through a microform supplement. In printed volumes, even those defined as *select*, the editor was obliged to publish a sample of both incoming and outgoing correspondence, of writings intended for publication as well as those that a literary critic would define as private.

The *literary* edition of a figure's *writings* was far more exclusive. Edited volumes of an author's works, of course, were an expected part of the process. However, when the editor approached private documents, he defined his task as editing the author's *writings*, not his *papers*; thus literary editions of correspondence customarily printed only letters written by their central figure, not the letters that he or she received. Literary editors were not obliged to provide microform supplements of collected materials not included in edited volumes.

Historical and literary editors also took different approaches to the treatment of texts. Both groups recognized that the printed page could not reproduce all of the details of inscription and physical appearance of the original documents. However, historical editors customarily contented themselves with publishing a partially corrected reading text that reproduced only selected categories of such details, and most established general guidelines for the editorial emendation of archaic forms and punctuation in the originals. Such treatment was known as *expanded* transcription of the sources. Most literary editors were as ready to emend the documentary text as were historical editors, but the standards of the CEAA and the CSE meant that most of these emendations were recorded at some point in the edited volumes, even if it was in an appendix hundreds of pages away from the texts to which they referred.

And there were differences, too, in the nature and amount of informational annotation supplied by the two groups of editors. Historical editors tended to supply more such annotation than did their literary counterparts. And many historical editors supplemented footnotes and headnotes with elaborate indexing systems that enabled their readers to retrieve from their volumes almost any kind of information that might serve a scholarly purpose.

Some of these differences in technique and methodology can be traced to the editors' training. The models from which historical editors worked were those of historical documents of the nineteenth century. Those for literary editors were the textual apparatuses prepared for works in European literature, where it was often necessary to provide an eclectic text that combined, or *conflated*, elements from several sources.

Other differences arose from the editors' conceptions of the audience for their volumes. The historical editor assumed that the reader would need a text closely tied to the original—a heavily emended clear text for a document would serve no useful purpose for the historian-reader who wished to employ that text as evidence. The literary editor assumed that his reader would be concerned with evaluating the readability and literary merits of the letters and journals that he read; for such a reader, clear text was a standard convenience. The historical editor dealt with papers of public importance that could not be understood without annotation that fixed their historical context. The literary editor assumed that the writings that he edited would be viewed as expressions of a person's private feelings and internal development.

With the creation of an interdisciplinary forum in the Association for Documentary Editing, editors were forced to confront an embarrassing truth about their specialty: after thirty years, there were no generally applied standards for documentary editors, and those standards that existed were applied in an apparently haphazard manner. A purposeful and continuing discussion of the basic problems involved in presenting printed editions of documentary materials had never taken place. The body of critical literature was uneven and unsatisfying at best.

V. The 1950s: The Critical Reception of Historical Editing

At first, historical editors had left any analysis of methodology to their readers. Historians and laymen welcomed the *Jefferson* and *Rush* volumes of 1950 and 1951 with open and grateful arms. Announcements of other series in this mode brought cries of delight and, one suspects, of relief—relief at the prospect of having authoritative printed texts that would spare scholars the trials of visiting inconveniently located manuscript repositories or of squinting at scratched microfilms. In 1981 Gordon Wood characterized this pattern of response as "effusively laudatory, but critically unhelpful" ("Historians and Documentary Editing," *Journal of American History* 67 [March 1981]: 877).

This is not to say that historians and historian-reviewers did not raise questions about the editions whose volumes began to crowd other books from their shelves by the early 1960s. The quality and quantity of annotation were discussed with increasing concern, and the effectiveness of indexes and other finding aids was analyzed. But reviewers largely ignored any questions raised by the editors' methods in establishing the printed texts that they offered as authoritative. (For a useful bibliography of such criticism see Fredrika J. Teute's "Views in Review: A Historiographical Perspective on Historical Editing," *American Archivist* 43 [Winter 1980]: 43–56.)

In 1951 Theodore Hornberger's review of the first volume of the *Jefferson Papers* (*American Quarterly* 3 [1951]: 87–90) pointed to the birth of a tradition of variorum editions of American documents, and Hornberger even raised constructive questions concerning Boyd's choices of source texts and his treatment of works printed in Jefferson's lifetime. But with rare exceptions, reviewers ignored such broad considerations. Isolated critics (usually editors themselves) could be found to compare specific printed texts with their sources for transcriptional accuracy, but none posed even tentative questions about general textual standards for historical editions for more than a quarter of a century after Hornberger.

VI. THE AMERICANIZATION OF COPY-TEXT

While historians contended themselves with reviewing the footnotes of historical series, another editorial movement took root that eventually forced a reexamination of these methods. The year 1950 not only marked the appearance of the first volume of the *Jefferson Papers* and the era of Boydean historical editing but was the year in which *Studies in Bibliography* carried Sir Walter Greg's "The Rationale of Copy-Text" (3 [1950–51]: 19–36).

Greg's essay was an eminently clear and cogent summary of the experience of British scholars in editing the texts of Renaissance and early modern drama and literature. Greg described the false starts, intellectual detours, and careful experiments that had led him and his colleagues to codify and rationalize practical rules for the selection of the "copy-text." Greg distinguished between those elements in a printed work that could be termed *substantive*, those that directly affected "the author's meaning or the essence of his expression," and those that could be regarded as *accidentals*—spelling, marks of punctuation, and other elements "affecting mainly its formal presentation." Greg assured his readers that he was well aware of the fragile line between substantives and accidentals. "The distinction I am trying to draw," he warned, "is practical, not philosophic."

The "practical" use to which Greg put the distinction was a simple one. In the absence of an author's manuscript, it was usually possible to identify one edition of a published work (and that, usually, the earliest) that drew most directly upon that lost manuscript. Recognizing the human frailties of printers, Greg pointed out that the craftsmen responsible for later printings were likely to respect the *words* of earlier versions but were unlikely to feel themselves bound by what might seem old-fashioned or incorrect notions of spelling and punctuation in the edition that they reset. He also suggested that writers who had a hand in revising their own works for later editions were likely to concern themselves more with changing inelegant substantive elements in the old edition than with standardizing punctuation or correcting typographical errors.

Thus, when only one edition reflects the author's personal scrutiny, and later editions are merely "reprints," that early copy-text has an authority that extends, in Greg's words, "to substantive readings and accidentals." But he reminded his readers that "the choice of substantive readings belongs to the general theory of textual criticism and lies altogether beyond the narrow principle of the copy-text."

Greg hoped that this explanation would end what he termed "the tyranny of copy-text"—the reluctance of editors to substitute hard work and harder thought for an unquestioning reliance on one sanctified printed text. Indeed, the simplicity of Greg's essay makes it seem an odd candidate for a place in scholarly Holy Writ. But as one observer remarked, "When he [Greg] published 'The Rationale of Copy-Text' . . . more than fifty years of editing Renaissance plays had gone by without anyone's having codified a statement of principles" (Peter Shaw, "The American Heritage and Its Guardians," *American Scholar* 45 [Winter 1975–76]: 733–51).

It was no accident that Greg's exposition of copy-text was published in an American periodical. Literary scholars in this country were as eager as historians to see a more systematic and scholarly publication of American materials, and Greg's essay on copy-text became part of the theoretical basis for the movement's claim that it possessed *scientific* methodology that could ensure success in the quest for truly authoritative texts of American authors. The creation of the CEAA gave literary editors a chance to show the potential uses of this methodology.

VII. THE 1960s: EDITING AND RELEVANCE

The first volume to bear the CEAA emblem was published in 1963. American literary scholars and lay critics were more ready than observers of the historiographical scene to take issue with this new phenomenon. In one of the paradoxes common to the literature of American scholarly editing, the earliest and best-known public attack on CEAA methods in documentary editions concerned volumes that did not even bear the CEAA emblem.

In January 1968 the *New York Review of Books* carried Lewis Mumford's scathing review of the first six volumes of the *Emerson Journals*, as well as his laudatory words for the first two volumes of Emerson's *Early Lectures*. The *Journals* recorded details of the original manuscripts with such a wealth of symbolic brackets and arrows in their texts that Mumford titled his essay "Emerson behind Barbed Wire." The *Lectures* were in clear text, with omitted details of inscription recorded in back-of-book notes.

All eight volumes had been prepared before creation of the CEAA's program of inspection and award of its emblem, hence none bore that seal of approval. Still, Mumford used the *Emerson Journals* as a symbol of the evils he sensed in the CEAA program. He attacked the volumes on two scores. First, the editors had printed the journals in their entirety, "mingling the important with the inconsequential." Second, they had chosen "to magnify this original error by transcribing their notations to the very pages that the potential reader might wish to read freely, without stumbling over scholarly roadblocks and barricades."

As representatives of the Emerson edition and the CEAA quickly pointed out, Mumford had quite simply misunderstood the editors' aims and had not grasped the volumes' raison d'être. The only existing edition of the *Journals* comprised "selections" and rewritten snippets of the original source. There was hardly a need for another such contribution. Instead of continuing in this tradition, William H. Gilman and his colleagues had given their readers the complete texts of these important records. They realized that their contents were not of consistent interest to every member of their audience, but they realized, too, that it was impossible for them to anticipate the needs of the thousands of scholars from a dozen fields who required access to the journal entries. As for the *Journals'* textual methods, the edition was an *inclusive* text that recorded specific inscriptional details, not a literal transcription as Mumford seemed to believe. And there was good reason to make these texts more inclusive than the ones presented for the lectures, for the journal entries had no definable final form as did drafts of the lectures that were actually delivered to an audience.

Mumford's review took on added significance when it became part of Edmund Wilson's broader attack on CEAA principles. In

September 1968 the first of three essays by Wilson on the CEAA program appeared in the *New York Review*. Wilson admitted that the award of NEH funds to the CEAA represented a personal defeat for him. His own proposal for a series of editions of American classics had been turned down by the NEH in favor of the MLA plan. However, he did not challenge the authority or validity of the CEAA texts that he reviewed. Rather, he denounced both the expense involved in their preparation and what he considered their nonhumanistic tone and editorial procedures. Thus he echoed Mumford's earlier complaints of "technological extravagance" and "automated editing" in the *Emerson Journals*. Both critics were suspicious of the supposedly "scientific" methods of the CEAA approach, and Mumford even hinted at a parallel between editorial callousness and the Vietnam War when he cried, "The voice in which Emerson calls out to one is drowned by the whirring of the critical helicopter, hovering over the scene."

Wilson's essays were later published in pamphlet form as *The Fruits of the MLA*. MLA partisans, in turn, issued rebuttals to his and Mumford's attacks in *Professional Standards and American Editions*. Peter Shaw recalled the results of these articles at the MLA convention of December 1968: "The young antiwar professors who temporarily gained control of the organization . . . sold copies of Wilson's *Fruits of the MLA* and offered resolutions calling for both withdrawal from Vietnam and a cutoff of funds for the American editions" ("The American Heritage and Its Guardians," 735). Both the conflict in Southeast Asia and support for the CEAA survived these attacks, although neither escaped further critical scrutiny.

Historian-editors viewed the battles within the MLA with amusement. No one had yet examined their textual practices closely, and they quietly continued their work. In 1971, however, historical editions received their first broadside hit from Jesse Lemisch, a member of the American Historical Association's Committee on the Commemoration of the American Revolution. Lemisch's "preliminary critique" of the NHPC's publications program appeared in the November 1971 *AHA Newsletter* (9, no. 5: 7–27), with a candid announcement that his report "in no way represents the committee's viewpoint or policy." In "The American Revolution and the Papers of Great White Men," Lemisch forced the historical community to reexamine the priorities established for documentary publication. The NHPC focus on projects printing documents of "white male political leaders" was attacked on ideological and methodological grounds. The concentration of funds and public attention solely on such projects seemed to encourage the elitism that Lemisch and many of his generation decried. And by focusing on the collection and publication of the records of individuals who had distinguished themselves in politics and government, the NHPC appeared to slight some of the most lively and fruitful areas of research in American history. Such a program did little to provide easily accessible source materials for quantitative analysts or for the social and economic historians whose focus was, of necessity, upon groups rather than upon single figures, no matter how distinguished they might be.

—In the best tradition of consumers of historical papers projects, Lemisch raised no questions about the textual methods of existing editions, nor did he suggest that any new techniques might be required by the kind of historical editing that he proposed: projects that focused on the records of groups, not merely upon the documents left by the more literate men and women in America's past. However, he had unwittingly contributed to a silent revolution in textual methodology among historian-editors. The NHPC did re-spond to criticism from Lemisch and his allies. The 1970s saw an increased emphasis on creating projects with an organizational rather than an individual focus. Historians were encouraged to investigate new sources for documentary editions as well as new formats for presenting these materials. But the editors of these new projects found that they could not confine their innovations to the collection and organizational arrangement of their sources. They had no choice but to ignore the patterns of emendation and standardization accepted by earlier editors and instead adopted far more literal methods of presenting editorial texts. Unfortunately, they did not publish their reservations concerning the efficacy of the older textual tradition for documents of a later period and for authors of different backgrounds. On the surface, at least, historical editing in the Boyd-Butterfield tradition continued unchallenged.

VIII. The MLA and Private Writings

Had the CEAA and its successor, the CSE, confined their activities to the published works of American authors, their achievements and the debate surrounding their programs would be of marginal interest to the editors of documents. As William Gibson made clear in his 1969 statement "The Center for Editions of American Authors," the editor who adapted Greg's copy-text theory to American writings hoped to "achieve a text which matches no existing text exactly but which comes closer to the author's hand and his intent than any previously printed version," not to present a text that necessarily had documentary value.

Clearly this goal could not be achieved easily when letters, diaries, and notebooks were published as part of each author's writings, and CEAA editors ventured into the realm of documentary publication. To complicate the discussion of editing further, many literary editors transferred to these documentary materials the new set of conventions devised for CEAA editions of printed works. While some of these conventions concerned an edition's format, others concerned textual method itself. Certain categories of emendation and suppression of detail (such as slips of the pen and details of inscription like catchwords) in the source text of documents, like similar problems in editions of printed works chosen as copy-text, could be handled *silently*, that is, with no record in the edition, whether in the text, in footnotes, or in the editorial apparatus. Any editorial actions that fell outside these categories were to be reported someplace in any volume that received a CEAA emblem. The application of such methods to what the CEAA called *private* writings (those composed without the intention of publication) had become the target of bitter controversy with the appearance of the volumes of the *Emerson Journals* in 1968. Although the volumes under consideration did not bear the CEAA emblem, Mumford assumed accurately that their textual methods anticipated those that would be used in CEAA editions.

Paradoxically, once the CEAA had adopted its standards for private writings, those standards were critized by William Gilman, editor of the *Emerson Journals* assailed by Mumford. In his review essay, "How Should Journals Be Edited?" (*Early American Literature* 6 [Spring 1971]: 73–83), Gilman criticized what he saw as a slavish and ultimately futile attempt by the editors of the *Irving Journals* to meet the CEAA's demand that they "collate and report fully" any doubtful readings or peculiarities of inscription in the original manuscripts that they had translated to print. Readers of the Mumford essay and of Gilman's review were left to unravel the puzzle of Gilman's reasons for criticizing the pedantic reporting of textual details less than three years after he had been attacked for this same sin.

The mystery's solution was clear to anyone who gave a close reading to the introduction to volume 1 of the *Emerson Journals*. The reading text of those journals is, indeed, heavily peppered with the arrows and brackets of editorial barbed wire, and the volumes carry hundreds of additional textual notes recording editorial emendations and commenting upon the vagaries of the sources. However, the combination of text and notes does not add up to a complete report of the contents of the original manuscripts. The edition has several categories of silent emendations. The *Irving Journals*, on the other hand, provide the reader with a nearly literal, or *diplomatic*, transcription in which details recorded symbolically in the reading text are supplemented by descriptive footnotes that appear immediately adjacent to the text (*Irving Journals* 1:xxv).

Gilman's attack on the CEAA standards reflected in the *Irving Journals* sparked no continuing public debate among editors of private writings. Certainly the problem was not ignored by editors at work on these series, but their discussions of the special challenges at hand were confined largely to notes contributed to the short-lived *CEAA Newsletter* (1968–71), where one finds a discussion of the degree to which private writings demand the same scrupulous reporting of emendations and inscriptional details found in editions of published works. In public, literary scholars confined themselves to arguing the merits of imposing copy-text theory and the standards of the CEAA upon printed American works.

The special textual problems of documents in the history of American literature also received short shrift when the CEAA published its *Statement of Editorial Principles and Procedures* in 1972. Although this was described as a "revised edition" of the CEAA's original statement of 1967, it was in fact a new and far more explicit discussion of the CEAA's aims and requirements. In effect, it represented the CEAA's attempt to report upon the results of the first half-dozen years' experience of the CEAA and its editors. Its appendix on "Relevant Textual Scholarship" (pp. 17–25) was the most complete bibliography of writings pertinent to editing American literary works to that date. But the 1972 *Statement* paid scant attention to the variety of approaches that these editors had already brought to private writings. Its recommendations for inclusive textual treatment of such materials ignored the fact that the CEAA had given its emblem to volumes in the Mark Twain series that carried no textual record and to volumes in the *Hawthorne Notebooks* that approached clear text with an accompanying report of editorial emendations.

IX. Interdisciplinary Evaluations Begin

The first observer to attempt a comparison of the work of literary and historical editors was Peter Shaw in his "The American Heritage and Its Guardians." Shaw focused most of his attention upon inconsistencies in quality and textual methods in CEAA editions of literary works rather than upon the small but growing sample of edited private writings of American literary figures. Among historical editions, Shaw limited his discussion to "Founding Fathers" volumes, such as those of Jefferson, Adams, and Madison.

When the time came to evaluate the volumes in both traditions, Shaw concluded that historical editors had served their audience better than CEAA scholars, "not necessarily by common sense but by their fundamental respect for historical fact." Since 1975 Shaw has modified his own judgment, and he now suggests that NHPRC-sponsored historical series are, indeed, no better than those of the CEAA/CSE mold. In large measure, Shaw was forced to revise his estimate because of an essay published two years after his own.

The analysis that demanded this reevaluation was G. Thomas Tanselle's "The Editing of Historical Documents," which appeared in January 1978 in volume 31 of the University of Virginia's *Studies in Bibliography*. The literature of American documentary editing was changed irrevocably by that publication. Tanselle surveyed the post–World War II tradition of historical editing of documents and took its practitioners to task on two scores. He pointed out that the statements of textual method in these volumes were often maddeningly vague and occasionally self-contradictory. And he argued that the application of heavily emended expanded transcription instead of more conservative methods of literal transcription was a disservice both to the documentary sources and to their readers. In 1981 historian John Y. Simon gave this summary of the impact of Tanselle's article:

> Some reacted as if the Japanese had again struck Pearl Harbor; more sought to repair their damaged vessels by altering, improving, or explaining transcription policies with a clearer understanding that inconsistent or silent alterations designed for "the reader's convenience" more often represented the critic's opportunity. We may eventually come to regard Tanselle's article as the single most important step forward in American historical editing since the publication of the first volume of the Boyd *Jefferson* ("Editors and Critics," *ADE Newsletter* 3 [December 1981]: 3).

Widespread and immediate though the reaction to Tanselle's article was, it did not take public form for several years. In private, many historical editors grumbled at an "outsider's" criticism of textual methods for materials that they felt he did not understand or appreciate. At projects where the textual methods of Boyd and Butterfield had been imposed on the editors by their advisory committees, there was a sigh of relief. The heirs to such decisions offered private prayers of thanks to Tanselle for voicing their own reservations and either announced that their editions would henceforth abandon expanded methods for more literal treatment or quietly adopted more conservative methods and prayed that their editorial advisers would not notice the difference.

When public debate came, it emerged, fittingly enough, in a forum that owed its existence to the private discussion of documentary editing sparked by Tanselle's essay. In March 1978 the NEH and NHPRC announced plans for a conference on "Literary and Historical Editing" at the University of Kansas. That meeting in September 1978 was the first occasion on which representatives of the two editorial traditions met en masse and exchanged views. At the annual meeting of the Southern Historical Association a few weeks later the Association for Documentary Editing was created to provide an institutional setting within which historical and literary editors could learn about and from each other.

Still, another two years passed before the ADE saw formal debate of the issues that had made the association a necessity. It was not until the ADE meeting of October 1980 that Robert J. Taylor, Lyman Butterfield's successor as editor of the *Adams Papers*, publicly presented his position in "Editorial Practices—An Historian's Views" (printed in *ADE Newsletter* 3 [February 1981]: 4–8). Taylor conceded the strength of Tanselle's criticism of statements of method in many historical editions. Paraphrasing Samuel Eliot Morison, Taylor confessed, "An historical editor's real sin is saying carefully and explicitly what he is going to do and then not sticking to it. And here Dr. Tanselle has indeed struck home." However, Taylor challenged what seemed to him Tanselle's unbending standards for printed documentary texts. Taylor argued that it was impractical to adhere to diplomatic methods, whereby every detail of the original manuscript would be recorded in the editorial text. He contended that editorial judgment must be exercised and that inviolable rules could open the way to texts needlessly cluttered with the barbed wire of unenlightening editorial sigla. As an aside, Taylor attacked the notion that printed documentary sources—unique pieces of historical evidence that existed in typeset, not handwritten, form— should be given eclectic conflated texts like those literary works bearing the CEAA or CSE emblem.

Unfortunately, the exchange between Taylor and Tanselle was an unsatisfactory one. Tanselle did not address himself at length to the points that Taylor had raised, and his comments were too brief to warrant print publication in the *ADE Newsletter*. His audience had to wait until 1981, when the MLA's *Introduction to Scholarship in Modern Languages and Literatures* appeared with Tanselle's essay "Textual Scholarship." Here Tanselle made clear his agreement with Taylor on the special requirements of printed documents. He recognized the need for a "noncritical edition" of such works, one that "serves essentially the function of making the text of a particular document (manuscript or printed) more widely available" (p. 34).

However, many parts of the Tanselle thesis had not been clarified. Tanselle had not contented himself with pointing to the sins of historical editing; he had also suggested a path to salvation, and it seemed to be some single approach to documentary editing that would serve both literary and historical scholarship. Tanselle's long association with the CEAA led readers to assume that this single standard must be that of the CEAA.

The CEAA tradition in this regard had taken on added significance at the very time that Tanselle prepared his essay on documentary editing. With the CEAA's replacement by the CSE, the discussion broadened from one of historical and literary studies to cover every field of scholarly endeavor. The CSE hoped to provide reliable editions "to encompass more than American literature." The CEAA had already moved beyond purely literary works by awarding its seal to volumes in the *Works of John Dewey*. However, it had been forced to withhold its aid and formal approval from editions that could not be described as American in origin. The change in the name of the agency was accompanied by a change in its purpose, and the official declaration of this new policy appeared in 1977. The CSE's broadened field of interest was reflected in the enumerative bibliography that accompanied this statement. That guide now included works in textual editing that did not confine themselves to the problems of the Americanist. However, the statement of 1977 offered no additional guidance in noncritical documentary editing: its focus remained squarely upon the problems of the textual editor concerned with recovering authorial intentions to be published in an eclectic, critical text rather than upon the challenges faced by documentary specialists concerned with presenting inscribed historical realities.

The debate over the application of textual methods to documents proceeded sometimes in disjointed fashion. For example, in November 1979 David Nordloh, textual editor of the *Howells Letters*, delivered remarks entitled "The 'Perfect Text': The Editor Speaks for the Author" at the annual meeting of the ADE. As printed in the May 1980 *ADE Newsletter*, his remarks suggested that an editor's goals were to " 'make' it [the text] what its author 'wanted.' "

In this regard, Nordloh continued, "editorial corrections of spelling and punctuation errors and repetitions of words in sequence can be justified because such details can't be conceived, in most ordinary language contexts, except as mistaken departures from intellectual norms." There could be no mistaking Nordloh's meaning, for the practical results of his textual theory could be seen in the clear-text edition of the *Howells Letters*.

More than two years passed before Wayne Cutler, editor of the *Polk Correspondence*, challenged Nordloh in "The 'Authentic' Witness: The Editor Speaks for the Documents" (*ADE Newsletter* 4 [February 1982]). Cutler took an exceptionally conservative position on the textual treatment of documentary materials. "The historical editor," he wrote, "speaks only for one document at a time." He decried Nordloh's suggestion that documents such as letters or private journals could be emended or conflated for the sake of "perfection."

Here, of course, the positions of the representatives of the two editorial camps were reversed. It was Nordloh, a literary scholar, who justified editorial emendations of documentary sources, while Cutler, a historian, insisted that only fidelity to those sources was valid. Interested observers were left to their own devices to ponder this, for neither Tanselle nor Taylor indicated where he stood in this skirmish in the controversy over literary and historical methods. Still, there had been at least a beginning of exchanges of opinions and ideas on the central problem of documentary editing—the establishment of an authoritative editorial text. And historians and literary scholars in the ADE discovered that their independent pursuits had led them to the same conclusions on one central and pragmatic issue, the need for editors from all disciplines to recognize the wide and diverse range of responsibilities borne by any competent editor.

X. RELATED FUNCTIONS OF EDITING

Editors in all academic disciplines found themselves in agreement on one point: although, strictly speaking, editing is only the establishment of a text, the duties of a successful editor neither begin nor end with that process. Editors are seldom able to edit to the exclusion of many mundane though essential related tasks. The documents that merit critical attention must be assembled. Errors of fact or interpretation can be introduced into the documentary texts or their accompanying notes if there is no procedure for verifying and proofreading these materials. Publishers must be satisfied that an editor's design for his volumes is thoughtful and useful. And in all these areas, limitations of funds often force editors to accept expedients that result in products short of ideal goals.

Thus scholarly editors must be the most practical and hard-headed scholars in their disciplines. Such ruthless pragmatism may be unexpected in academic editors, who would appear to be the purest of modern scholars. They focus their attention on original sources, not on the conclusions stated by others in secondary works. Theirs is a professional obsession with the best evidence that is to be had. And their goal is to communicate that evidence to others in a clear and accurate form. But every editor soon learns that all the scholarly dedication and critical insight in the world will not compensate for inattention to the practical considerations involved in preparing a documentary edition.

Here, too, editors have seldom written about what they do. The first and last published description of the process by which an editorial project establishes *control* over thousands of manuscripts and photocopies appeared thirty-five years ago in the *American Archivist*. Discussions of the problems encountered by modern literary editors in proofreading editorial texts were published only in the *CEAA Newsletter*, a periodical that survived for but three years and whose circulation was largely confined to editors of CEAA series.

Documentary editors have much to share in this area, not only in their specific methods but also in the general rules that they have come to observe. Any edition's success will be directly related to the degree to which the editor has planned and anticipated the problems that he meets. And that planning and organization must take into account what is both the delight and the curse of the trade—the appearance of the unanticipated problem or unexpected scholarly bonus.

Beyond having an aptitude for careful planning, the editor must be able to establish clear lines of responsibility for any project at its outset. It is not enough to outline an exhaustive search for source materials unless the editor ensures that each step in that process takes place. The most meticulous scheme for proofreading transcriptions of sources is useless unless the editor establishes pedestrian bookkeeping procedures to record each step in such verification.

Finally, the editor should be prepared to expose his planning and execution of the considerations related to the act of editing to public view. His printed volumes should not only explain his methods for establishing documentary texts but also inform his audience of the scope of his search for materials, his standards for annotation, and his proofreading methods. All editors should be bound by standards for full disclosure, and the editor's organizational plan and table of responsibility and authority should be published as part of the edition itself.

Recent technological advances now test every editor's organizational skills and require him to establish new patterns of responsibility for his edition. Modern scholarly editing was made a practical possibility by technological advances in one area—photoduplication—and the field is now being transformed again by the technology of computer systems. Over the past thirty years editors have been required to master the mysteries of photoreproduction ratios, the comparative prices of "copy-flo" Xerox prints, and the merits of various microform reader-printers. Now the editor must face the challenge of learning the jargon and the equipment of computer systems.

Scholarly editors first investigated the promise of computerized technology in the 1960s. At first such exploration was confined largely to computer-assisted collation of literary texts, but now editors in every field are learning how to make computers work for them. Several projects have computerized systems for indexing their collections of source materials. Others are ready to present their publishers, not with typed copy, but with magnetic tapes containing symbols that can be translated into printed pages by a computer composition system.

Despite this revolution in editorial methods, it is difficult for an interested scholar to find reports of these changes. One pioneer in computerized editing recalled, "When we started, there were no models and no literature. Now we have plenty of models, but there's still precious little literature in the field." Editors have been too busy learning to exploit computer equipment to publish accounts of their experiences. Here, as elsewhere, the interested observer of the editorial game is left without convenient summaries of editorial experience.

XI. THE RATIONALE FOR A GUIDE TO DOCUMENTARY EDITING

The modern specialty of scholarly editing in America has reached a critical point in both intellectual development and technological advances. Volumes of novels, letters, diaries, statesmen's papers, political pamphlets, and philosophical and scientific treatises have been published in editions that claim to be scholarly, that is, with texts that have been established and verified according to the standards of the academic community. Yet the field of scholarly editing has grown so quickly that many of its principles have been left implicit in the texts or annotation of the volumes themselves.

This lapse is most painfully apparent in the area of noncritical, documentary editing, where editors have been peculiarly reluctant to publish discussions of their own goals and methods. This book attempts a beginning of a remedy to this pattern. On-site visits to editorial projects, lengthy correspondence, and telephone conversations have been used to supplement the information that American editors have offered in formal, printed terms.

The volume is organized in terms of a rough chronology of the physical and intellectual tasks that confront any editor, beginning with the collection of sources and ending with the final review of materials as set in type by the publisher. As any editor knows, such organization is a polite fiction. The considerations of any edition must be regarded as a whole. A project's plan for collection (chapter 2) is inevitably influenced by the projected scope of the print edition (chapter 3). Methods of transcription (chapter 4) must take into account the standards of the printed editorial text (chapters 5 and 6). Error or miscalculation in one area can guarantee disaster in another, and the editor's failure to assign or to assume responsibility for discharging each aspect of the plan will delay or even doom the whole edition.

Documentary editing, although noncritical in terms of classical textual scholarship, is not an *uncritical* endeavor. It demands quite as much intelligence, insight, and hard work as its critical counterpart, combined with a passionate determination to preserve for modern readers the nuances of evidence that exist in the sources on which the printed documentary editions are based.

Suggested Readings

The books and articles cited below may seem to belie the statement that American documentary editors are not fond of writing about their specialty. However, many of these writings are concerned with textual rather than documentary issues, and many more address themselves to the history of American documentary editing rather than to its contemporary problems and issues. In addition to the Teute and Tanselle essays cited in this chapter, students interested in the bibliography of the field will wish to consult Ross W. Beales, Jr., "Documentary Editing: A Bibliography," *ADE Newsletter* 1 (December 1980): 10–16. Many scholars who have taught documentary editing in a classroom setting have compiled their own reading lists, and one of the most useful of these is Harold Moser's

"Documentary Editing: A Working Bibliography." The only attempt to present editing principles in a "textbook" format is Ross W. Beale, Jr., and Randall K. Burkett's *Historical Editing for Undergraduates* (Worcester, Mass., 1977), a brief pamphlet of limited scope.

American editors in the literary and textual tradition have compiled a rich literature, well described in the Tanselle essays cited in this chapter. Some of the most useful essays are included in Ronald Gottesman and Scott Bennett, eds., *Art and Error: Modern Textual Editing* (Bloomington, Ind., 1970). The reader can also consult the conveniently collected essays of two of the country's most prolific writers on American textual editing in Tanselle's *Selected Studies in Bibliography* (Charlottesville, 1979) and Fredson Bowers's *Essays in Bibliography, Text, and Editing* (Charlottesville, 1977).

Documentary editors in the historical tradition are represented in Leslie W. Dunlap and Fred Shelley, eds., *The Publication of American Historical Manuscripts* (Iowa City, 1976). The papers presented at the interdisciplinary University of Kansas conference in 1978 are published in George L. Vogt and John Bush Jones, eds., *Literary and Historical Editing* (Lawrence, Kans., 1981).

I. There are many entertaining essays on the beginnings of documentary editing in the United States. Some of the most valuable are: Lyman H. Butterfield, "Archival and Editorial Enterprise in 1850 and 1950: Some Comparisons and Contrasts," *American Philosophical Society Proceedings* 98 (1954): 159–70; Lester J. Cappon, "American Historical Editors before Jared Sparks 'they will plant a forest . . .,' " *William and Mary Quarterly* 30 (July 1973): 375–400; Philip M. Hamer, ". . . authentic Documents tending to elucidate our History," *American Archivist* 25 (1962): 3–13; Lee N. Newcomer, "Manasseh Cutler's Writings: A Note on Editorial Practice," *Mississippi Valley Historical Review* 47 (June 1960): 88–101; Newman F. McGirr, "The Adventures of Peter Force," *Records of the Columbia Historical Society* 42 (1942): 35–82; Richard N. Sheldon, "Editing a Historical Manuscript: Jared Sparks, Douglas Southall Freeman, and the Battle of Brandywine," *William and Mary Quarterly* 36 (April 1979): 255–63; and Fred Shelley, "Ebenezer Hazard: America's First Historical Editor," ibid. 12 (January 1955): 44–73.

The history of efforts to organize a nationwide program of documentary publication in the early twentieth century is described in Theodore C. Blegen, "Our Widening Province," *Mississippi Valley Historical Review* 31 (June 1944): 3–20; Clarence E. Carter, "The

United States and Documentary Historical Publication," ibid. 25 (June 1938): 3–24; Worthington C. Ford, "The Editorial Function in United States History," *American Historical Review* 23 (1917–18): 273–86; J. Franklin Jameson, "Gaps in the Published Records of United States History," ibid. 11 (1905–6): 817–31; Waldo Gifford Leland, "The Prehistory and Origins of the National Historical Publications Commission," *American Archivist* 27 (1964): 187–94; and Fred Shelley, "The Interest of J. Franklin Jameson in the National Archives: 1908–1934," ibid. 12 (1949): 99–130.

II. The Holmes, Beales, and Teute essays cited in this chapter offer good guidance in the literature of historical editing. The initial volume in each historical series customarily offers a rationale for that editing project, and many of these can be consulted with profit.

Some of the most useful essays on the evolution of post–World War II historical editing are Julian P. Boyd, "God's Altar Needs Not Our Polishings," *New York History* 39 (January 1958): 3–21; Robert L. Brubaker, "The Publication of Historical Sources: Recent Projects in the United States," *Library Quarterly* 37 (April 1967): 193–225; and Lyman H. Butterfield's "The Scholar's One World," *American Archivist* 29 (1966): 343–61. Lester J. Cappon offers instructive comments in his three essays "The Historian as Editor" (*In Support of Clio: Essays in Memory of Herbert A. Kellar*, William B. Hesseltine and Donald R. McNeil, eds., [Madison, Wis., 1958], 173–93); " 'The Historian's Day'—From Archives to History" (*The Reinterpretation of Early American History: Essays in Honor of John Edwin Pomfret*, Ray Allen Billington, ed. [San Marino, Calif., 1966], 233–49); and "A Rationale for Historical Editing Past and Present" (*William and Mary Quarterly* 23 [January 1966]: 56–75).

The bibliography in this area continues with Oliver W. Holmes, "Documentary Publication in the Western Hemisphere," *Archivuum* 16 (1966): 79–96. Richard H. Kohn and George M. Curtis III provide a harsh critique of the NHPC and NHPRC programs in "The Government, the Historical Profession, and Historical Editing," *Reviews in American History* 9 (June 1981): 145–55. More favorable surveys of government-related documentary publication programs appear in Richard W. Leopold, "The Historian and the Federal Government," *Journal of American History* 64 (June 1977): 5–23; Richard B. Morris, "The Current Statesmen's Papers Publication Program: An Appraisal from the Point of View of the Legal Historian," *American Journal of Legal History* 11 (1967): 95–106; and Robert Rutland, "Recycling Early National History through the Papers of the Founding Fathers," *American Quarterly* 28 (Summer 1976): 250–61. The Holmes and Butterfield essays appear in a 1966 issue of *Archivuum* that presents several of the papers delivered to an Extraordinary Congress on documentary publication in May 1966.

The claims and methods of documentary editing of the Boyd-Butterfield era should be contrasted with the discussion in Clarence E. Carter's comparatively modest *Historical Editing* (Washington, D.C., 1952), number 7 in the National Archives *Bulletins* series.

III.   The reader may wish to consult G. Thomas Tanselle's "Literary Editing," in Vogt and Jones, *Literary and Historical Editing*, 35–56.

V.   Teute's "Views in Review," in the *American Archivist*, provides a useful guide to patterns of reviewing American historical editing.

VI and VII.   Tanselle's articles in the 1975 and 1981 volumes of *Studies in Bibliography* are an invaluable guide here. Hershel Parker and Bruce Bebb provide useful material in "The CEAA: An Interim Assessment," *Papers of the Bibliographical Society of America* 68 (1974): 129–48, and the reader will profit from Peter L. Shillingsburg's down-to-earth "Critical Editing and the Center for Scholarly Editions," *Scholarly Publishing* 9 (October 1977): 31–40.

Perhaps the last word on the controversy sparked by Edmund Wilson appears in Michael Mancher's amusing "The Text of *The Fruits of the MLA*," *Papers of the Bibliographical Society of America* 68 (1974): 411–12. Less widely publicized, but more serious, challenges to the CEAA program appear in the *New York Public Library Bulletin* 75 (1971), with informative contributions to the debate on pp. 147–53 (March), 171–73 (April), 337–44 (October), 419–23 (November), and 504–5 (December). Quite as valuable is the group of essays in *Studies in the Novel* 7 (Fall 1975): 375–406, where Bruce Bebb, Hershel Parker, Vinton A. Dearing, Thomas L. McHaney, Morse Peckham, and G. Thomas Tanselle provide a "forum" on the CEAA in response to John Freehafer's "Greg's Theory of Copy-Text and the Textual Criticism in the CEAA Editions." More recently, Tom Davis raises many thoughtful points in "The CEAA and Modern Textual Editing," *Library* 32 (1977): 61–74.

The issues raised by Lemisch and others for historical editing in the 1970s are summarized in Simone Reagor, "Historical Editing: The Federal Role," *ADE Newsletter* 4 (May 1982): 1–4, with a response from John Y. Simon on pp. 5–6. Simon deals with many related points in his "Editors and Critics," ibid. 3 (December 1981): 1–4.

VIII and IX. Followers of the impact of Tanselle's 1978 attack upon historical editing will profit from Don Cook's useful summary of the issues in "The Short Happy Thesis of G. Thomas Tanselle," ibid. 3 (February 1981): 1–4.

X. The reader who longs for some humor in the discussion of American editing will welcome Donald Jackson's "The Editor's Other Functions" in Dunlap and Shelley, *Publication of American Historical Manuscripts*, 69–76. Stanley Idzerda's "The Editor's Training and Status in the Historical Profession," ibid., 11–29, offers a more serious discussion of the attitudes and talents demanded of the documentary editor.

A growing body of literature is available on computerized methods. Vincent J. Ryan and Vinton A. Dearing recall their own introduction to the use of such systems in "Computerized Manuscript and Index Processing," *Scholarly Publishing* 4 (July 1973): 333–50. Lawrence F. Buckland's *State-of-the-Art Report: Data Input for Publishers* (Littleton, Mass., 1980) is a useful introduction to computerized book production. Two other books attempt to address the problems peculiar to the scholar in the humanities: Susan Hockey, *A Guide to Computer Applications in the Humanities* (Baltimore, 1980); and Robert L. Oakman, *Computer Methods for Literary Research* (Columbia, S.C., 1980). Briefer discussions of the use of such systems in preparing scholarly editions appear in *Scholarly Publishing*: Marilyn Frankenthaler, "Utilizing the Computer to Prepare a Manuscript," 7 (January 1976): 161–68; Constance Greaser, "Authors, Editors, and Computers," 12 (January 1981): 123–30; and John M. Strawhorn, "Word Processing and Publishing," ibid., 109–30. T. H. Howard-Hill's "Computer and Mechanical Aids to Editing," *Proof* 5 (1977): 217–35, is also useful and readable.

The *ADE Newsletter* offers discussions of the experience of two historical editors in Larry I. Bland's "The Editor and Word Processing Equipment" and David Chesnutt's "Comprehensive Text Processing and the Papers of Henry Laurens," in the May and September 1980 issues, respectively. The May 1981 issue provides a helpful summary of the papers presented at a conference on modern technology and historical editing in a report entitled "Goodbye Gutenberg." "Electronic Editing and Publishing: Miscellaneous Sources," in the September 1981 issue, is an excellent introductory bibliography.

Reports on the electronic systems that now revolutionize documentary editing will appear in both *Scholarly Publishing*, where the reader can expect to find explanations in layman's terms, and *Computers and the Humanities*, where such discussions tend to be in more technically sophisticated terms.

In all of the areas treated above, certain periodicals are likely to provide continuing coverage of the problems addressed in this chapter. The *ADE Newsletter*, with its "Exemplary Citations" column, provides a guide to recent books and articles in all fields related to documentary editing and publishes original essays and reviews. The *American Archivist* continues to provide articles on documentary editing, and its annual bibliographical review is invaluable. The periodicals that traditionally have offered their audience perceptive articles on textual and literary matters should be consulted regularly, and the reader must add to that list *Text*, the organ of the Society for Textual Scholarship.

CHAPTER 2

Initiating an Editorial Project

In initiating a project, an editor employs skills demanded of any responsible scholar. He must look ahead to anticipate the problems he will encounter, and he must make decisions at this early stage of his research that will allow him to complete his work as efficiently and thoroughly as possible. Many of the decisions to be reached at this time will concern the collection of the materials on which to base a scholarly work, in this case an edition of documentary sources. Editors must provide for some system of *control* over the materials that they collect so that none of their work will be wasted or duplicated.

The documentary editor must exhibit these skills more intensively than more conventional scholars, and he must often sustain his powers of careful scrutiny and meticulous planning for a longer period of time than the historian or literary scholar who prepares a monographic study. For the documentary editor, planning can never begin too early, and his responsibility for putting his plans into effect never ends. The discharge of these responsibilities is all the more difficult because the modern editor also needs to assess the value of various technological aids for his own project. In earlier decades editors might fulfill such duties by weighing the costs and advantages of manual typewriters versus those of electrically powered office machines. Today editors need to master not only the mysteries and prices of computerized equipment (hardware) but also the value of various programs for the use of such equipment (software).

Perhaps the most common problem for editors with funds available for computerization is choosing between using dedicated *stand-alone* equipment and sharing the resources of a large *mainframe* computer. Stand-alone units are independent microcomputers especially designed for certain tasks. For the editor, the stand-alone equipment of choice is the *word processor*, which is designed to meet the needs of manipulating written language. Word processors are generally limited to handling files of 100 pages or less, although some sophisticated units can store the data required for an entire printed volume. Mainframe computers are full-scale electronic data-storage and data-manipulation units that retrieve and process thousands of pages at a time. Through *time-sharing*, dozens or even hundreds of users can be tied to a central mainframe, each user employing a separate terminal with a keyboard to enter data or call up material from the computer's storage facilities.

Each system has its merits. The word processor's greatest advantage is its independence. The editor with such a unit is not at the mercy of a central computer whose time must be shared with others and which can "go down," or be out of operation, for hours or even days. Of somewhat less importance is the word processor's specialized design. Intended primarily for the manipulation of verbal symbols, it is easier to use for editing tasks than the terminal of an all-purpose mainframe.

Editorial projects blessed with access to a mainframe have usually found it cheaper to pay fees for the rental of a terminal and the use of computer time than to buy or lease a word processor. The computer terminal may not manipulate words as gracefully as a word processor, but it will allow a project to sort and arrange the units of information in the project's *data base* (the cumulative record of all entries made by the project) more effectively. A central computer can store far larger amounts of information than a word processor, and it can index and catalog this information more efficiently. Further, it can offer *random access* to everything that the project has stored in the system; information stored in a word processor is divided among *diskettes*, whose capacity is far smaller than that of the computer's memory.

Ideally, an editorial project would have both an independent word processor and access to a larger computer unit with which the stand-alone unit can communicate, but this happy circumstance is rare. For now, most editors must content themselves with one system or the other, not the combination of stand-alone and mainframe equipment, although the development of the smaller *personal computer* has led some editors to useful experiments with this new alternative. Further, the computer will make an editor's life easier only if he is willing to take the time to investigate the hardware and software available to his project, to ask embarrassing questions of the salesman who offers these wares, and to be fearless in admitting his own ignorance in the face of technological advances.

Editors with computer experience offer the novice five pieces of advice: (1) Always explain clearly to an equipment vendor or computer technician just what tasks the project needs the computer to perform. (2) Make sure that the vendor or technician understands that explanation. (3) Never take at face value the word of a vendor who promises that his new toy can do everything that the project requires; demand a demonstration. (4) Whenever possible, consult an editor who has already worked with computer equipment. (5) Never stop thinking of new ways in which computerized equipment can assist the editorial process.

The editor should bear these rules in mind as he contemplates the entire course of his project. Consideration of the virtues of computer equipment or manual methods in collecting and controlling the materials on which the edition will be based is only the first step in planning the project in theoretical and practical terms.

The mere fact that a particular documentary edition is considered necessary should alert the modern editor to the inadequacy of the existing body of knowledge concerning the source materials on which that edition will be based. If all the variant versions of the correspondence or papers of a given writer were in one convenient location, there would be little need to fund a project for their location and cataloging. If all such materials were adequately arranged and described in a published finding aid, there would be no cry to appoint an editor to assume the burden.

Thus there is little chance that the editor can escape becoming an expert in the collection, care, retrieval, and cataloging of documentary materials. In all likelihood, he will be called upon to create an entirely new archive. That editorial archive may include photocopies, original manuscripts, and microfilm reels that together can be called "the Papers of X," "the Records of Y," or "the Writings of Z." It is the editor's responsibility to make sure that this archive is as complete as possible and that he and his staff, through intelligent cataloging procedures, will be able to find what they need there.

I. COLLECTION OF SOURCES

No *authoritative edition* is possible without a thorough canvass of source materials that may deserve a place in it. No documentary edition can be any better than the collection of materials on which it is based, and projects that misplace or lose documents or photocopies often waste more than time and money. Long before scholars begin to edit, they become tracers of lost documents and masters of archival management.

Most editors must collect photocopies of documents from a variety of sources. This phase of editing may be the most physically taxing, but the rewards of discovery and victory over the vagaries of time and chance, the accidents of war and natural disasters, and the carelessness of heirs are often the sweetest that editors taste.

The work of collection begins with a survey of what is already known about the body of documents to be gathered. The editor combs footnotes for citations to original materials, noting the date, description, and location of every document that earlier scholars have unearthed. The editor should also enlist the cooperation of scholars who have shown an interest in his project's subject. Even if these men and women have published the findings of their earlier research, their notes on sources and their experience in canvassing the same repositories that the editor must visit will be of invaluable assistance.

Since his primary concern is the location of original materials, the editor must establish a file that will allow him to draw up lists of the pertinent holdings of given repositories. If he is limited to manual methods, this can be done by preparing a series of slips or cards where the symbol for the owner-repository of each document appears in the upper lefthand corner, so that the slips can be easily sorted according to *location*. Editors fortunate enough to have access to data-processing equipment are not so limited. Using a standard set of repository abbreviations, the editor can enter the information and then quickly retrieve a printout arranged by repository.

Earlier editions of the correspondence, journals, or personal or organizational papers to be edited should also be checked carefully, and their contents indexed for use in the collection phase of the new edition. Although such printed texts may be flawed, some may prove to be the only ones that survive. For this reason, it is wise to prepare the cataloging slips, or the computer system used for such an index, in the format that will be used for the project's permanent control files. In this way, the slips can remain part of that permanent file should the printed texts represent the only sources available for individual items. And during the search, the new editor can exploit these editions' clues to patterns of correspondence: the very identities of correspondents as well as geographical and chronological patterns of an individual's letter-writing.

The editor will also, of course, check indexed and unindexed back runs of periodicals likely to furnish articles bearing on the subject of his project. Special attention should be given to those scholarly or antiquarian journals that customarily publish special sections of printed documents or routinely publish portions of the collections of a historical society or other special library. Journals that consistently publish articles and documents related to the editor's subject are excellent candidates for notices of the inauguration of the editorial project. Unfortunately, editors of scholarly journals have recently adopted stricter policies on accepting such advertisements. Some may refuse to print any such announcements, while others may demand a fee. Still, every attempt should be made to advertise the project as early as possible in such journals, as well as in newspapers like the *New York Times* and the *Washington Post*, which boast a nationwide audience, and in newspapers whose readers live in regions where the project's subject flourished.

A. DEFINING THE SCOPE OF THE SEARCH

The editor's preliminary files will indicate the names of the individuals and organizations whose papers are likely to contain materials for the project, as well as those collections sure to contain material for his edition. He must now compile lists of the repositories that are certain—or merely possible—sources for the new editorial archive that his project will create.

1. Manuscripts

For American manuscript material, four reference series offer the best guides for the editor's outline of his search for documents. Each of these has special limitations and individual virtues, and the editor must use all of them. The following summaries of the formats and scope of this quartet may prove useful:

(1.) The *Hamer Guide*, Philip M. Hamer's *A Guide to Archives and Manuscripts in the United States* (Washington, D.C., 1961), appeared as part of the NHPC program of which Hamer was executive director. It lists 1,300 repositories, giving the address and telephone number for each. Descriptive entries for each source vary, depending upon the information supplied by the repositories and upon existing catalogs of their collections. However, the entries are usually generous enough to make clear the major focus of each archive and to list its major collections by name. When printed catalogs for a repository or one of its collections exist, these are noted.

(2.) *NUCMC*, the *National Union Catalog of Manuscript Collections*, has been published periodically by the Library of Congress since 1962. The volumes contain reduced photoreproductions of the cards prepared by the library for its union catalog of American manuscript collections. These cards are based upon data furnished by each manuscript repository, and their thoroughness and accuracy vary greatly. The entries are arranged in the order of their accession by the library's staff, but the indexes to each volume and the periodic cumulative indexes to the series enable the determined reader to locate entries that contain information on specific persons, groups, or topics, as well as to pinpoint collections reported by a given repository.

(3.) *American Literary Manuscripts* is the familiar name for J. Albert Robbins's *American Literary Manuscripts: A Checklist of Holdings in Academic, Historical, and Public Libraries, Museums, and Authors' Homes in the United States*, 2d ed. (Athens, Ga., 1977). This guide reports the holdings of only 600 repositories, but these are described in great detail. The entries are based on canvasses of the holdings of manuscripts written by 2,750 men and women deemed of special significance in the history of American literature. The entry for each such individual includes Library of Congress codes for each institution whose holdings include his or her manuscripts, for the size of these collections, and for any finding aids that may exist.

(4.) The *NHPRC Directory* is the commission's *Directory of Archives and Manuscript Repositories in the United States* (Washington, D.C., 1978). Although it covers more repositories than any of the others (2,675 in all), its descriptions of individual collections are spare. The entry for each library or archive offers the institution's address and telephone number as well as information on policies for access and photocopying and a very general description of the focus of these collections. The *Directory* cites manuscript catalogs and calendars published since the appearance of the *Hamer Guide*, but it does not repeat information given in that earlier commission publication. However, the entries in the *Directory* give generous cross references to fuller descriptions of institutional holdings that may appear in the *Hamer Guide*, *NUCMC*, *American Literary Manuscripts*, and other printed sources.

Few significant American figures confined their correspondence or their professional activities to the United States, and their heirs did not confine their sales of family papers to American collectors. Thus editors must be equally cosmopolitan in searching for their surviving papers. The best guide to published catalogs and other finding aids for materials in foreign repositories is the excellent section on "Foreign Archives of Interest to American Historians" in the *Harvard Guide to American History*, rev. ed. (Cambridge,

Mass., 1974), 100–107. Perhaps because this is such an obvious source, too many editors have neglected it in planning their collection of materials. It remains the most logical and comprehensive survey of such literature, although it is now a decade out of date. To supplement the *Harvard Guide*, editors should consult recent issues of the *American Archivist* and *Writings in American History*.

2. Printed Documents

Most individuals significant enough to warrant an edition of their letters, journals, or other papers have written works for publication, which editors must also collect and evaluate. At this early stage, the editor can confine himself to the basic methods and terminology of *enumerative* and *descriptive* bibliography. *Enumerative bibliography* deals with the preparation of reliable and comprehensive listings of printed works and their various editions. Obviously, the editor of the papers of any public figure or organization must compile such a bibliography of the printed works produced by that author or group. The editor's preliminary inventory of "known" writings will allow him to compile a skeletal enumerative bibliography. To expand it, he must consult a wide variety of reference works and published catalogs that apply to the period and the field in which his subject was prominent. For the eighteenth century, as an example, scholars must consult Charles Evans's *American Bibliography: A Chronological Dictionary of All Books, Pamphlets and Periodical Publications Printed in the United States of America from the Genesis of Printing in 1639 down to and Including the Year 1820*, 13 vols. (Chicago, 1903–34; Worcester, Mass., 1955), which serves as a chronological dictionary of imprints through 1800, as well as Roger P. Bristol's *Supplement to Charles Evans' American Bibliography* (Charlottesville, 1970). Students of American bibliography of the early nineteenth century must refer to the series familiarly called Shaw-Shoemaker, namely, *American Bibliography: A Preliminary Checklist for 1801–1819*, compiled by Ralph R. Shaw and Richard H. Shoemaker, 19 vols. (New York, 1958–63), which has been continued as *A Checklist of American Imprints* for the 1820s and 1830s as compiled by Shoemaker and other scholars. The most convenient source for guidance to such reference tools is G. Thomas Tanselle's *Guide to the Study of United States Imprints*, 2 vols. (Cambridge, Mass., 1971).

Bibliography for the editor does not stop with an enumerative listing. Catalogs of rare books and pamphlets employ the vocabulary of *descriptive bibliography*, which pinpoints the physical differences among various editions, *impressions*, *states*, or *issues* of the same work. The editor must master this terminology so that he can determine whether he has located all the pertinent variants for such printed documents. The standard works in this field, such as Fredson Bowers, *Principles of Bibliographical Description* (Princeton, 1949), and Philip Gaskell, *A New Introduction to Bibliography* (New York, 1972), can intimidate the novice, who may wish to introduce himself to the field by first reading Terry Belanger's helpful essay, "Descriptive Bibliography," in *Book Collecting*, Jean Peters, ed. (New York, 1977), 97–115.

Planning a search of periodical literature is exceptionally challenging. While most magazines publish a cumulative index—or at least a table of content—newspapers represent a greater problem. For an author's contributions to newspapers, earlier biographies and the writer's own correspondence may offer clues to the editor for his search for pertinent issues. The editor whose study focuses on the pre-1820 period has the great advantage of access to Clarence Brigham's *History and Bibliography of American Newspapers, 1690–1820*, 2 vols. (Worcester, Mass., 1947), plus his *Additions and Corrections* published in 1961. Unfortunately, there is no comparable guide for the later period. The *Harvard Guide* and pertinent sections in Tanselle's *U.S. Imprints* offer the best discussions of finding aids. In some regions, surviving WPA guides supplement these sources, and checklists of newspapers in microform will allow the editor to identify those periodicals that can be obtained in microfilm or microfiche on interlibrary loan.

No two editors will be able to follow the same line of attack, but all have found it useful to consult colleagues who have completed a search similar to the one they project. The editors of the *Frederick Douglass Papers*, for instance, had to reconstruct the runs of antebellum newspapers that Douglass edited and published, and they first sent letters of inquiry to all American historical societies, as well as to colleges founded before 1860. Appeals went to dealers as well, and at the same time the editors communicated with all public libraries founded before 1860 in states where most of the newspapers' subscribers had lived, as well as to all libraries and historical societies in the United Kingdom and Jamaica. This mail canvass located 60 percent of the missing issues, and the editors then sent out a new mailing that covered all American libraries in states where subscribers had lived.

Few editors will be able to afford the kind of search required of the Douglass editors, but their methods furnish good guidelines. In searching for printed documents, as for manuscripts, the law of diminishing returns applies. The editor should first make contact with the repositories most likely to have the materials that he needs. Only after these returns have come can the editor decide whether the first canvass was fruitful enough to justify a second and wider appeal.

3. *Dealers and Collectors*

Unless an editor chooses as his subject a recently deceased and obscure figure, he is probably not the first to show an interest in collecting documents relating to his subject. Tracing the course of materials that have passed into the hands of dealers in rare books and manuscripts is one of the most time-consuming and frustrating tasks an editor must confront. The editor should gauge carefully the time that he allots to searching for the records of such transactions, and he must accept the fact that he will never unravel every mystery concerning such sales. In the words of one experienced editor, "You do the best you can with the time and money available."

Perhaps the most valuable lesson that an editor can learn in this area is how to sense when to call a halt to his detective work, for such a search can be disappointing and unrewarding. Even a project with an unlimited budget and an open-ended schedule cannot hope to locate every copy of every dealer's catalog, nor will it be able to establish contact with every purchaser of such documents. Careful planning is essential so that the editor makes the best possible use of the weeks or months allotted to this aspect of the research.

Records of sales of documents fall into two categories: auction catalogs and dealers' listings. Catalogs list only items to be offered for sale to bidders at public auctions. Generally such catalogs receive a wider distribution than the periodic issues of listings prepared by individual dealers and circulated among special libraries and the dealers' longtime customers. These listings generally quote the prices asked for individual items, and sales are concluded by mail or telephone contact between the purchaser and the dealer.

The wider circulation of auction catalogs ensures that they are more likely to survive and to be available to editors. Consulting such catalogs is simplified by the existence of the yearly volumes of *American Book-Prices Current (ABPC)*, which since 1895 has provided an indexed, comprehensive listing of manuscripts and rare books sold at auction in the United States. Volumes after 1956 also cover materials sold at London auction houses. Cumulative indexes to back issues of the *ABPC* simplify the editor's work in recovering listings of the sales of materials central to his project.

The *ABPC* is only a starting point for the editor. Its descriptions of items do not always reproduce completely the information offered in the original auction catalogs. The *ABPC*'s format does not, for instance, permit the reproduction of photographic facsimiles that may have accompanied the original auction listing. Using its references, the editor should obtain the auction catalogs from which the *ABPC*'s notices are drawn. Here George L. McKay's *American Book Auction Catalogues, 1713–1934: A Union List* (New York, 1938) is an invaluable finding aid.

Although post-1956 *ABPC* listings include London auction sales, the editor whose subject maintained a considerable correspondence abroad or whose papers are popular among European collectors must weigh the need for a search of foreign dealers' records. Unfortunately, the autograph and rare book trades of the Continent have not felt the need to create regular national listings comparable to the *ABPC* or the British *Book-Prices Current* and *Book Auction Prices* series. (A notable exception is the German *Jahrbuch der Auktionpreise*.) Some American auction houses maintain in-house files of European catalogs, and the Grolier Club of New York City and the British Library in London boast generous holdings of these records. Before venturing outside the records of the American market, the editor should consult a dealer who specializes in manuscripts and books relating to the project's focus. Expert advice can save the editor months of wasted effort, particularly if the advice is, "Don't bother. It won't be worth your trouble."

Dealers' listings, because of their irregular publication and limited circulation, suffer a higher mortality rate than do auction catalogs. If the editor can identify dealers who have consistently specialized in materials of interest to his work, he may be able to gain access to their back files of lists and offerings. Failing that, there are several other choices. Any repository with a large collection of the papers or writings of a prominent figure will be on the mailing lists of dealers who frequently offer these materials for sale. Such a library customarily keeps these circulars on file, and they are available to scholars. Similarly, an individual collector with an interest in the editor's subject will have shared a place on those same mailing lists. If such a collector can be enlisted in the project's campaign, he may be able to provide such listings. Libraries like the one at the Grolier Club also boast files of such publications.

The editor whose manuscript materials fall in the period 1763–1815 has a great advantage: Helen Cripe and Diane Campbell's *American Manuscripts, 1763–1815: An Index to Documents Described in Auction Records and Dealers' Catalogs* (Wilmington, Del., 1977). This monumental work indexes entries in auction catalogs before 1895 (the year of the inauguration of the *ABPC*) as well as dealers' listings through 1970. Entries are indexed by date, name of correspondent, or author, and name of dealer. Even editors whose projects fall outside the 1763–1815 period must consult *American Manuscripts*. Part 3 of the massive volume provides the only extant published inventory of dealers' listings (with repositories owning these items), and its surveys of periodicals in the autograph- and book-collecting trades are invaluable. Like the *ABPC*, *American Manuscripts* is only a starting point. The editor will find only the dates and titles of manuscript materials. The bibliographical information offered in the volumes permits him to locate the rare and scattered copies of dealers' lists and catalogs where the full descriptive entries appear.

As he plans his search, the editor will file and index copies of notices from auction catalogs and dealers' listings, just as he has done with earlier printed versions of documents. These records can reveal patterns of correspondence of which earlier researchers were completely unaware, and they will ensure that the project pursues all fruitful leads in consulting guides to manuscript repositories and in making on-site searches of collections. Once the search is completed, the editor will often find that these listings are the only surviving evidence that X wrote to Y on a given day. And notices that offer précis, lengthy extracts, or photographic facsimiles of these "lost" documents will be an important addition to his files.

B. COLLECTING PHOTOCOPIES: THE MAIL CANVASS

Depending on the project's scope, weeks or months may pass before the editor completes the preliminary inventories of primary and secondary sources that will allow him to plan his search for source materials. When his notes are arranged properly, they will reveal the patterns of repositories that require investigation. After consulting his budget and his timetable, the editor can then begin the process of locating the original materials and, where appropriate, of obtaining photocopies for the project's archives. It will be apparent that some institutions contain so much material that only a personal visit from the editor or his deputies will ensure a complete search. However, a good part of an editor's search will probably be conducted by mail.

The scope of that mail canvass will be dictated by several factors: the era in which the project's figure lived; the nature of the subject's prominence; and the history and geographical distribution of the personal or organizational records involved. At one end of the spectrum are the papers of men or women who (1) maintained meticulous files of their own papers, (2) spent a relatively obscure life unlikely to make their manuscripts attractive to autograph dealers, and (3) died within the previous decade, before their fame could spread and their papers could be dispersed. Here the editor can assume that his figure's personal archive represents copies of all or nearly all the materials to be located and that there has not been time or reason for recipients' copies of letters to be scattered or destroyed. The search can be confined largely to the subject's correspondents (or their heirs) and to the files of the businesses, educational institutions, or government agencies where that figure performed his or her professional work.

There is a correspondingly greater challenge for the editor of the papers of a more conventionally "famous" individual whose personal papers have been dispersed in the decades or centuries after his or her death. In such a case, the editor may find that he cannot confine his contacts only to repositories where there are known to be collections of papers likely to produce materials for his project. He must also conduct a *blind search*, one that extends to institutions where there is no reason to suspect that such documents survive. Editors must observe the law of diminishing returns in conducting such canvasses. Letters of inquiry should go first to libraries known to own materials of interest to the project. Here the editor knows that photocopies must be made, bills must be paid, and questions must be answered. Obviously it makes sense to begin this chain of correspondence as soon as possible.

The form letter for the blind search will be the basis for the entire mail canvass. (A sample of such letters appears in the Appendix.) It should include (1) a description of the project's scope and an indication of its scholarly credentials in terms of sponsorship or endorsement, (2) a clear statement of the types of materials needed by the project, and (3) an indication of the editor's businesslike attitude toward library procedures. When the form letter is modified for an institution where materials are known to exist, the editor should not only list the materials in question but also provide the sources that led him to believe that these documents are part of the repository's collections. In such cases, he should always make it clear that his interest is not confined to the list offered, since additional acquisitions or improved cataloging may have enlarged the list of the repository's holdings.

The reasons for these elements in a project's appeals by mail are self-evident. A letter from an editorial project is only one of dozens of time-consuming inquiries that a librarian or curator will receive each week. That letter must convince its recipient that the project is recognized as a worthwhile scholarly endeavor whose request merits the time and trouble it will demand. A specific description of the materials needed will spare the curator unnecessary work and will ensure that the editor receives all the information and documents that he needs from an individual repository. A list of known materials will assist the librarian in locating items in the same collections that may not be cataloged. A statement of the editor's realistic attitude toward library procedures will assure his correspondent that the letter comes from an experienced professional, not an inexperienced or amateur researcher.

The mail canvass can be eased considerably by the use of a word processor or similar equipment. The word processor was originally designed for business offices, where such form letters are routinely required. For blind search letters, the machine can be instructed to reproduce the body of the letter as many times as necessary, with the operator making the necessary changes in the inside address and dateline. For those libraries where there is known to be material for the project, the operator simply adds a paragraph listing specific items. The editor will then need to proofread only those sections of each letter that are unique to it, not the paragraphs and sentences that have been placed in the word processor's memory.

As noted above, the editor should first dispatch letters to institutions that are certain to possess materials essential to the edition. If foreign repositories appear in this list, then letters to their librarians or curators should precede those to domestic institutions. The rule of thumb for the mail canvass is to establish contact first with institutions that may require more time to answer the editor's request. Clearly it will take longer to obtain photocopies from abroad than to obtain them from a neighboring state. And it will take longer for librarians at institutions that have a dozen manuscripts to locate and photocopy those items than it will for librarians whose collections contain no pertinent manuscripts to respond to a blind search letter with a polite note indicating that their institution cannot be of help.

The scope of the blind search will depend not only upon the project's budget and schedule but also upon the prominence of the figure or organization central to the project's work. For an exceptionally celebrated figure, that search may have to extend to every institution listed in the current edition of the *American Library Directory* that admits to having a manuscript or special collections division, as well as to all historical societies in the United States. For less well-known subjects, the editor can confine his blind search to institutions whose focus of collections (as described in the *Hamer Guide* or the *NHPRC Directory*) or geographical location makes it likely that their holdings will include items of interest to the project. In general, it is better to cast the collecting net too widely than too narrowly. Veterans of one decade-long search remind us, "A vacuum cleaner is more efficient than a broom and a dustpan."

C. ON-SITE SEARCHES

The editor's preliminary research will give him a list of repositories whose holdings require a personal search. Responses to the project's mail canvass will often reveal that the resources of another institution are so limited that even a search for a half-dozen known items cannot be done by the library's staff. The wise editor will first turn for advice to other scholars who have visited the institution in question, relying on the personal experience of veterans of a given library's procedures.

Beyond this, no personal search should be undertaken without first confirming that such a visit will be convenient for the institution and its staff. Budgetary considerations, local holidays, and even the opening of a new exhibition can force a library to modify its days or hours on a permanent or temporary basis. Some of the collections to be consulted may be temporarily unavailable or housed in a separate facility with access limited to those who have made appointments in advance. Aside from such practical considerations, the editor must remember that his search will place far greater demands upon a library than the appearance of more conventional scholars. The editor who arrives unannounced to canvass three dozen collections at a historical society will receive the cold welcome that he deserves.

The effective editor appears promptly and as well-prepared as possible, and upon his arrival, he asks whether the library has unpublished finding aids to the collections to be consulted. (He will, of course, already have studied any published finding tools.) He should never assume that he understands the workings of one institution's card catalog merely because he has already consulted those in other libraries. Direct questions about any peculiarities in filing methods will spare unnecessary anguish and ensure that the editor finds everything that there is to find. The definition of a cataloged or an indexed manuscript collection, for instance, can differ from one repository to another. Some archivists may consider a group of manuscripts to be completely indexed if there is a file of catalog cards that indexes alphabetically the *authors* of pieces in the collection. When this proves to be the case, the editor must have at hand an alphabetically arranged enumeration of his subject's most constant correspondents. Working from this list, he will consult index files, alphabetically arranged "miscellaneous" folders, and collections of autographs for letters written by these men and women to or about the subject of his project.

Since most editors conduct their searches with a view to placing orders for *hard* photocopies (Xeroxes or other paper prints) or microfilm, these special considerations must be kept in mind during the on-site search. Before beginning work, the editor should ask the curator of a collection if there is a preferred method of marking or flagging items for photocopying. If the appropriate marker, usually a piece of labeled acid-free paper, can be placed immediately with the appropriate document, the original materials will be spared unnecessary handling, and the editor will not have to go back through the collections to insert these markers.

A running list of such materials must be kept whether or not markers are placed. This list should indicate each item's description and its precise location. The description in this list should record pertinent information about the document's physical appearance, indicating whether it is an original or a photocopy, a recipient's copy or a draft of a letter, a *fair copy*, or a preliminary version of an author's work. It should also indicate the number of pages and details such as address leaves or endorsements. This list will serve as the basis of the photocopy order itself, and it will allow the editor to check the completed order. And since it may be necessary to consult the original manuscript or printed materials again, the detailed list will make it easy to retrieve the items a second or third time.

If the editor has special requirements for photocopies, he should explain these to the staff of the library or archive before placing his order. Many projects seek negative microfilms that can conveniently produce positive paper prints for their files, while many libraries prefer to keep the negative of any microfilm made from their collections as a *security* or *record* copy. In such a case, the library may be willing to furnish the editor with a *direct-image* duplicate negative. If the library's laboratory facilities do not permit such processing, the editor must be sure that the positive film he receives will meet the requirements of the outside laboratory that will make the necessary conversion. Should the project plan a comprehensive microform edition as a supplement to its printed volumes, the reduction ratio in any films made for the project should be roughly the same. Most microfilm cameras can be adjusted to a range of reduction ratios, but instructions for a special reduction must be given in advance. The editor with a microform edition in mind should also attempt to obtain as many of his project's hard copy prints as possible in positive rather than negative hard copy form, ⸺ since these will reproduce more clearly in the next generation of photoduplication.

The editor must accept as immutable law any special policies a library may have for photoreproduction. Generally there are good and sufficient reasons for rules of this kind. If a library demands that it retain a negative of microfilms, it is only because of concern for security of the original materials. Libraries that demand the eventual return of any photocopies of their materials do so only because researchers have donated such photocopies to other research centers without the permission of the owner-institution. Restrictions on Xeroxing bound volumes and fragile manuscripts exist for the protection of these source materials. Curators of rare material are usually only too happy to explain the reasons for these and other rules.

D. A WORD ON RESEARCH ETIQUETTE

Curators of rare materials respond favorably to kind and courteous treatment as well as to intelligent questions. The librarian who answers a blind search letter deserves a personal note of thanks. The curator who provides photocopies by mail or who extends hospitality to on-site searches deserves even more praise and gratitude. The editor who makes himself memorable for his good manners will be kept in mind when any institution acquires a new collection or catalogs an existing one and discovers unsuspected riches for the editor's project. A long-term project may have to conduct several canvasses. If the editor needs to visit any such libraries in the future, he will need a warm welcome and the staff's full cooperation, not a cold shoulder and the brusque dismissal, "If it's not in the card catalog, we don't have it." Should the project need to hire searchers on a free-lance basis to canvass distant collections, these deputies should be drilled in the project's practical requirements and in the standards of proper scholarly behavior.

An even greater degree of diplomacy must be exercised by the editor who hopes to establish a working relationship with autograph dealers and collectors. The prudent editor exploits the results of his canvass of sale records for manuscripts and printed materials beyond planning his search and supplementing his files of documents. In reviewing the records of these transactions, he may see that a small number of dealers specialize in the subject of his research. At the least he can ensure that he is put on these dealers' mailing lists for future offerings. If lucky, he will find among these dealers a friend to advise him and to offer introductions to private collectors and to other dealers who will lead the editor to more original materials.

If the project's subject has been a popular one for collectors, it will pay the editor to pursue this tactic. He may even find a dealer or auction house willing to open its old records so that he can consult inventories of collections sold decades ago for which there is no published listing of their contents. Dealers may even be willing to disclose the identities of institutional purchasers (though not of private buyers) of specific items. In some cases, the editor may find it worthwhile to consult books about patterns of collecting in his field. Working from published catalogs of auctions and from dealers' listings, he may be able to guess which collectors (or their agents) were likely to have purchased certain items. He can then begin discreet and tactful approaches to those collectors or their heirs.

Rare book and autograph collectors frequently choose not to advertise the existence, much less the extent or nature, of their collections because (*a*) they have no wish to be troubled by inquiries from hordes of scholars and (*b*) they are well aware that their collections can be the targets of theft. Dealers who wish to stay in business are conscious of their clients' concern for privacy. A dealer promises confidentiality to those individuals who purchase rare materials, and he will not and should not violate that promise to assist any editor. When an individual collector shares the contents of his collection with an editorial project, his wishes must be honored to the letter. Should he direct that his name not be given as the owner of any documents used in the edition, then the source line for these texts should read "in a private collection." If there is public access to project files, correspondence with private collectors should be kept in a section of the office where security can be assured.

Some collectors and dealers voice concern that print publication of the text of a manuscript will lessen its market value. The editor can often persuade them otherwise by pointing to what Katharine Kyes Leab calls the "imprimatur value" that the original material receives by being chosen as the source for all or part of a definitive edition. Happily, there is one group of collectors unlikely to be concerned about devaluing their collections by authorizing publication: specialists in the collection of stamps and other materials relating to postal history. Frequently the items purchased because of their philatelic interest (envelopes and address leaves) are accompanied by the letter covered by that significantly franked or postmarked material. Not only is the postal collector more willing than the autograph specialist to share his collection with the editor but he is also a potentially valuable consultant to the project. His expertise in the mechanics of the transmittal of correspondence can save an editor countless errors in dating materials and in assessing the significance of details of postal markings.

Journals directed to collectors will, of course, carry notices announcing the project's creation, but the editor need not content himself with waiting for responses to these advertisements before establishing contact with dealers. During the project's life, his staff must review current auction catalogs and dealers' listings for items of interest to the edition. When such notices appear for an auction house in the vicinity of the edition's offices or in the neighborhood of a friendly editorial colleague, a member of the staff or other deputy can usually view the document while it is on public display before the auction. Although dealers frown on the use of cameras during these viewing periods, few object to an editor's taking notes or even discreetly making a handwritten transcript of the letter.

Even if the editor is able to obtain a transcript of a manuscript being offered for sale, he will prefer to have a photocopy of the original for his files. When it is impossible to have such a transcription made, it is essential that the editor make every effort to persuade the manuscript's purchaser to make such a copy available. No responsible dealer will disclose this information to an editor. A pair of form letters must be prepared to meet this exigency: one letter addressed to the dealer and the second directed "to whom it may concern" and accompanied by a stamped, self-addressed envelope, to be forwarded to the item's purchaser. (Samples of such letters appear in the Appendix.)

If a collector fails to respond to such appeals, the editor should not curse him for insensitivity. Collectors of manuscripts of recent date are a sophisticated lot who understand the niceties of copyright law. Although they can claim physical ownership of the inscribed paper of interest to the editor, they hold no literary rights to the text embodied in that document. In these cases, a responsible collector cannot and should not authorize further dissemination of the document without the permission of the author or the author's heirs or any others with copyright claims.

II. Cataloging and Control

Even while the search continues, photocopied documents arrive on the doorstep of the collecting editor. He must master the art of cataloging and the control of documents, and he must, again, plan his methods well in advance. The most comprehensive search is wasted if the editor and his staff are unable to retrieve individual items or groups of items that they have collected.

The editorial staff should also guard against wasting precious time by cataloging documents that are not of interest to the project's scope or by miscataloging pertinent items. The process of authenticating documents by handwriting, signatures, and literary style begins now. To these methods of identification the editor must add his sense of logic and historical context to assign dates and authors to undated or unsigned materials. Lester Cappon reminded editors, "Authenticity of the document is the cardinal rule, axiomatic by the very nature of historical method" ("A Rationale for Historical Editing Past and Present," 57); it is never too early for an editor to begin applying this rule to his burgeoning collection.

In comparatively rare cases, the editor will be not only the publisher of printed texts of original source materials but also the temporary curator of these documents during the project's life. Some large-scale documentary projects, such as the Adams Papers at the Massachusetts Historical Society and the Benjamin Franklin Papers at Yale, have files that include both photocopies gathered throughout the world and original manuscript collections at their sponsoring institutions. However, it is more likely that the editor will serve as a manuscript or rare book curator when his edition is an *archival* one, that is, an edition limited to a specific group of manuscripts or printed works owned by the institution that sponsors his project.

If the editor is not an archivist or rare books librarian by training, he must learn the rudiments of these professions so that the unique materials entrusted to his care do not suffer. Even the editor who does not have this responsibility is wise to learn the tricks of these trades, for the knowledge will serve him in understanding the methods of the repositories that he will search and in devising a system of cataloging the new editorial archives created by his research.

Should an original collection be completely uncataloged before it is assigned to an editor, he should consult the curator of the institution's other holdings to make certain that the methods he employs for arranging the editorial collection will be compatible with those used for other materials at the repository. Such consultation will ensure that the project uses document boxes and folders of both the proper dimensions and the proper quality for the protection of the original documents. For planning the arrangement and description of these materials the best introductory guide is David B. Gracy II's *Archives and Manuscripts: Arrangement and Description* (Chicago, 1977), part of the Society of American Archivists' Basic Manual series.

A. ACCESSIONING MATERIALS

Any project that is likely to deal with variant versions of the same documents from several sources must devise a system for identifying the source of each copy or original. The simplest and most straightforward method is to assign each an identifying number (usually called the accession number) that indicates the order in which the document or its copy is added to the project's files. Projects that need to maintain separate files for discrete groups of materials can use two or more sequential series. One series may contain the number 01, 02, 03, and so on; the second can begin with 001, 002, 003; and the third, with 0001, 0002, 0003.

For photocopies, these accession numbers can be stamped or written by hand on the back of the reproduction. If a document is represented by more than one page of photocopy, sequential page numbers are a convenience, and the leaves of the copy might be labeled 017.1, 017.2, and so on. Of course, no such stamps or written numbers should be imposed on original materials; identifying numbers on their individual folders must suffice. Should the project's collection include such materials as letterbooks or ledgers containing dozens of items of varying dates and titles, it is usually preferable to assign the same accession number to the entire volume and to file the photocopied leaves together rather than to separate individual items. The chronological and alphabetical sections of the project's control files will furnish access to individual entries, and the integrity of the original will be preserved.

The staff member responsible for accessioning materials must also check photocopies for completeness. If the copies result from an on-site search, the searcher's descriptive list is the basis for comparison. Should the copy have been received as the result of a mail canvass, the cataloger must check closely for possible omissions—margins cut off by careless photocopying or the absence of endorsement or address leaves whose existence can be deduced from *show-through* on another page of the copy. Any questions concerning such imperfections should be raised immediately in a letter to the curator of the original material.

B. LABELING AND ARRANGING FOLDERS

Once an item has been assigned its identifying number, a file folder can be prepared. The folder label should contain the following information: accession number, date, and a brief version of the document's title. This label should be placed where it can be seen easily when the editor flips through the shelved folders. Arrangement of this information on the label should reflect the organizing principles of the project's archive, and the arrangement must be consistent. Whatever element of information will determine the document's location in the file should appear at the top of the label. For collections focusing on correspondence, this will usually be the date. For collections of technical material that is to be arranged topically, a key word in the document title may be the cue for filing. When several items exist for the same date or topic, a system of subclassification may be necessary. For correspondence, the most convenient subheading will be the name of the correspondent who has sent a letter to or received a letter from the project's subject. For subclassifications within a topic, either the document's date or the name of its author may prove most useful.

The document title should be given as briefly as possible. It is usually wise to abbreviate the name of the project's subject in all records, and this begins with the folder labels. Thus, a letter from George Washington would be labeled "George Washington to H" in the Hamilton Papers archive, but it would bear the label "GW to Alexander Hamilton" at the Washington Papers project. If the folder contains a copy of a printed pamphlet, government report, or other published writing with a long and complicated title, it is not necessary to reproduce the complete title on the folder. Such bibliographical details are better recorded in the control file entries for the document.

Before the first document folder can be filed, the editor must establish guidelines for chronological arrangement of materials at the project. Most editors follow the principles of archivists and file undated material to which it is impossible to assign even a month or year at the very end of the collection's chronological series. However, there is less agreement on the arrangement of partially dated material and of documents that bear inclusive dates. Some projects file documents that bear only a fragmentary date, such as the year or the month of the year, at the end of the period recorded in that date. All materials dated simply 1771 would follow items dated 31 December 1771; all materials dated March 1771 would follow items dated 31 March 1771. Other projects adopt precisely the opposite course, placing partially dated materials at the beginning of the period into which they fall: here materials dated 1771 would precede those dated 1 January 1771. Whichever method the editor adopts, he must follow it scrupulously. The same general principle applies to documents with inclusive dates. Some projects file such items at the first date that appears: a ledger sheet with entries for 1 January 1771 through 2 March 1775 would be placed at the beginning of the year 1771. Others, of course, would file the item at the end of materials for 2 March 1775. The editor should choose the method that best serves his archive.

Even during the initial processing of materials, the staff will be able to supply some details of authorship and dating that do not appear on the document itself. When the cataloger, through comparison of handwriting, can identify as John Smith the correspondent who has signed himself "John," the full information should appear on the folder. And if the cataloger, through the use of a perpetual calendar or the application of common sense, can establish that a note dated "Wednesday, February 3" was written in 1808, then the full date should find a place on the folder.

C. CONTROL FILES

Access to these folders depends on a consistent and clear indexing system. This is furnished by the project's control files, which are of special importance to the collecting project. Any editor who has imposed order on thousands of sheets of hard copy and dozens of reels of microfilm from hundreds of sources can testify to the aptness of the term *control* for the means used to achieve mastery over an editorial archive.

In general, control files must give the editor ready access to at least four types of information:

1. The location of the original of each photocopy or the name of the collection that is the source of an original manuscript
2. A record of the photocopied materials furnished by each repository owning materials of interest to the project
3. A chronological list of cataloged materials
4. Some form of alphabetical index to the documents titles

In addition, some projects may be able to afford the luxury of subject indexes to the contents of the documents that they collect and catalog. Recent developments in such indexing procedures are discussed below.

In the earliest documentary projects, control files took the form of multiple copies of index slips typed for each item in the project's collection. This process is described in Lyman Butterfield's "The Papers of Thomas Jefferson: Progress and Procedures in the Enterprise at Princeton" (*American Archivist* 12 [1949]: 131–45). If manual methods are used, this means that after each photocopy or original has been given its accession number and safely placed in its labeled folder, a member of the staff must prepare entries for the control files.

Traditionally, entries are typed on self-carbon packs of slips or upon a group of slips between which pre-cut sheets of carbon paper have been sandwiched. Information needed for sorting the slips for insertion into the various files is typed near the top of the slip for easy visual reference. In its classic form, the model for such slips was the one devised by the Jefferson Papers project more than thirty years ago:

```
date      place      location symbol:   accession
                                        number

                      name of the collection in
                      which the original is located

document title

MS version of the original.  Additional details
of the original or the photocopy, such as number
of pages, lists of enclosures, or cross refer-
ences to related documents.
```

Today, of course, an increasing number of editorial projects use computer technology to prepare control files (see sec. E, below). With either manual or computerized methods, the editor may need to refine or expand the information provided in the control slip or the computer entry. For instance, when several letters to the same correspondent or several documents with similar titles bear the same date, it is wise to add to the control entry the first half-dozen words of the text of the document.

And even at this early stage of the project, the editor and his staff will begin a preliminary analysis of the materials they collect. An examination of the manuscripts and photocopies will allow them to assign dates to undated materials, to correct the dates on misdated items, and to determine the author of an unsigned letter or the intended recipient of one whose address has been lost. Whenever the editorial project is able to correct or supplement a document's date or title, the control file should contain a *dummy* slip under the date, author, or recipient that had been erroneously attributed to the item, as well as a slip for the accurate date or title. This will prevent confusion over just which items from a given repository have been cataloged, so that two orders are not placed for the photocopy of a manuscript that has been cataloged under a corrected date or description.

Document files and control files are closely related. The control slip will use the same abbreviation for the project's subject that appears on the file folders. If the control slip contains editorially supplied information, such as full names and complete dates that the cataloger was able to provide, such letters, words, or numerals should be enclosed in square brackets ([ ]) on the control slip just as they are on the document file folder.

Once the slips have been typed and checked for accuracy, they will be separated and interfiled in their appropriate places in the project's various control series. The degree of use that a file receives determines which of the multiple typed copies is placed there. For projects where documents and photocopies are arranged chronologically, the chronological control file is the *master*, and the ribbon copy of the typed set is reserved for this series, because it is likely to be consulted most frequently. The second slip (or group of slips, if there are two or more authors or recipients of a letter from the subject) is placed in an alphabetical control file, and additional copies of the slips may be reserved for files that give a record of accession numbers and of the contributions of various repositories.

D. ARRANGEMENT OF CONTROL SLIPS

The arrangement of the control slips must be coordinated with the arrangement of folders in the editorial archive. If letters of the same date are arranged alphabetically by the name of the sender or recipient, then the chronological slips must be arranged in the same order. If such letters are instead filed first by letters from the project's subject and then by letters to him, the same method must be used in the chronological control series. The alphabetical control file should also be planned in relation to the methods of arrangement for the editorial archive. If folders for the same date are arranged in one alphabetical series, then the slips for each correspondent should be arranged in a single chronological series. If folders of materials for the same date are subdivided between materials *to* and *from* the project's subject, then the alphabetical index slips for an individual should reflect this same method. And, of course, the methods adopted for arranging file folders that bear partial dates or inclusive dates must be followed in the control files as well. Using a single set of organizing principles for both folders and control slips means that members of the staff need memorize only one set of rules, not two or three.

Although the need for control by date and alphabetical cues is obvious, the other elements on the control slips require some explanation. Location symbols for American repositories that own the original materials are commonly based on the ones devised for the Library of Congress's *National Union Catalog*. This standardized system has the great advantage of avoiding possible duplication of symbols invented on the spot by the editor, and it is easily mastered by the editorial staff. The system consists of a code that contains two or three elements, each of which begins with a capital letter. The first element stands for the state of the union where the repository is located, the second represents the city or town, and the third stands for the repository itself. If this is the official repository of records for a state or city, then not all elements are used. Thus "N" stands for the State Library of New York at Albany, "NBu" represents the archives of the city of Buffalo, and "NBuHi" stands for the Buffalo and Erie County Historical Society. Should the project need to devise symbols for libraries not listed in the *National Union Catalog*, the same principle can be used for these institutions.

Projects whose limited funds or limited space rules out the creation of hard copy from microfilms must take special care in indicating location on their control records. The slips should carry not only the code for the owner-repository but also the full title and reel number of the film where the text of the original can be consulted by the editorial staff. If the film's frames are numbered, then these references should also appear on the control slip. Indeed, the editor whose archive will include a substantial number of filmed reels should establish a separate system of control for these spools. Each can be assigned an identifying number reflecting the order of the film's acquisition by the project, and this can be included in the location information on control slips. If this is cumbersome, the films themselves should be arranged in rational and consistent order that will make their retrieval easy: this might involve shelving the reels in the order of the Library of Congress location symbols for the sources of the films' contents.

The location symbol is followed immediately by the accession number. Additional information on the specific location of the original is usually placed below the location-accession entry. If it is necessary to give more detail than the name of an individual collection, such information can be typed further down on the slip, along with remarks concerning the physical appearance of the original. Commonly, a project will use the same symbols for manuscript versions of original materials ("ALS" for "autograph letter signed," and so on) in the control files as will be employed in the printed edition. Again, this reduces the number of abbreviations and codes that the staff must master.

Control over accession numbers and lists of repositories' contributions to the project need not be part of a card file. Pages in a loose-leaf binder for each owner-repository can carry lists of the accession numbers assigned to that institution's cataloged holdings. Sequential records of the accession numbers themselves could be entered in the same form, but it is just as convenient, and far less time-consuming, to save the last copy of the typed control slip for an accession control file. As soon as each item has been cataloged, the accession slip is simply added to those already in the accession drawer, with no need for interfiling.

E. COMPUTERIZATION AND CONTROL FILES

The disadvantages of manually created control files are obvious. The correction of typographical errors on multiple carbon copies is time-consuming and unsatisfactory. The hours spent in filing and interfiling such slips are a drain on the project's time and energies. And only one set of each control series results: drawer upon drawer of easily misfiled slips that cannot be removed from the project's office for the use of on-site searchers or of interested scholars who have questions about specific groups of holdings. The designers of the traditional control file system were the first to welcome computerized methods—only veterans of this agonizing manual process can fully appreciate the benefits of more modern systems techniques. Since the mid-1960s editors have experimented with the use of computers in the creation of control files. Today, of course, more and more editorial projects have access to a mainframe computer or a word processor sufficiently "smart" to aid in control. For these projects, the final version of the control file can be computer print-out sheets, not drawers of slips or cards laboriously typed and filed by hand.

Even for the project with computer capability, the process of maintaining control remains the same in principle; only the methods of entering and sorting the data and the form of the file itself have changed. Documents must still be assigned identifying numbers, and individual folders with appropriate labels must be prepared. However, instead of typing multiple copies of slips containing the information required by the control file, a staff member enters the data on the keyboard of a terminal or on a data information sheet that is later entered at the terminal. Instead of a carbon pack, one record is created for each document. Within that record, each element of the control system is entered in a designated position called a *field*. One field will carry the document's date, another its title; others will carry the accession number, the location, and the number of pages. Still another can be reserved for special comments such as the existence of enclosures. Once a record for each document has been created and stored in the computer system, the system can be instructed to arrange the information according to the demands of traditional control files: a chronological series, an alphabetical series, a series arranged by source-repository, and a series showing sequential accession numbers. Periodically, the editor can request sets of printouts that will provide complete and convenient records of any or all of these series, and the computer can provide as many of these copies as desired.

An early experiment with these methods has been described fully in "Computer Applications for Historical Editing Projects: The Joseph Henry Papers Index of Documents," an unpublished report by James H. Hobbins and Kathleen Waldenfels. At the Henry project, information was entered in coded form on standardized sheets whose contents were later keyboarded. The task of data entry and retrieval can be simplified by using pre-packaged computer programs like SASS and SPSS or the standard in-house *sort* packages that are part of the general software system of every computing system. In recent years, mainframe access through time-sharing or through telecommunications from stand-alone devices like word processors has made the use of coding sheets almost obsolete. With a stand-alone device, the control file is created by a member of the office staff, and the file is stored in the word processor's diskettes. When the control file needs to be sorted, it is moved to a mainframe that sorts the file and generates a printed index based on it.

Despite the pioneering work of the Henry editors and the new techniques available, comparatively few projects have adopted these methods. In large part this is because it is seldom wise to convert an existing manually prepared control file to computerized data. When thousands of documents have already been recorded on typed slips, and the editorial collection is all but complete, it may be impractical to incur the expense of conversion or to risk the introduction of error through new keyboarding for the computer.

The experience of some projects suggests that the resourceful editor can exploit electronic systems less elaborate than a full-scale mainframe unit. The editors of the Samuel Gompers Papers have devised a method using a word processor for control purposes, hitting upon this as a solution to the problem of creating a control file for a project that will eventually have direct telephonic communication with a mainframe computer. The method can also serve the needs of a small project that can never look forward to mainframe access. The word processor can be equipped with a printer that accommodates rolls of five-inch-wide paper perforated at three-inch intervals for separation into control slips. The operator enters the necessary information for each accessioned item, checks the entry for accuracy, and then instructs the machine to print the number of slips necessary for the several control elements. The word processor formats the information in the design of the control file and spaces multiple printings of the same information appropriately so that each slip has a complete control entry.

Word-processor diskettes provide a permanent memory for the accessioned items in the order of their cataloging. No additional accession file is necessary. Although the Gompers project's word processor was a comparatively "smart" one, it was not used to arrange the chronological and alphabetical entries represented in the control slips. These were still sorted and filed manually. However, in the near future, the Gompers project will be able to communicate the information stored on its diskettes to a central computer, and the data entered now can then be stored in a central data base along with later control entries. A small project with only a few thousand documents to be controlled and with a "smart" word processor may be able to handle all its control functions—the sorting and arrangement of data as well as their entry and storage—on the machine's diskettes. And a larger project with the prospect of mainframe computer access can use this method to ensure that cataloging of documents goes ahead until that access is established, creating a machine-readable set of files that can later be fed into the larger unit.

III. SPECIAL PROBLEMS OF COMPUTERIZED SYSTEMS

If the scale of the editorial archive makes some form of computerized control a necessity, the editor's planning must be even more meticulous than for a manual system. The correction of an inadequate computerized system will require rekeyboarding data and the use of expensive computer time for reentry and resorting. The degree of foresight needed for a computerized system is demonstrated by the methods used by the editors of the Edison Papers, described in their unpublished reports on "Word Processing and Computer Support for the Edison Papers." The project is both an archival and a collecting endeavor, for there are more than 3 million original documents at the Edison laboratories in Orange, New Jersey, to be cataloged along with a projected additional mass of 100,000 photocopied documents from other sources. To complicate the problem, the Orange, New Jersey, facility is not tied to the computer center of Rutgers University, which serves the main offices of the Edison project.

During the period in which control files are established, one group of Edison editors remains at the Orange laboratories, entering data for the cataloged manuscripts on standardized coding sheets. These are periodically taken to the project's office on the Rutgers campus, where the data are entered on the project's sophisticated word processor. Photocopied materials are, of course, cataloged on that word processor as they are received. From time to time, the records for both manuscripts and photocopies are communicated to the computer center, where a comprehensive data base of all Edison materials is created. Periodically, the computer provides the Edison offices with the necessary printouts of chronological and alphabetical listings of both originals and photocopies.

The editor should bear in mind that computerized facilities may create special problems in establishing control over his editorial archive. Manual control methods, although more time-consuming, have one great advantage over the use of a central computer: manually created and filed control data are immediately available to the editor in their most up-to-date form. Data stored in the central computer become available only when the editor issues orders for a complete sorting and arrangement of recently entered data and for sheets of printout that embody this new information along with earlier cataloged materials. Sorting the data and obtaining current printouts will naturally be more frequent during the early months of a project, when the collecting process is at its height. Clearly, the need for frequent reviews of such data is most acute when new accessions are being cataloged at the rate of hundreds of items a week rather than in later periods, when the project may catalog only two or three new documents a month and the cost of new printouts must be taken into consideration.

Further, while awaiting cumulative printouts, the editor needs to have on hand some current file that does not depend on the computer's schedule or mood—either the folders of cataloged documents themselves, arranged in chronological order, or the running record of accession numbers. The special nature of some projects may not allow the creation of a single master file of cataloged items. The best example of this is the project whose archive is reels of film rather than individual photocopies. For the editor with a filmed archive, an ever-ready and up-to-date control file, whether in file drawers or in computer printout, is essential so that individual items can be located among the dozens of reels of film that form the core of this kind of project.

Still, for most editors, the electronic recording of control information is not only quicker and cheaper than the manual creation of such files but, quite simply, better. The computer printouts of data will expand the codes for names, dates, and subjects to the full words and numerals they represent. Unlike carboned multiple slips, each printout is accurate and clean. The computer can produce special, selective printouts such as lists of all documents accessioned from a special collection at the given library (a boon for searchers) or lists of all known correspondence between the project's subject and an individual or group (a godsend to inquiring scholars outside the project). And these printouts will provide a complete control file, if such is needed, for every member of the project's staff.

A. SUBJECT INDEXES OF CATALOGED MATERIALS

The efficiency of computerized cataloging and the ease of entering subject entries and sorting the results of these classifications allow many more projects the luxury of creating rough subject indexes simultaneously with establishing the control file itself. Indeed, the editors of the Joseph Henry Papers were admittedly more dogged in their pursuit of a computerized system precisely *because* a subject index to their documentary collection was essential to their edition.

If a project is to experiment with subject indexing, still more planning is required. Not every topic or every proper name should be indexed; veterans in this field advise a firm limit to the number of subject entries that can be made for a given document. The computerized index will be only a rough one that will guide the staff in later editorial work, and it is foolish to waste valuable human and computer time on an overdetailed index. In the words of the Henry editors, "The object is not to produce a definitive index at this pre-editorial stage. The purpose is to establish a rough content control, in addition to traditional controls."

In cataloging, a staff member not only enters conventional control information such as date, document title, and details of provenance but also codes for references to themes and individuals whose importance warrants a place in the project's list of approved subject entries. Although the number of entries that can be made for a given document will depend on the design of the computer being used, no more than seven or eight of the fields should be reserved for subject entries. The codes employed are absolutely arbitrary: three-digit numbers suffice for subject entries; three-character sets of letters of the alphabet represent persons.

A *content control* system can be initiated during the cataloging process itself or later in the project, prior to the selection of materials for publication. The early scheduling of such an index provides a subject guide to the project's collection from its initial stages. It will slow the process of cataloging somewhat, but for an experienced cataloger working from a limited number of subject entries, it probably does not add more than a few minutes to cataloging even the longest document. Even this delay may be important for the project for which cataloging must proceed as quickly as possible. Such an occasion might arise when so little is known about the patterns of an individual's correspondence that it is imperative that materials be cataloged with the greatest haste so that planning of the search can progress. For most projects, however, a rough content control file can be created simultaneously with cataloging control if the catalogers are experienced and if the editor has provided them with an intelligent and workable system of subjects and codes.

B. A NOTE ON COMPUTERIZED CONTROL

The experience of the editors who have used computers for control purposes leads to the following conclusions:

1. It is unlikely that any documentary project can consider on-line entry of control data into a mainframe computer. This would be possible only if the project has no competitors for use of the central unit. Most projects will vie for seconds and minutes of computer time with other offices or agencies at the institution where they have a time-sharing arrangement. And, of course, no data can be entered when the central computer is *down*, a word that strikes

fear into the hearts of all parties to a system of shared time.

2. Ideally, the control data should be entered on a word processor or other stand-alone unit that can communicate this information periodically to a mainframe unit. This eliminates the introduction of error in keyboarding data from coding sheets, and it can also be less costly. Although the *connect* time used to enter data is comparatively cheap, it will be more economical to communicate those data in the seconds needed by a linkup between a word processor's diskettes and the central computer than in the hours needed to enter the coded data from sheets prepared by members of the editorial staff.

3. The editor must be careful to budget the processor time that he will use to sort and arrange the data that he enters in the computer's memory. This time is far more costly than that used for the mere entry of data, and most institutions with time-sharing arrangements for computer use charge higher rates during conventional business hours. The editor can usually instruct the computer center that serves his project to perform these processing functions in the evening hours, when costs are lowest. The schedule of the computer center and the efficiency of its printout facility will dictate the speed with which the project receives the information that it needs. All concerned should be prepared to wait for several days for complete printouts of the control files at times of year when the computer center is busiest.

4. Computerized control methods have become more attractive and efficient as the scope of a project's holdings and the sophisticated needs of its indexing increase. For only a few hundred documents, traditional manual methods will probably remain the most convenient and inexpensive. For a project of moderate size, a combination of word-processor entry of data and manual sorting may be best. But for massive projects, with hundreds of thousands of documents to be cataloged and with a need for a subject control of the documents' contents, a control file grounded on a data base stored in a mainframe computer is a necessity.

5. A project that plans a microform or other variety of nonprint supplement to a selective book edition has an added incentive to investigate computerized control methods. The data entered at the time that individual items are cataloged can serve as the basis of the indexes that will appear in the guide to such supplements if they are stored in the computer. When the time comes to prepare such a guide, special instructions can be given to the computer so that its printout will be in a format suitable to such a finding aid.

These guidelines are only a beginning. The new editor's best source for both caution and encouragement in creating control files, just as in planning his search, is the experience of other editors who have survived the ordeal. Although editors have seldom put their wisdom in this area on paper in the form of published monographs, they are willing to share their knowledge informally. There is no substitute for a personal visit to an old and established editorial firm where working control files can be examined. And both the NEH and the NHPRC can refer an editor to projects in his geographic neighborhood or his documentary specialty that have had experience in using either manual methods or computerized systems for purposes of control.

Suggested Readings

Most American editors have confined their writings on the technical problems of collection and control of sources to memoranda whose circulation is confined to the editorial office. The most exhaustive series of this kind is Lyman Butterfield's "Directives" for every aspect of the operations of the Adams Papers at the Massachusetts Historical Society. These are a model of the sort of planning and assignment of responsibility for which every project should aim. Many other projects have prepared less comprehensive descriptions of procedures, and these can be obtained by individual editors whose projects resemble the older undertaking in scope or focus. Helpful published materials are noted below.

I. The experiences of nineteenth-century editors in retrieving materials for their editions are recounted in Galen Broeker, "Jared Sparks, Robert Peel, and the State Papers Office," *American Quarterly* 13 (1961): 140–52; and William B. Hesseltine and Larry Gara, "The Archives of Pennsylvania: A Glimpse at an Editor's Problem," *Pennsylvania Magazine* 77 (1953): 328–31.

Essays that give some notion of the challenges facing the collector of American historical materials are Francis Berkeley, Jr., "History and the Problem of the Control of Manuscripts in the United States," *American Philosophical Society Proceedings* 98 (June 1954): 171–78; and Leonard Rapport, "Dumped from a Wharf into Casco Bay: The Historical Records Survey Revisited," *American Archivist* 37 (1974): 201–10. James E. O'Neill's "Copies of French Manuscripts for American History in the Library of Congress," *Journal of American History* 51 (December 1965): 674–91, adds some useful information to older, more comprehensive listings of these materials.

Although modern American editors have tended to write about their projects in anecdotal rather than technical terms, some of their essays in this area are very helpful in describing collection and control. Among the best are Whitfield Bell, "Franklin's Papers and *The Papers of Benjamin Franklin*," *Pennsylvania History* 22 (1955): 1–17; Leonard Labaree, "In Search of B Franklin," *William and Mary Quarterly* 16 (April 1959): 188–97; Howard C. Rice, "Jefferson in Europe," *Princeton University Library Chronicle* 12 (Autumn 1950): 19–35; Albert E. Van Dusen, "In Quest of That 'Arch Rebel' Jonathan Trumbull, Sr.," in Dunlap and Shelley, *Publication of American Historical Manuscripts*, 31–46; and Ralph L. Ketcham, "The Madison Family Papers: Case Study in a Search for Historical Manuscripts," *Manuscripts* 11 (Summer 1959): 49–55.

Special problems in provenance and bibliography that confront scholars at these projects are discussed in Paul G. Sifton, "The Provenance of the Thomas Jefferson Papers," *American Archivist* 40 (1977): 17–30; Kate Stewart, "James Madison as an Archivist," ibid. 21 (1958): 243–57; and Edwin Wolf II, "The Reconstruction of Benjamin Franklin's Library: An Unorthodox Jigsaw Puzzle," *Papers of the Bibliographical Society of America* 56 (1962): 1–16. Although it does not concern a modern editorial project, Thomas C. Reeve's "The Search for the Chester Alan Arthur Papers," *Manuscripts* 25 (Summer 1973): 171–85, is a valuable description of a related challenge.

The best description of the spirit and tenacity required of a searching editor is the collection of letters printed in *Butterfield in Holland: A Record of L. H. Butterfield's Pursuit of the Adamses Abroad in 1959* (Cambridge, 1961). Review essays that point to the unfortunate effects of an inadequate editorial search include George A. Billias's critique of the *Naval Documents* volumes in *American Historical Review* 73 (October 1967): 216–17, and T. Harry Williams's study of the *Collected Works of Abraham Lincoln* in the *Mississippi Valley Historical Review* 40 (June 1953): 89–100.

The editor who must introduce himself to the different phases of scholarly bibliography as well as manuscript research should read Fredson Bowers's two essays "The Function of Bibliography," *Library Trends* 7 (April 1959): 497–510, and "Four Faces of Bibliography," *Papers of the Bibliographical Society of Canada* 10 (1971): 33–45. The special bibliographical problems in American government publications are dealt with in J. H. Powell's *The Books of a New Nation* (Philadelphia, 1957).

Three useful articles dealing with the collection of materials for editions of the papers of British authors appear in J. A. Dainard, ed., *Editing Correspondence: Papers Given at the Fourteenth Annual Conference on Editorial Problems, University of Toronto, 3–4 November 1978* (New York and London, 1979): Alan Bell's "The Letters of Sir Walter Scott: Problems and Opportunities," Wilmarth S. Lewis's "Editing Familiar Letters," and John Matthews's "The Hunt for the Disraeli Letters."

Issues involved in working with manuscript and rare book dealers and collectors are addressed in B. Richard Burg, "The Autograph Trade and Documentary Editing," *Manuscripts* 22 (Fall 1970): 247–54; H. Bartholomew Cox, "Publication of Manuscripts: Devaluation or Enhancement," *American Archivist* 32 (1969): 25–32; Leonard Labaree, "350 Were Approached, Only Three Said 'No,' " *Williams Alumni Review*, February 1967, 11–12; and Claude M. Simpson, William Goetzmann, and Matthew J. Bruccoli, "The Interdependence of Rare Books and Manuscripts: The Scholar's View," *Serif* 9 (Spring 1972): 3–22. The June 1970 *CEAA Newsletter*, pp. 21–23, presents summaries of papers on the "collection of manuscript information" in both libraries and private collections. Herman Herst, Jr.'s "Philatelists Are the Luckiest People," *Manuscripts* 32 (Summer 1980): 187–90, is an informal introduction to the field of postal history.

II. On the subject of control, editors have confined their wisdom almost completely to unpublished, in-house memoranda. Scholars may wish to improve their vocabulary in this area by consulting Frank B. Evans et al., "A Basic Glossary for Archivists, Manuscript Curators, and Records Managers," *American Archivist* 37 (July 1974): 415–31. A useful lesson in the analysis of handwriting to date manuscripts appears in *The Letters of Charles Dickens*, Madeline House and Graham Storey, eds., vol. 1 (Oxford, 1965), xxiv–xvi. And a classic demonstration of historical method and common sense in authenticating manuscripts is recounted in Arthur Pierce Middleton and Douglass Adair, "The Mystery of the Horn Papers," *William and Mary Quarterly* 4 (October 1947): 409–45.

The student who would keep abreast of writings on collection and control faces a considerable challenge. Editors who write brief histories of their projects, including summaries of their experience in searching out sources, are as likely to publish these reminiscences in journals issued by their collegiate alma mater or the library of their sponsor-institution as in scholarly journals such as the *American Archivist*. In the past, they have shown no inclination at all to publish factual accounts of their methods for control. Should they reverse this trend in the future, their essays will probably appear in the *American Archivist*, the *ADE Newsletter*, or *Computers and the Humanities*.

CHAPTER 3

Organizing a Documentary Edition

Sharing the resources collected by a project in documentary editing can be one of the greatest intellectual challenges that editors face. Most feel a moral obligation to communicate as much as possible of the data compiled in reconstructing the writings or papers of their subject; some are even under explicit directions to publicize their findings under agreements concluded with their sponsoring institutions. In deciding how best to communicate the contents of the editorial archive, the editor is faced with two questions: What material will be published? and How will it be published? The first question is reflected in establishing the scope of the edition and in planning accompanying finding aids or supplementary microforms; the second, in organizing the documentary texts chosen for publication and setting the standards for their textual treatment.

The considerations of an edition's scope and organization are addressed in this chapter. Preliminary decisions in this area will already have affected details of the project's collection methods and cataloging procedures. The editor's definition of the papers, writings, or records of his subject are reflected in the breadth or narrowness of the search. The cataloging and control strategies for projects whose printed volumes are to have a chronological framework will differ from those to be arranged topically.

Editors cannot, however, make final decisions concerning the edition's size and organization, much less initiate transcription of the source texts that meet these criteria, until collection is well under way and the control files have revealed the editorial archive's patterns. Once their thoughts turn to the nature of the project's publication, editors can never forget that theirs is a scholarly service function. They work to provide others with the documentary basis on which analytical and historical monographs can rest. It is their

66

duty to give their special public what it needs in terms of careful selection and painstaking transcription.

I. SCOPE

Considerations far more prosaic than the intellectual requirements of the edition's audience may dictate whether it is *comprehensive*, or inclusive of all the materials defined in the project's rubric, or merely *selective*, representing but a fraction of the materials that the search has uncovered. Before examining the patterns of organization adopted by modern documentary editions, it may be prudent to clarify the distinctions between these two terms and the terms *definitive* and *authoritative*. *Comprehensive* and *selective* have quantitative meanings only—they refer to the editor's decision to publish all or merely some of the documents that could be considered appropriate for the volumes that he prepares. *Definitive* and *authoritative*, on the other hand, have qualitative meanings. A *definitive edition* of an individual's writings must be not only all-inclusive in scope but also so rigorous in its textual methods that the reader will have no reason ever to recur to the original materials on which those printed texts are based. In dealing with manuscript or typescript sources, definitive printed texts, even when they are part of a comprehensive edition, are often a practical impossibility. At best, such an editor can offer his readers an *authoritative edition*, a collection of accurate and reliable printed versions of those elements of the sources that can be either translated into printed symbols or adequately described in editorial notes. Some details of inscription, some nuances in the sources, will resist the most ingenious editor. Scholars whose interests demand access to these details will be forced to consult the original materials or their accurate photoreproductions.

Editors routinely provide a statement of the limits of their textual methods so that readers can judge when the printed texts are inadequate to their purposes, and the quantitative process of choosing materials for a selective edition requires an equally straightforward explanation. The process of selection can be an interpretive tool, and any bias inherent in the standards for inclusion in the printed volumes must be addressed openly in the edition's introduction.

A. COMPREHENSIVE AND SELECTIVE EDITIONS

Few editors claim that theirs is a truly comprehensive edition. The editor of the published works of a well-known literary figure may achieve this goal, and so may the editor of a small archival edition of documents. However, most editors know better than to accept such a challenge. The realistic editor frankly states his standards of selection and devises methods that will give readers clues to both the nature and the location of the materials that do not appear in print.

In his initial volume of the *Jefferson Papers*, Julian Boyd outlined a plan that has become common among historical papers series. The Jefferson volumes print both letters and other documents addressed to Jefferson and those written by him. Certain categories of routine materials that do not warrant full print reproduction are noted in calendar entries that summarize the documents' contents and indicate the repositories where the originals can be consulted. In addition, the volumes carry entries for *letters not found*, letters of specific dates mentioned in surviving Jefferson documents for which the full texts have vanished, entries that may contain information from Jefferson's own register of his personal and official correspondence describing these now-vanished letters. The documentary texts, the calendar entries, and the notes of letters not found appear in a single chronological sequence. Thus, though the volumes do not provide texts of all the materials that are known to have once comprised Jefferson's papers, they do attempt a comprehensive *record* of those papers. A similar combination of the full texts of significant documents with letters-not-found entries for missing items and calendar entries for routine administrative papers has been employed by the editors of the Hamilton, Franklin, Madison, and Adams papers. A variation on the technique of combining printed texts and calendar entries is to print in full only documents deemed of the greatest significance. Brief calendar entries are provided for documents of still slighter interest (see, for example, the *Calhoun Papers*).

Although volumes in the tradition of literary scholarship seldom provide descriptive calendar entries for letters of secondary interest or records of letters not found, it is not uncommon for such series to furnish a list of surviving letters not selected for publication in the modern print edition. An important difference between such records in literary and historical editions is that the literary editor imposes a parallel order, placing such a list in an appendix to his volumes, while the editor with a historical background is more likely to integrate calendar entries, notices of letters not found, and so on, into the same chronological sequence in which the complete documentary texts appear. This is more than accidental. Generally, the editor of the correspondence of a literary figure can assume that his readers will use these volumes as much for their aesthetic value as for biographical or broader historical research: in such a design, calendar entries and the like may seem intrusive. On the other hand, the historical editor assumes that his reader will approach the volumes with a historian's bias toward chronology: such a reader will be best served by a format that allows him to see readily a listing of all documents written on a given date.

Editors of a new enterprise should launch their work only after giving careful thought to the consequences of having to revise their policies of selection when faced with changes in the nature of the records that they publish. The editors of the *Laurens Papers* were able to follow a near-comprehensive policy of publication for the first nine volumes of the series, but with volume 10, which brings Laurens to the forefront of the Revolution in South Carolina, the printed texts become highly selective. Microfiche supplements offer complete transcriptions of the documents omitted from the volumes. And the editors of the *Franklin Papers* have recently devised a new system of calendar entries and the publication of samples of certain types of routine materials to meet the explosion of documents created by Franklin's appointment as American commissioner to France.

Other editors eschew any attempt at a comprehensive chronological record of the editorial archive in the printed volumes but instead attempt to offer a guide to the broader collection in annotation to selected documents. In editions confined to letters written by a given author, a responsible editor always supplies complete data on the location and contents of letters to the author that have evoked the correspondence published in his volumes. Footnotes in selective editions of both sides of a correspondence customarily indicate the location of surviving related materials not printed in full. If a covering letter is printed without its enclosure, editorial notes must identify that unpublished document and sometimes summarize it in detail.

All of these methods try to make the selective edition, in the words of Wayne Cutler, a "window to the larger collection" from which its printed texts are drawn. There are times, however, when a printed format cannot provide adequate and convenient access of this sort. The comprehensive-record technique led the reviewer of one volume of statesmen's papers to remark, "The calendar has become the text" (John A. Munroe, *Mississippi Valley Historical Review* 50 [September 1963] :306). If the printed edition draws on only one chronological period in its subject's life, or if it focuses on but a single area of concern in his or her correspondence and papers, then the published volumes and the footnotes to the items chosen for print publication cannot serve as the clear "windows" for which editors like Cutler strive. When confronted by such problems, the editor must consider the publication of separate finding aids or other supplements to the printed volumes.

B. MICROFORM SUPPLEMENTS

Microforms of the editorial archive are the most common supplement to a selective print edition. If a comprehensive microform publication precedes the book edition, the need for a calendar of unpublished documents vanishes, for scholars will already have access to complete microform versions of these texts. Some editors have announced plans to publish such microforms of the documents or their transcriptions after completion of their book edition. While this method ensures that all the project's collected materials are available in one microform series, it can delay publication of the microform for a decade or more, and scholars harbor the lingering suspicion that any editorial enthusiasm for compiling a microform will vanish after the last printed volume appears.

Traditionally, editors have published micrographic supplements on 35-millimeter film that meets the standards of the NHPRC for such editions. However, the editors of the *Latrobe Papers* successfully experimented with a microfiche edition of Latrobe documents—a format with special advantages for the reproduction of the graphic documents of Latrobe's career as an engineer and architect. The editors of the *Charles Willson Peale Papers* selected this format for the same reasons, and the editors of the *Lydia Maria Child Papers* successfully used microfiche for more conventional documentary materials.

Microfilm and microfiche each have special advantages and disadvantages that any would-be microform editor must weigh carefully. Microfilm allows a more flexible use of reduction ratios and density values that may be needed to reproduce legible versions of mutilated or faded originals or less than perfect photocopies. Microfiche cards provide less opportunity for such camera adjustments because the apertures on such cards are of standard size. Oversized documents can be legibly reproduced on fiche only by a complicated and expensive paste-up process or by transcribing the documents to produce typed sheets that the fiche aperture can accommodate.

In general, microfilm is preferable for documents that antedate the late nineteenth century. The editor will find originals or photocopies from that period to be of widely varying dimensions and even shapes. The longer passage of time since the inscription of the originals will have produced greater ranges of discoloration or fading, problems better solved with the more flexible microfilm camera. Materials of the modern era, however, tend to be inscribed or printed on paper whose size can be accommodated easily by the fiche format without any distorting reduction. Recently generated original materials, too, have been subject to less wear and tear of the years, and they are more likely to be of a consistent level of legibility. And fiche is the microform of choice for collections of comparatively short printed documents such as pamphlets and published short stories and essays.

Modern film and fiche editions provide convenient formats for indexing. Early microfilm indexes such as those provided for the Library of Congress's Presidential Papers series were forbidding and cumbersome. Index entries offered references only to the dates of letters and papers, and the user was hard put to take notes from these pages before consulting the film reels to which they referred. The automatic frame-numbering attachments now available with most microfilm cameras ensure that each image on a reel is numbered in sequence. For microfiche, the alphanumeric reference system of location employed by the Latrobe editors is an easy and practical solution to this reference problem, although it can be used only on fiche readers equipped with an appropriate grid locater. Editors of the Child Papers assigned identifying sequential numbers to each document in the fiche, and index entries refer to these document numbers.

With any or all of these techniques, a microform index can be as compact and readable a finding aid as one to a printed volume. Entries for a correspondence series can be offered with each item's full date, or a "letters" entry for a correspondent can be broken down into subentries "letters to" and "letters from," with only the year given for each letter or group of letters. Rough subject indexes are common for microforms, and the mass of material likely to appear on fiche or film makes some sort of subject control essential. With careful planning and homework in the art of indexing, the editor of a microform supplement can provide his audience with a streamlined and efficient finding aid. The index to the *Papers of Aaron Burr*, for instance, furnished a correspondents index to letters, a plaintiff-defendant index to legal papers, a subject index to the records of Burr's professional career, and a personal-name index to Burr's journals in one hundred printed pages which cover twenty-seven reels of microfilm. The guide to the Latrobe fiche edition, using a different format, provides similar depth of indexing for 315 fiche cards in ninety-four printed pages.

C. OTHER SUPPLEMENTARY FORMS

Some editorial projects do not pretend to comprehensive publication in the form of record, calendar entries, or microform supplements. Editors of the correspondence of literary figures, for instance, customarily confine their editions to the letters written *by* their subjects. In most such cases, the editorial office's control files are available to those scholars who can travel to the project site, but the printed volumes themselves seldom carry a calendar of unpublished materials, and no project with the CEAA or CSE emblem has ever published a microform supplement to a selective edition.

Projects outside the tradition of historical editing, however, are increasingly aware of their responsibility to provide students with an independent, interim published record of their collections during the years that the preparation of annotated volumes takes place. The *Mark Twain Papers* project, for instance, plans a computerized compilation of a "Union Catalog of Clemens Correspondence," soon to be published for the convenience of Twain scholars who would otherwise have to wait decades for the completion of a selective edition of Clemens letters.

Even a moderately sophisticated word processor can ease the pain of indexing a microform or a catalog of unpublished documents. Access to a mainframe computer is almost essential for any project contemplating the preparation of an index to a large body of materials. If the editor knows that his printed volumes will be accompanied by a microform or that he will be obliged to issue a complete catalog of the materials that he does not publish in full, he should investigate the use of electronic systems. Fortunately, many editorial projects with access to mainframe computers are willing to act informally as service bureaus for other projects, processing raw index files prepared on stand-alone units.

D. THE PITFALLS OF SELECTIVITY

Microform technology, computer-generated checklists, or other finding aids to the editorial collection as a whole do not excuse the editor from responsibility for making an intelligent and fair selection of materials for print. The indexed bound volumes will be used more often and more thoroughly, and even the editor whose annotation carries generous quotations from unpublished materials or pointed references to documents in a supplementary microform must confront this problem. Scholars are as lazy and hedonistic as other mortals. Most are accustomed to the convenience of a book format, and they will avoid reference to unprinted materials at all costs. The editor's standard for selection in the printed volumes remains crucial.

Pressured to streamline his volumes, conscious of his publisher's pleas for an interesting series, the editor risks distorting the documentary record in the process of selection. One of the most tempting sins of omission is that of printing only one side of a figure's correspondence. The interpretive bias that results from this policy is discussed in James B. Stewart's review of the *Garrison Letters* (*Reviews in American History* 4 [1976]: 539–46). While this source of unintentional "interpretation-through-selection" is easily recognized, others are more subtle but just as dangerous. Another reviewer has pointed out that "different editorial frameworks and the decisions made within them affect the reader's picture of the subject to a far greater degree than he [the reader] probably imagines" (ibid. 1 [1973]: 519–23).

As an example, consider the decision of the editors of the papers of statesmen to provide calendar entries for materials that appear routine. Such a plan can gravely distort the picture of the overall collection. Since correspondence of a routine or administrative nature occurs with varying frequency during the life of a public figure, calendaring such documents means inconsistent degrees of comprehensive publication from one volume to another in an edition. Paradoxically, it will result in publishing the complete texts of all or nearly all the correspondence and papers for years when a statesman is in private life, while printing only a percentage of such materials in their entirety for periods when the same man holds an important public office. (Examples of such fluctuation are evident in the Clay and Calhoun editions.) Similarly, a decision to give preference to the records of a figure's public or professional life will inevitably slight the needs of scholars interested in the wide varieties of social history and intimate human experience recorded in that figure's private correspondence.

The bias inherent in omitting materials from the edition is obvious, but editors have also weakened the appeal and utility of their work by including trivial or inappropriate materials. Even the most restrained editors can be guilty of an occasional lapse. With the advantage of hindsight, the editors of the *Woodrow Wilson Papers* suggest that they erred in printing the complete texts of reviews of Wilson's published writings in their early volumes; they believe that their readers would have been satisfied with a complete checklist of such critiques.

Perhaps the greatest temptation in setting selection standards is that of giving the reader what he expects to find in the edition. The discovery of the unexpected is the basic justification for appropriating time and money to a systematic search for materials, and the editor must be wary of establishing the final organizational plan for his volumes too soon. If he bases his plan on the findings of earlier scholars, he may assume that a given chronological period in his figure's life will be too dull or insignificant to warrant extensive attention. The documents gathered in the project's search can put the lie to such an easy assumption. Letters scattered in two dozen repositories may show that an apparently minor correspondent was, in fact, a constant and regular part of the letter-writing life of the project's subject. It is the editor's duty to make sure that his modern edition reflects the most current knowledge of the documentary record that he has reconstructed, and it is his duty to be an honest and accurate reporter of the results of the expensive and time-consuming search on which his volumes are based.

II. ORGANIZATION OF THE PRINTED EDITION

Selectivity versus comprehensiveness is not the only choice that the editor faces in determining the format of his printed volumes. Nor are these the only preliminary editorial decisions that can have interpretive effects upon an edition: the arrangement of the documents selected for print can also be important.

The intellectual ancestor of modern American papers editions, the *Correspondence of Horace Walpole*, grouped Walpole's letters by his major correspondents. Thus, Walpole's exchanges with the Reverend William Cole are contained in volumes 1 and 2; his exchanges with Madame du Deffand and her circle appear in volumes 3–8; and so forth. This is one example from the Walpole edition that American editors—of all traditions—have chosen not to imitate. In volumes of correspondence, all items selected for full publication are generally printed in a single chronological sequence, although sometimes groups of related documents are printed as special sections. (For examples of such variations see the treatment of diplomatic correspondence in volumes 16–20 of the *Jefferson Papers*.)

Any departure from chronological organization—indeed, the violation of any general principle of an edition—should be taken only after serious thought. A printed volume of correspondence should provide readers with a full index that will allow them to make their own arrangement of related materials for their personal research purposes. The casual destruction of the general organizational pattern can make the volumes less, not more, useful. Haphazard topical arrangement can make it more difficult for the reader to reconstruct the patterns that meet his or her needs.

What is just as important, editorial arrangement can distort and interpret the documents as effectively as a biased choice of documents for printing. This fact has been remarked upon at length by American editors in the history of science. The Joseph Henry and Thomas Edison editors have consciously broken with the European tradition of publishing scientific documents in topical groupings. Modern intellectual historians, whether their interest be science, philosophy, or the arts, realize that such a pre-packaging of source materials makes it virtually impossible for the reader to understand the context within which each step of the intellectual process involved occurred. History, whether of politics, painting, or technology, places a premium on time as an organizing principle, and only the most urgent considerations should persuade the editor to ignore this fact.

There are, of course, groups of documents that defy a unifying chronological organization. The records of a lawyer's practice, for instance, would be unintelligible were the editor to print all legal documents in one time sequence. Pleas, depositions, subpoenas, and affidavits that relate to a given case must be grouped together if their contents are to make sense. The principle of organization by case has been adopted consistently by all modern editors of legal materials. *Freedom: A Documentary History of Emancipation* combines topical and chronological arrangement to enable its readers to sift through a vast bureaucratic archive to uncover a wealth of social history. Here, as in most editorial decisions, intelligibility and utility are overriding considerations.

A. SOME CONVENTIONS OF DOCUMENTARY ORGANIZATION

Modern documentary editors have adopted certain conventions for the subdivision of the papers or writings of their subjects. All CEAA/CSE editions, for instance, publish works composed for publication separately from private writings such as letters and journals. No one quarrels with this division for authors, whose works were designed for independent consumption by a wide audience quite different from the one to which letters and journals were addressed. Each group must be studied separately; however, further subdivision should be undertaken only for compelling reasons, and any editor who publishes documents in separate series or subseries must be prepared to devise different, though equally clear and cogent, standards of selection for these groups.

This problem is addressed at length in the introductions to the *Adams Family Correspondence* and the *Papers of John Adams*. Indeed, the rationale for the series organization of the Adams Papers may be instructive for all editors. When editorial work began, some advisers suggested that all the correspondence and papers of three generations of the Adams Family be published in one chronological series, with even diary entries broken up and interspersed among letters, state papers, legal records, and literary works. This plan was quickly vetoed. The Adamses' diaries were major autobiographical writings that deserved to have their integrity preserved in discrete volumes. Aside from this consideration, the editors realized that one chronological series of Adams family papers, public and private, would make the edition less useful than one with carefully designated divisions. Comparatively few readers would approach the volumes with the intention of studying the Adamses as a family; rather, readers would come to the volumes with an interest either in personal interrelationships among family members or in some family member's professional activities in law or literature or public service. Thus the Adams edition appears in three series: Diaries and Autobiographical Writings; Family Correspondence; and Papers, which include letters and other writings bearing on the Adamses' professional and public careers.

B. DIARIES AND JOURNALS

The common practice of publishing diaries and journals separately from other papers has been criticized by Arthur S. Link, who feels that diary entries should be printed in the same chronological sequence with the rest of a figure's papers unless overriding considerations call for a discrete series. This was seconded by Lyman H. Butterfield, even though his four-volume edition of John Adams's *Diary and Autobiography* might hint at a difference of opinion on this point. Both men agree, however, that there are certain factors to be weighed before deciding on the appropriate format for diary publication. A separate series for diaries presupposes that their contents are so full and so interesting that readers will need to study them as an independent work: the Adamses' diaries clearly fall within this category.

Before choosing to have a special series for a group of diaries, the editor must weigh the relationship between the contents of the diaries and those of the diarist's other papers. Some diaries are little more than appointment books. No useful purpose would be served by printing them separately. They do not stand alone in any way; their only purpose is to illuminate the fuller exposition of the diarist's life as represented in his correspondence and other papers. If only scattered leaves of a diarist's memoirs survive, it would be foolish to allot them a separate series. Thus the editions of Cooper's *Letters and Journals* and Robert Morris's records of the Revolutionary Finance Office integrate surviving scattered journal entries into the chronological series of correspondence for the same period. Whenever the writer is an intermittent record-keeper—making such entries only during extended trips—his travel journals may also benefit from incorporation into the general series of his writings.

For some diarists, a personal journal may represent a life quite distinct from that reflected in correspondence and other records. Many literary figures of the nineteenth century, for instance, used their journal less as a record of daily events than as a literary daybook in which they jotted down ideas for stories or essays and even used some pages to draft their skeletal inspirations into fully developed literary passages. Were daily entries from such journals interspersed with their authors' correspondence for the same period, the editors would destroy the intellectual integrity of the sources to no useful purpose. Every reader would have to reconstruct the sequence of journal entries from the volumes in which they were scattered among letters and other papers. There is no question about the ability of such journals to stand alone in terms of literary quality, length, and subject matter. And their editors have no reason to hesitate before printing them as separate series.

There may, of course, be other, less lofty considerations behind an editor's decision to publish journals or diaries separately. The repository owning the original manuscript may withhold permission for its publication unless the printed volumes preserve the integrity of the original. The editor may be under pressure to begin publication of part of his edition as early as possible, in which case easily located journals and diaries can be prepared for print publication while the project completes its search for correspondence and other papers. And there may be, quite simply, some overwhelming public expectation of separate publication of a series of diaries.

Whatever the external or internal pressures determining the organizational format and scope of a series, the editor must remember that these decisions are not casual or unimportant ones. The scope of the edition and the arrangement of its contents may determine how widely the volumes are used—or whether they can be used at all.

Suggested Readings

The body of literature in the field of selection and organization of materials in documentary editions is generous, though scattered. The introductions to selective and topically organized editions cited in this chapter should be supplemented by the chapter on selection in *Editorial Specifications: The Papers of George Catlett Marshall* (Lexington, Va., 1982). This pamphlet, published by the George C. Marshall Research Foundation, is an excellent summary of the manual and computerized methods used by the Marshall project for all aspects of the editorial process from selection of documents through the final paste-up of copy for book composition.

I. Fredrika Teute's "View in Review: A Historical Perspective on Historical Editing" offers guidance to further essays and reviews that address themselves to editions' policies of selection and organization. Useful discussions of the general problem appear in Gerald Gunther's review of John Adams's *Diary and Autobiography*, in *Harvard Law Review* 75 (1961–62): 1669–80. Patricia Galloway's "Dearth and Bias: Issues in the Editing of Ethnohistorical Materials," *ADE Newsletter* 3 (May 1981): 1–6, concerns the problem in a specific scholarly area. John Brooke's "The Prime Ministers' Papers," *Journal of the Society of Archivists* 3 (April 1969): 467–69, presents a British view of the issues of selectivity and comprehensiveness.

The reviews of specific editions often raise helpful issues. For the *Adams Papers* see William L. Joyce's review in *American Archivist* 41 (1978): 189–91, and James Hutson's essay in *William and Mary Quarterly* 31 (April 1974): 326–27. The selection policies of the Calhoun edition are discussed in reviews in ibid. 21 (April 1964): 315–17, *American Historical Review* 69 (October 1963): 166–67, and *Mississippi Valley Historical Review* 50 (September 1963): 306–7.

Charles Grier Sellers raised pertinent points in his review of the Clay edition, *Journal of Southern History* 26 (1960): 238–40. The standards of the editors of the *Jefferson Davis Papers* are questioned sharply in David Donald's review in *American Historical Review* 77 (December 1972): 1506–8. Nathan Huggins's review of the *DuBois Correspondence*, ibid. 80 (April 1975): 512–13, and Max Savelle's review of the *Franklin Papers*, ibid. 66 (April 1961): 750–52, should also be consulted. Two essays in *Reviews in American History* by Aileen S. Kraditor (1 [1973]: 519–23) and James Brewer Stewart (4 [1976]: 539–46) analyze the policies of the *Garrison Letters*.

The selection standards of the Madison edition are examined by F. Gerald Ham in *Papers of the Bibliographical Society of America* 58 (1964): 309–10. And the policies of the John Marshall volumes are examined in Robert Faulkner's reviews in *William and Mary Quarterly* 33 (January 1976): 154–56 and 36 (October 1979): 646–48.

Louis Morton's review of the *George Mercer Papers* in *Mississippi Valley Historical Review* 41 (March 1955): 692–93 catalogs a multitude of editorial sins. The *Naval Documents of the American Revolution* are examined harshly in reviews in *William and Mary Quarterly* 22 (October 1965): 660–63 and *American Historical Review* 77 (June 1972): 831. John Garraty is somewhat more charitable in his review of the *Theodore Roosevelt Letters* in *American Quarterly* 6 (Fall 1954): 281–84. The *Webster Correspondence* receives close attention from reviewers in the *New England Quarterly* 50 (1977): 349–51 and the *American Archivist* 38 (1975): 557–59.

Although reviewers of literary editions of documents are less likely to examine policies of selection, a notable exception is William J. Gilmore in his review of the *Whittier Letters* in *Journal of American History* 63 (1976): 672–73.

Two essays by Barbara Oberg in the *ADE Newsletter* discuss the question of editorial responsibility in selection: "Selection and Annotation: Deciding Alone" (2 [February 1980]: 6–9) and "Interpretation in Editing: The Gallatin Papers" (4 [May 1982]: 7–9).

General problems in the publication of documentary microforms are discussed in Sam Kula, "The Preparation of Finding Aids for Manuscript Material on Microfilm," *Canadian Archivist Newsletter* 1 (1964): 3–10; Charles E. Lee, "Documentary Reproduction: Letterpress Publication—Why? What? How?" *American Archivist* 28 (1965): 351–65; Albert H. Leisinger, Jr., "Selected Aspects of Microreproduction in the United States," *Archivuum* 16 (1966): 127–46; Ian Montagnes, "Microfiche and the Scholarly Publisher," *Scholarly Publishing* 7 (October 1975): 63–84; and Fred Shelley, "The Choice of a Medium for Documentary Publication," *American Archivist* 32 (1969): 363–68. Elizabeth L. Hill offers a straightforward discussion of "Descriptive Guides for Publications on Microfilm" in ibid. 34 (1971): 318–23.

The experience of specific microform programs is discussed in Lyman H. Butterfield, "Vita sine literis, mors est: The Microfilm Edition of the Adams Papers," *Library of Congress Quarterly Journal* 18 (February 1961): 53–58; Whitfield Bell's review of the Latrobe edition in *William and Mary Quarterly* 36 (January 1979): 134–37; Howard M. Levin and Wendy J. Strothman, "Introducing

Text Fiche," *Scholarly Publishing* 7 (July 1976): 321–32; and David Ammerman's review of *Province in Rebellion* in *William and Mary Quarterly* 33 (July 1976): 536–38. For a form of an independent microform supplement to a "literary" edition see the Bruccoli-Clark edition of the facsimile of Stephen Crane's *The Red Badge of Courage* (*A Facsimile Edition of the Manuscript. Edited with an Introduction and Apparatus by Fredson Bowers*, 2 vols. [Washington, D.C., 1972–73]).

The editor who needs guidance on the preparation of a microform edition should address his questions to the NHPRC and the NEH. Staff members there can refer him to a project that has anticipated some of his problems in this area.

The use of nonmicroform supplements to selective editions has not been examined closely. Worthington C. Ford's essay "On Calendaring Manuscripts," *Papers of the Bibliographical Society of America* 4 (1909): 45–56, is still worth study. And Kenneth Curry's "The Text of Robert Southey's Published Correspondence: Misdated Letters and Missing Names," ibid. 75 (1981): 127–30, offers a striking example of an economical method of correcting and supplementing an unsatisfactory documentary edition.

II.   The reader who wishes models of varying organization formats has many choices. For examples of the organization of legal papers in documentary editions see the appropriate volumes in the Adams, Hamilton, and Webster series. The best example of a series format with a fully realized system of cross references is that described in the introduction to volume 1 of the *Papers of John Adams*. And the techniques of the new *Freedom* edition are models for topical organization. The editions of journals and notebooks in the Emerson, Thoreau, Hawthorne, and Mark Twain series present examples of editorial treatment of literary daybooks.

CHAPTER 4

Evaluating and Transcribing the Source Text

Documentary editing is most clearly distinguished from critical textual editing by its customary reliance upon a single handwritten, typed, or printed document (the *source text*) for each editorial text. Although documentary editors occasionally use such tools of textual editing as conflation to establish a text (see chap. 7, below), their general rule must be that one source text, whether an original document or its photocopy, will be the basis of one printed editorial text. Even though variants between the source text and other versions of the same document will be recorded in editorial notes, it is the words, phrases, and punctuation of the source text that will be readily and conveniently available to the reading audience. Thus, the selection of that source text and its accurate transcription are crucial matters for any editorial project.

Only after collecting and cataloging are complete can the editor begin to assess the special problems that his sources will present. It is the individual documents or groups of documents themselves that will dictate the best textual approaches. And before the editor can determine what that textual treatment should be for his edition, he must have at hand accurate transcriptions of carefully selected source texts as working copy for his editorial project.

Early nineteenth-century American documentary editors like Jared Sparks did not concern themselves with the labor of transcribing the manuscripts whose texts they wished to publish; instead, they simply used those original manuscripts as *printer's copy*. The autograph letters of Gouverneur Morris and George Washington bear mute and mutilated witness to the method, their pages filled with Sparks's penciled "corrections" of the author's style and punctuation. Modern editors must show more self-restraint, and modern photocompositors are less obliging in accepting handwritten materials as the basis for their typesetting. Even though photocopies of some printed documents can serve as the editor's copy, most items must be transcribed to produce working copy for the editor and the printer.

The problems of transcribing an edition's source texts fall into two obvious categories: what to transcribe and how to transcribe it. Most editors will frequently have to choose from among several candidates for a document's source text. Once the source texts for an edition are identified, they must be transcribed in a fashion that will expedite rather than impede later editorial work. Even modern technology will not shield the editor from this labor. Although word processors and other computer devices enable the editor to make extensive changes in the initial transcription without the need for complete rekeyboarding, it is vastly more efficient—and more re-liable—to choose the correct source texts and transcription methods at the outset.

I. Choosing the Source Text

The rules adopted to designate source texts, like all editorial pro-cedures, should be stated clearly in the introduction to any edition. The criteria used to establish these rules generally involve little more than common sense. The following guidelines apply to the major categories of documentary materials for the modern period.

A. HANDWRITTEN OR TYPEWRITTEN MATERIALS

1. The manuscript or a reliable photocopy is to be preferred over any later scribal copies or transcriptions as the source text.

2. If the original has been lost or destroyed, contemporary copies are preferred over later ones unless evidence survives to demonstrate that later copyists (*a*) had access to the now-vanished original and (*b*) were more accurate than the earlier scribes.

3. In general, the most nearly final version of a document is the preferred source text. Editors can take comfort in the thought that variants can and should be noted in the editorial apparatus. Signif-icant differences between different versions of a document will not be denied the reader by choosing one of them as source text. That source text is simply the version that serves as the best working basis for the edition.

Other priorities are listed below.

1. Letters

The first order of preference is given to a version of the original letter (preferably signed to denote authorial approval) that is known to have been received by its addressee. The best evidence for identifying a recipient's copy of a letter can be an attached address leaf, the recipient's endorsement, the presence of a mailing envelope, or the location of the letter in the addressee's papers. Although editors of many categories of materials will seldom find an attached address to prove the receipt of a particular copy of a letter, fold patterns and other physical evidence will often mark a particular document the recipient's copy, and the editor who has familiarized himself with his subject's letter-writing habits generally will be able to identify "finished" versions with little trouble.

A special problem may arise with the correspondence of statesmen assigned to foreign posts in times of national emergency. At such periods, diplomats frequently sent duplicate or even triplicate or quadruplicate signed copies of their dispatches to their home government. When two or more such multiple addressee's copies survive, the editor may have to make a subjective decision concerning the best version or source text. The basis for such a judgment can include the completeness of the variant copies and the care that the letter's author or his secretary used in copying the dispatch. A duplicate letter in which words are carelessly omitted or in which the handwriting reflects haste would be a less desirable source text than the quadruplicate of the same letter in which the text is complete and the manuscript shows that it was copied more accurately than the duplicate. However, nontextual considerations may be decisive. If, for example, the carelessly copied duplicate reached the Department of State in June and became the basis for a foreign-policy decision, while the elegantly inscribed quadruplicate was not delivered until several weeks later, the duplicate may be a better source text.

A second order of preference is given to copies of the letter in the hand of the author or someone under his direction that were not received by the addressee. Such versions fall into four categories:

(a) Drafts
(b) Letterbook copies
(c) Copies that present fairly exact facsimiles of the recipient's version, such as letterpress copies (see below), carbon copies, and so on
(d) Independently prepared loose file copies

Preliminary draft versions on separately inscribed sheets are easily identified, but some of the other categories are not mutually exclusive. In the eighteenth century, bound blank volumes were used to record outgoing correspondence. Many authors used such letterbooks as a convenient place in which to draft their correspondence, recopying the final version on a separate sheet for mailing. Others copied texts into their letterbooks from the final version of the letter. Thus some letterbooks represent bound volumes of drafts, while others are assemblages of file copies of the recipients' correspondence.

Documents that represent contemporary facsimile versions include letterpress copies, carbon copies, and, in our own time, photocopies. The efforts of American letter writers to provide themselves with files of their outgoing correspondence without retranscribing such materials is a tribute to Yankee ingenuity. In the late eighteenth century such American statesmen as Thomas Jefferson enthusiastically experimented with every invention that could ease their burden. Stylographic pens and pencils, which produced primitive carbon copies for holograph materials, were employed. Correspondents purchased devices that made two pens move simultaneously to produce two copies of each letter, one for transmittal and one for filing. And last, but not least, there was the letterpress. In the earliest letterpresses, a thin, nearly transparent sheet of paper was moistened and pressed against the inscribed surface of handwritten material. Ideally, enough ink was transferred from the original to the back of the blank sheet that the handwritten words showed through, giving a legible and complete copy. In practice, most such letterpress copies were fragile, smudged horrors for the editor before the midnineteenth century, when more sophisticated letterpresses produced more satisfactory copies.

The invention of the typewriter and the use of carbon paper added still another form of simultaneously created facsimile copy. Despite the fact that the carbon copy of typed materials has been part of American life and American language for more than seventy-five years, editors have seldom written on the problems of rendering intelligible versions from uncorrected carbon copies, much less on those created by photocopying techniques that generate files of retained copies. A notable exception to this rule is Fredson Bowers, "Multiple Authority: New Problems and Concepts of Copy-Text," *Library* 27 (June 1972): 81–115. Until more such literature appears, an editor who confronts these issues must use common sense, and his experience will be his guide.

A third order of preference is given to transcriptions and printed copies. Editors commonly designate as *transcriptions* copies made substantially later than the document's composition and executed by someone acting without the authority or assistance of the author. As source texts, such transcriptions and printed versions of letters rank far below a contemporary copy.

If more than one transcript version survives and the original material has disappeared, the editor may have to resort to some of the basic practices of textual filiation to determine which offers the soundest source text. *Filiation* is the determination of the *families*, or groups, to which the copies belong in order to isolate that copy closest to the archetype or original. The editor of modern documents will seldom have to employ the more complicated techniques by which the classicist uses filiation to identify the scribal copy closest to the vanished archetype, but the commonsense rules of filiation apply to modern as well as to ancient materials. These rules require of the editor (a) an attempt to learn something about the copyist for each scribal version and (b) an attempt to date the variant transcripts. The skills of the scribe and the circumstances under which he made his transcription may offer a key to the most reliable transcript in the group. For modern materials, evidence for dating can include patterns of handwriting, results of chemical tests of paper, and a comparison of typefaces in printed sources.

When nothing useful can be learned from such historical evidence, the methods of classical filiation should be employed. Perhaps the most useful for the modern documentary editor is the comparison of variants to detect clear and recurrent patterns of error or miscopying. Transcripts that contain the same errors are likely to be part of the same family, one descended from the other in order of transcription.

Like handwritten transcriptions, earlier printed versions of a letter can reflect the interpretation and even the style of a later copyist, not the author's intentions. The problem addressed here is not that of establishing the preferred text of a work written for publication and printed during an author's lifetime but that of reproducing printed versions of letters or other private materials for which the original has disappeared and only the version printed in some earlier documentary edition survives. When more than one such printed text survives, the editor must determine which has the greatest claim to authenticity and accuracy. Some of the techniques of choosing among several handwritten or typewritten transcriptions should be applied here. Obviously the editor has an advantage in establishing chronological patterns among printed texts that is absent when manuscript transcripts are involved, for the printed text usually bears a date of publication. Even this is not always a determining factor in selecting a printed source text, for the editor must remember that earlier editors may have prepared their printed versions of the same original source by independent reference to an archetype. The eye of the editor who published a text in 1830 need not have been more reliable than that of the editor who prepared a new text in 1880. When the evidence indicates that two printed versions or two transcripts of original materials were both based upon the same archetype, then the editor must make his choice on the basis of such internal evidence as faithfulness to known patterns of the author's spelling, punctuation, and capitalization, as well as the accuracy of the copyists' readings of proper nouns. Many such printed versions dating from the nineteenth and early twentieth centuries appear in editions that carry no statements of editorial policy, and the modern editor must often resort to playing his hunches in selecting a source text.

2. Papers

In general, the rules that apply to an individual's correspondence also apply to selecting source texts from variant versions of his or her *papers*, unprinted records of professional activities or public life that cannot be defined as any form of letter. This category would include such documents as the legislative reports of a lawmaker, the technical notes of a scientist, the general orders of a military commander, or the lecture notes of an educator.

Sometimes, special considerations may arise that make the best source text something other than the most nearly final version that survives. These considerations are very practical ones that relate to the availability of reliable printed versions of these final versions and the absence of such printed sources for preliminary versions that may display significant variants. This problem arises frequently in the papers of men and women who held public office. Official government publications often contain adequate versions of the texts of legislative committee reports and formally adopted statutes. Given the limits of his schedule and his budget, the editor may hesitate to give the world still another, identical printed version of such materials. But if he discovers manuscript or typewritten draft versions of such reports or preliminary versions of legislative bills, he may find that these better serve his reader as source texts, directing scholars to the location of the printed "final" versions so that readers can use the two as parallel texts of the stages in the evolution of the same document.

B. PRINTED WORKS

The *works* of any writer, prose and poetry composed for publication and issued in print more or less as intended by the author, present special problems to the documentary editor. Of these, the first is the choice of that version of the published work that will be used as the basis of the text to appear in his edition.

The editor who aspires to the CSE emblem must naturally refer to the guidelines of that organization before choosing a version for transcription. His choice will be the most appropriate copy-text, not a source text, and the criteria for its selection lie outside the modest boundaries of this volume. The copy-text will be the foundation of an emended critical text, whose aim is the representation of the author's final intentions, intentions that may or may not appear in all respects in any one surviving copy of the work in question. The *critical edition* itself may be a new document, recording the best judgment of the editor, not the words or punctuation of any version of the work published in the author's lifetime or available to any earlier reader. However, a *documentary edition* of a work should be a noncritical one based on a single version that was actually read by the audience for which it was intended.

The differences between the goals of a textual and a documentary editor, then, are not confined to varying textual treatments. They also extend to the choice of the version of the work that will be transcribed for the editor's use. In general, the textual editor will prefer that printed version that reflects the author's most fully expressed intentions. The documentary editor must weigh other factors. He must also consider the historical impact of various editions of the same book or essay, not merely the edition's reflection of the author's most clearly refined literary art. As an example, textual and documentary editors might make very different decisions were they faced with the problem of choosing between two versions of a pamphlet originally published in Boston in 1773 and then revised by its author for a new edition a year later. An editor concerned with the author's literary intentions might conflate elements of the two into a critical edition, but the documentary editor would weigh the influence of each edition. If the 1773 printing was an important factor in rousing public opinion in Boston during the Tea Party crisis, and the 1774 revision had languished unread in a limited edition, the documentary editor would choose the earlier version. The pamphlet's significance for political history is its impact in 1773. The author's later improvements would be recorded as variants in footnotes, but it would be nonsensical to use the 1774 edition as a source text, forcing the reader to reconstruct laboriously the more significant 1773 version through reference to footnotes or tables of emendations.

The CSE's guidelines are designed for the works of published authors. To the readers of some such materials, importance lies in the development of the author's literary craftsmanship, which is often reflected by his correction of earlier printed errors. The works of nonliterary figures may owe their significance to other considerations—which can make something other than the final version in a set of printed variants far more important than the later, more polished edition. Whether literary or historical values are the primary reason for rereading a printed document, the choice of a source text or copy-text must involve a thorough knowledge of the document and its author. An editor must assume the role of historical bibliographer to master the story of a work's composition and publication before deciding on the appropriate basis for his new edition. And the technology of publication methods must be a part of this newly acquired skill.

Newspapers present a special editorial challenge, for pieces published in this medium are peculiarly affected by changes in the mechanics of dissemination. In the early period of American history, the newspaper that first printed an author's essay or articles can be assumed to be the one to which the writer submitted his manuscript version, and its columns are likely to carry a version that received some attention from the author himself. Later newspaper printings customarily drew on the first, and the variations that appear are likely to be typographical errors that can be noted, if significant, in the editorial apparatus.

However, this rule of thumb breaks down in the late nineteenth century, when the syndication of works in newspapers developed. If an author's article or story was published in syndicated form, the editor's research expands to the methods used by the news syndicate in question to determine which newspaper version has special claims to notice.

II. Transcribing the Source Text: Methods of Inscription

The same factors that determine the choice of source texts will dictate the appropriate method of their transcription. The means used to record that documentary evidence are often the primary factor that an editor considers in determining standards of transcription and, indeed, in settling on the final textual method. Certainly it is always the first factor to be weighed. Only after the editor has mastered the intricacies of all the methods used to inscribe the sources that he will publish can he begin to rule out textual practices that would distort the details of those sources. The form of documentary evidence represented by each source text—letter, diary, state paper, scientific treatise—will raise another set of questions. The editor should consider the method of communication that each embodies before he comes to a final decision on their treatment in his edition.

Literary editors have quite rightly stressed the need to present the publishing history of any critically edited work. The need to master the *inscriptional* history of unprinted documentary sources, as well as the history of printed materials that will be the basis of a documentary edition, is just as great. As he makes a choice among competing source texts, the editor learns as much as possible about the methods by which these variants were produced. The knowledge may run the gamut from the practices of a group of clerks in the same office to the peculiarities of a particular eighteenth-century letterpress or the details of book production or newspaper composition.

Unfortunately, there are few secondary sources to which an editor can refer. In European medieval studies, there is the recognized academic discipline of *diplomatic*, which offers systematic studies of record-keeping methods of important groups of clerks or administrators. There are no such formal courses from which to learn how the secretary of the American Continental Congress maintained his records in 1785 or how elementary students were taught to standardize the forms of personal correspondence in 1830. Each editor must learn these methods for himself. Often the best introductions appear in edited volumes that draw on sources similar to the one that the novice hopes to publish. Documentary editors who have survived the agonies of learning the intricacies of American inscriptional history frequently share this wisdom in their own edited series. The general rules to be drawn from their experience are summarized in the pages that follow.

A. HANDWRITTEN SOURCE TEXTS

Anyone who has transcribed handwritten materials or proofread the resulting copy knows that no typewriter or typeface can reproduce all the subtle distinctions in such originals. Any typed or printed transcription of such a source is a *critical* one in that it silently incorporates dozens of editorial judgments and decisions. The editor cannot indicate every instance in which experience allows him to recognize a scrawled mark as a period instead of a comma nor every occasion when skill and training enable him to recognize a slightly inflected line as an *n* instead of an *m*. Indeed, the experienced editor may exercise such judgment quite unconsciously. Knowing this, the editor should choose a textual policy whose conventions do not conceal additional subtleties in a source that has already been transformed from script to type. Such *normalization* should always be avoided.

Only a careful analysis of the sources at hand will enable the editor to decide which emendations and conventions will least distort his source. Some writers may employ one method of punctuation in correspondence with close friends and another, more formal system in letters to strangers and professional colleagues. Obviously the standardization of such marks would conceal important evidence of the author's relationship with each correspondent. Still other writers vary the length of a standard mark of punctuation such as the hyphen for different functions. In such instances, the editor must mark his typed transcription not only for hyphens but for one-en and one-em dashes or even double dashes to reproduce the author's consistent, if idiosyncratic, patterns. Individual patterns of capitalization, the use of contractions, and care or carelessness in spelling often provide unexpected insights into an author's state of mind. The editor cannot responsibly ignore such slips of the pen until he is certain that they do not represent significant patterns in his writer's orthography.

The age and condition of the manuscripts that bear the author's script may make even a rough transcription of their contents difficult. In such cases, the editor must verify his transcriptions against the originals before even beginning his assessment of the importance of each detail of inscription. And he may have to refer to those originals again and again during the period in which he labors to establish their texts for his edition.

It is difficult enough to discover such patterns in the handwriting of a single individual: they can change with the writer's progressive education or with advancing age. However, the possibility of distinguishing and analyzing such patterns in a group of documents representing a number of authors is nearly impossible. The editor who imposes arbitrary, often modern, notions of punctuation or spelling to normalize both sides of a handwritten correspondence or original records that include journals kept by a dozen scribes or reports and papers from a hundred contributors is advised to reconsider his hasty decision.

Adding liberal editorial emendations to the conventions of printing imposed on handwritten source texts jeopardizes a documentary edition and can even invalidate the undertaking's justification. And modern technology may make possible even more faithful transcription and publication of handwritten sources in a print edition. Traditionally, such details of inscription as superscript letters have been standardized to reduce the costs of producing the print edition. Computer composition has made the retention of such details a practical possibility, and many of the traditionally necessary emendations of handwritten sources such as lowering superscript letters or expanding the "tailed *p*" will no longer be an economic necessity. Source texts should be transcribed as literally as possible to take advantage of this technological blessing.

B. TYPEWRITTEN DOCUMENTS

Only in recent years have documentary editors confronted the textual problems created by modern office machines. A signed typewritten recipient's copy of a letter or other communication presents few problems: no matter what its flaws, it should be considered to represent the author's final intentions. If the typescript carries handwritten corrections or revisions by the author, those with substantive meaning must be indicated by textual symbols, special typefaces, or annotation. Often the same methods that the edition adopts to meet the needs of handwritten sources (see chap. 6, sec. I) can be modified for typed sources. In the absence of such symbols, the editor may choose a special typeface to be reserved for handwritten additions to typed pages, and if such authorial revisions occur but rarely, footnotes can explain these occasional details of inscription. In any case, the initial transcription must indicate these details.

A *retained* typescript in the form of an uncorrected carbon copy creates new problems. Faced with file drawers of such uncorrected copies of outgoing correspondence, the editors of the *Woodrow Wilson Papers* announced that they would assume that the ribbon copies of these letters had been corrected before dispatch, and texts are emended accordingly. Of course, this assumption was made only after comparing surviving carbon and ribbon copies of the same letters to verify that Wilson himself routinely made such corrections. The editor of late-nineteenth-century typescripts can make such an assumption only if his emendations accurately correct errors likely to have been made on the keyboard of the machine employed. Decades passed before these keyboards were standardized, and emendations can occur only with full knowledge of the particular instrument involved.

Transcriptional and textual policies for typed sources should reflect not only that medium of inscription but also the basic nature of each source. A typed draft letter with handwritten or typed revisions has requirements quite different from a nonauthorial transcription from a handwritten source. Editors who ignore this rule and lump together typed letters, retained carbon copies, typed transcriptions, and printed transcriptions of lost sources into one textual category compromise their product before the process of transcription even begins. Typewriting must be regarded as merely an exceptionally legible form of inscription, and the appearance of a typed document should not mislead one into ignoring other factors that may dictate editorial treatment.

C. PRINTED SOURCE TEXTS

The editor who establishes the text of a published work for the purposes of a critical edition may sometimes legitimately depart from the substantives and accidentals of any single surviving printed copy of that writing. However, the noncritical documentary editor views print as merely another way to inscribe a document, and the surviving copies of a given source must be evaluated to determine which is the best *document*, the one that is a unique, authoritative source with evidentiary value. Once that source has been identified, it must be printed without being subject to emendation, conflation, or the other heavy artillery of textual editing.

The noncritical editor of printed sources should not, however, be *un*critical in his methods. Many printed items can be viewed as documents: official government publications, pamphlets, essays, books. Within each category, the editor must become familiar with all the tools of historical and critical bibliography, even though the editorial product itself will not be a critical one. To edit printed sources noncritically, the editor must investigate their printing history with all the care employed by an editor hoping for a CSE emblem. Various—and variant—printings of the document must be collated as rigorously as for any MLA series. And the results of that historical research and the mechanical collation must be analyzed scrupulously.

Neglecting the tools of sophisticated bibliography for documentary editions can have embarrassing results. The editors of the *Laurens Papers* admit openly, if not happily, to having committed such a blunder in the fifth volume of their series, where they present a scrupulously printed facsimile of Laurens's 1767 pamphlet *A Representation of Facts*. Variant readings from all surviving copies of the pamphlet are recorded in textual notes. But the introduction to the document states that the editors were unable to discover the precise order in which the two latest versions of the pamphlet were issued. Had the editors used the tools of modern bibliography to compare the variant printings for such clues as broken type, they might have determined the sequence in which the versions of the pamphlet were run from the same standing type.

In documentary editing, the compositor's typefont should be regarded as a method of inscription that requires as careful an analysis as a scribe's copying practices or the keyboard of a typewriter of the 1880s or Woodrow Wilson's use of Graham shorthand. The editor of printed documents cannot assume that his task is easier because his sources already exist in typeset form. Instead, he must make himself an expert on the vagaries of this method of documentary inscription. Fredson Bowers's *Principles of Bibliographical Description* will disabuse such an editor of the notion that editing printed sources is simple, and the members of the CSE are ready to offer advice and encouragement to novices in their fields of specialization.

D. GRAPHIC ELEMENTS IN DOCUMENTS

The editing of completely nonverbal documents has not yet been addressed by editors in the NHPRC or CSE traditions. However, many editors have had to solve the problem of presenting scattered authorial illustrations and even doodles that are part of a more conventionally inscribed text. When such elements have recognized equivalents in type, the transcriber can enter such ready-made symbols from the printer's font in good conscience. Thus the editors of the *Hawthorne Notebooks* translate the author's hand-drawn marginal "fists" into the existing standardized type unit for this symbol (☞). The editors of the *Emerson Journals* employ the conventional typeset caret (∧) for Emerson's mark for interlineation. And Mark Twain's editors translate Clemens's autograph proofreading symbols in his *Notebooks* into the printer's symbols for these marks.

Writers seldom, however, confine themselves to such easily translated marks. The expensive photoreproduction of sketches, drawings, or maps in a printed volume of documents should be undertaken only when their literal presentation is essential to understanding the documents' verbal elements. The diagrams and schematic drawings of great figures of science obviously fall into this category. Joseph Henry's sketches and diagrams are conscientiously reproduced in the *Henry Papers*, and the forthcoming edition of Thomas Edison's papers will imitate this model.

The graphic records of great artists and illustrators introduce a new dimension to the problem. Reproduction of such records for author-artists must meet higher technical standards than the ones adequate for the comparatively simple line drawings of a scientist. More sophisticated and costly reproduction techniques are necessary in the editions of the papers of figures like Benjamin Henry Latrobe and Charles Willson Peale. The process needed to reproduce such sketches as a physical part of a printed page may be prohibitively expensive. For artists of this caliber, a separate microfiche supplement can provide the reader with a comprehensive reproduction of such graphic materials, while the print edition may reproduce selected drawings and sketches on plates inserted as illustrations to the printed text.

The nature of the sketch or drawing may be essential to the reader's understanding of the document's verbal elements even when literal photoreproduction of the sketch is not required. In such cases, the transcriber should note the drawing's existence so that the editor can fulfill his responsibility by describing it in a note adjacent to the text. If such graphic materials are common to the group of documents being edited, the editor can fulfill this responsibility more completely by issuing an accompanying microform where the reader can consult the unprinted, and even unprintable, elements of the documents.

E. TRANSCRIPTIONS OF UNLOCATED ORIGINAL DOCUMENTS

Whether handwritten, typed, or printed, transcriptions of unlocated original documents must be regarded as scribal copies—or recopied copies—of the documents that they represent. They should be transcribed literally for the modern edition, and any later emendations should be as sparing and carefully considered as possible.

Frequently, the editor will be able to second-guess the earlier transcriber, recognizing that the scribe has consistently read the author's *a* for *o* or his *r* for *n*. Such systematic mistranscription by a specific copyist can and should be emended, but only after the editor has provided his readers with adequate warning in notes that both explain the reasons for his decision and pinpoint the areas in the edition where emendation has occurred. Similarly, typographical errors in printed transcriptions based on unprinted transcriptions or upon the lost originals can be corrected sparingly if such emendation is needed to make the transcriptions intelligible. Here, too, the editor should furnish notes explaining his decisions in any substantive emendations.

The transcriptions' punctuation and other accidentals should stand without any attempt to make them conform to conventions established for original source texts in the new edition. Second-guessing an earlier transcriber does not extend to mind reading.

III. Source Texts Requiring Translation

Traditionl textual methods of transcription and emendation cannot convert some source texts into editorial texts intelligible to their intended modern audience. Even though transcribed accurately and published in special typefaces, these materials would be printed sources of bafflement and not enlightenment. Much foreign-language material, as well as material written in authorial shorthand or cryptography, will remain of little use to most readers unless it is translated.

A. SOURCE TEXTS IN A FOREIGN LANGUAGE

Editorial policy concerning source texts in a foreign language may depend upon the amount of foreign-language material that will appear in the edition and upon the intended audience for the newly edited volumes. Some editors choose to present all documents in their original languages. A single volume for Woodrow Wilson's presidential years may include materials in French, German, Spanish, and Japanese as well as English. In such cases, the sources must be transcribed literally. The foreign-language materials that qualify for inclusion in the Wilson edition form but a small percentage of the whole, and the editors have assumed that diplomatic historians interested in specific documents are already masters of the languages in which these letters and state papers are inscribed.

The Lafayette editors were forced to follow another course. Lafayette's papers for the Revolutionary era include so many documents in French that only bilingual American readers could have employed the series had all documents appeared in their original tongue. Thus the editors chose to translate the materials into English, the language of the audience to whom the edition is primarily addressed. These translations are clearly labeled as such, and they appear in the annotated, chronological series of editorial texts in the Lafayette volumes. An appendix to each volume carries transcriptions of the original French texts for easy reference. Stanley Idzerda, editor of the Lafayette edition, admits, "No translators' apologies or rationales have ever been convincing to those who can read the language that is being translated." However, he recognized that the Lafayette materials, "untranslated, would be either a closed book or very poorly understood by too many readers who might otherwise find them interesting and useful." Here translation was the only way to furnish an effective editorial text for the edition as a whole.

When translated documents are printed as part of a documentary edition, the reader *must* be given a chance to consult the materials in their original languages. For editions that prefer not to imitate the Lafayette example of appended untranslated transcriptions, an accompanying microform may suffice. And any translations should be prepared by linguists familiar with the usage of the era in which the documents were inscribed. An expert in twentieth-century Spanish literature may not have the skills needed to translate adequately the records of an early eighteenth-century mission in New Mexico. And the editor and his translator must work out a careful policy on the reproduction of the accidentals of the original text. Many of these elements perform no useful function in an English translation (for example, German punctuation and capitalization), while devices that indicate special emphasis (such as underlined phrases or words rendered in block letters) should be reproduced literally in the translation.

The edition's general policies in recording deletions and insertions (see chaps. 6 and 7, below) must be honored in translated editorial texts. Whenever the treatment of accidentals, substantives, or format in translations differs from the accepted standards of the edition, such a departure must be described in the volume's introductory statement or in source notes for the translated sources.

B. AUTHORIAL SHORTHAND

The writer who employs either a personal or a standardized form of shorthand leaves his later editors with a very special problem. Moreover, the editor who deals with this problem should take care lest the method he chooses to solve the specific puzzle at hand distorts his overall textual policy. The ease with which this warning can be ignored was demonstrated by no less an editor than Julian Boyd. In expounding the merits of editorially emended expanded methods of transcription (see chap. 5, below), Boyd explained in volume 1 of the *Jefferson Papers*,

> If presented literally, what Jefferson wrote as he took down hasty notes in a congressional investigating committee in the busy summer of 1776

would read as follows: "Carleton havg hrd yt we were returning with considble reinfmt, so terrifd, yt wd hve retird immedly hd h. nt ben infmd by spies of deplorble condn to wch sm pox had redd us." Such a passage, by the conventionalization to be followed in these volumes, will read: "Carleton having heard that we were returning with considerable reinforcement, [was] so terrified, that [he] would have retired immediately had he not been informed by spies of [the] deplorable conditions to which small pox had reduced us."

In using this extract from Jefferson's notes in the Continental Congress to justify expanded method, Boyd loaded the argument in his own favor. The extract given reflects accurately Jefferson's methods of informal note taking, but Jefferson did not employ the same system of idiosyncratic shorthand in making fair copies of letters dispatched to correspondents, in writing legislative reports, or, indeed, even in making entries in his famed "Anas." There were good reasons to emend Jefferson's shorthand notes, but the same considerations did not apply to his other writings, public or private. Editors since Boyd have come to recognize this distinction.

Most of the source texts that serve the *Woodrow Wilson Papers* are printed in a very conservatively emended form, but Wilson's editors would have served no purpose by publishing handset printed facsimiles of the notes and drafts that Wilson made in Graham shorthand. Instead, such source texts were translated, and they appear in the Wilson volumes in English, not in Graham symbols. Since Wilson usually indicated his preferred marks of punctuation and paragraph breaks in his shorthand materials, these are honored in the editorial texts. Still, the editors do not pretend that they have guessed all of the author's intentions for translation from Graham, and their standard for the treatment of shorthand materials differs from that given to materials drafted by Wilson in clear English. A statement of these special methods appears in editorial notes in volume 1, pages 8–19 and 128–31, and notes to individual documents alert the reader to the use of translated shorthand source texts.

Even writers without Wilson's stenographic skills can lapse into unusual abbreviated forms when taking notes or drafting letters or other documents. The editor will have the opportunity to compare and analyze a wide selection of such idiosyncratic shorthand to determine the meaning of these forms, while scholars without access to the project's editorial archives are denied this luxury. In such cases, it is the editor's duty to determine the meaning of such forms and to represent them verbally in the editorial text for the convenience and enlightenment of the reader. As with Wilson's formal shorthand, the editor may often have to present a more heavily emended editorial text than is usual in the series. If the nature of the shorthand allows the expansion of alphabetic contractions within square brackets, the editor's responsibility is fulfilled. If the symbols make such expansion and explication within brackets impractical, the document may be presented in something approaching clear text. In either case, the notes accompanying the document must indicate that a departure from the usual editorial practice has occurred, and the edition should include an editorial statement of the techniques used to translate the shorthand symbols or abbreviations into readable English. Responsibility for such emendations belongs to the editor, not to the initial transcriber.

C. CODES AND CIPHERS

Coded and enciphered communications present many textual problems analogous to those presented by materials recorded in any standardized system of shorthand. In both cases the editor must make every effort to translate the symbols into verbal equivalents that can be comprehended by the modern reader. In the case of codes, as in that of shorthand records, he is obliged to share with the reader the details of the method by which he has established that clear reading text.

Codes and ciphers introduce their own special problems, however. Systematic codes and ciphers are customarily employed to ensure confidentiality in the writer's communications with a second party; they are not used in shorthand records for the author's own use. Such cryptic passages usually appear in communications of considerable historical significance, such as diplomatic dispatches or private correspondence between political leaders. These documents are in the form of communications between two parties. Not only must the translated clear text of coded documents enable the reader to see just which sections were entered in code and cipher, but the text or the accompanying notes must also record how fully the communication's recipient was able to master the ciphered passages.

The indication of which words, phrases, or sentences were significant enough to deserve encoding allows the reader to judge exactly which information in the letter was judged confidential and which facts the writer felt free to leave open to prying eyes. The author's skill in encoding his own words and his correspondent's accuracy in using the key to the same code are both critical in showing the effectiveness of the transmission of the ciphered information.

For modern American editors, these textual problems have occurred most frequently in the writings of statesmen of the Revolutionary era. Many of these leaders established personal codes or ciphers for use in private correspondence during their public service in wartime, and the same men often received diplomatic appointments that required them to use official government ciphers for their correspondence. Historical series for such statesmen offer the best examples of the treatment of codes and ciphered documents.

The source texts may survive in several forms. A draft letter can bear interlined symbols for passages that the author entered in cipher above their verbal equivalents in the copy actually dispatched later. The author's file copy may carry interlined cipher equivalents, or it may be copied directly from the final recipient's version, with only numerical symbols or hieroglyphics for the coded passages. In the papers of such letters' addressees, the editor may find a recipient's virgin copy, with or without an accompanying sheet of the deciphered lines. At other times, the recipient may have translated cipher passages interlineally on the pages of the letter that he received.

The textual treatment of such documents depends on the survival of the keys to the modes and ciphers employed. If the ciphered materials survive only in encoded form, and no key exists, the editor must admit defeat and offer his readers what little he has to provide. With brief and scattered coded passages, it may be simplest to print the numerical or alphabetical symbols within the unencoded portion of the text, warning the reader of the existence of such untranslatable codes in the document's source note. However, if the coded sections are lengthy, it is pointless to reproduce them in the reading text. Instead, the editor should omit them, indicating an ellipsis followed by a superscript number keyed to an explanatory footnote or by a bracketed editorial interpolation in the reading text (e.g., "[ten lines in cipher are omitted here]").

Should the editor have copies of the document that carry the author's or recipient's decoded version of cryptic passages, he must decide how to represent these sections in his reading text. Modern documentary editors generally eschew the use of brackets to enclose such passages. Instead, they use either footnotes or special typefaces to indicate the cryptic writing.

In his introduction to volume 6 of the *Jefferson Papers*, Julian Boyd objected to any "fixed method" for indicating coded passages. Instead, he employed italicized characters in letters "having one or two words or a number of widely-scattered words in codes," and he employed numbered textual footnotes when "the coded passage [could] be precisely and conveniently described" by that method. However, he assured his reader, "every word and passage in code will be indicated" in one fashion or the other. Unfortunately, Boyd sometimes combined these two methods within the same document, and the reading text of Jefferson's cipher letter to Madison of 14 February 1783 (vol. 6, pp. 241–44) requires the reader to flip back and forth to numbered footnotes that designate some coded passages while remembering that other cipher sections in the same letter appear in italic type. A similar method is employed in the *Robert Morris Papers*, although the editors of that series do not combine the two methods of distinguishing cipher from clear passages in the same document. Instead, they use italics to indicate encoded passages in some letters (see vols. 3, pp. 518–20, and 4, pp. 242–45) and employ explanatory, numbered footnotes to indicate encoded sections in others (see vols. 2, pp. 90–92, and 4, pp. 386, 438, 441, 550).

The editors of the *Madison Papers* discarded this dual system for designing encoded sections. In their edition, only italic type is used to signal ciphered passages. However, this system has its drawbacks, for any words underlined in clear passages of an enciphered letter must be followed by a superscript number leading the reader to a note explaining that these words were not enciphered by their writer (see vol. 6, pp. 177–79). A far more effective solution was chosen by the editors of the *Jay Papers*: ciphered passages are printed in small capital letters, which do not appear elsewhere in the editorial texts of handwritten sources. Selection of such a neutral style for *all* ciphered passages eliminates the need for additional footnotes and ensures that the reader cannot confuse it with any other textual device.

The editor with access to a cipher's or code's key has a responsibility beyond the choice of an appropriate typeface for encoded passages. He must also check both the author's accuracy in enciphering the passages and the recipient's skill in decoding them. Once this is done, the editor decides how best to share such knowledge with the reader. He may find, as did Madison's editors, that a recipient's errors in deciphering the coded text led earlier, less conscientious editors to publish inaccurate versions of significant political correspondence (see vol. 6, pp. 177–79). Or he may discover, as did Jay's editors, that the inventor of a code misused his own system so badly that his correspondent was unable to decipher his letters (vol. 2, pp. 117–18). When there is a significant difference between what the author intended his correspondent to read and what the second party was, in fact, able to comprehend, the editor must make this clear. The simplest solution to this problem consists in offering an editorial text that approximates the author's intentions, no matter how badly he fulfilled that wish or how poorly his correspondent-audience managed to grasp his meaning. Numbered footnotes can describe variants between intentions and perceptions. (A detailed analysis of a cipher document representing the full array of such problems of communication can be seen in the *Madison Papers*, 6: 177–79.)

With ciphers, as with shorthand, it may be impossible to guess at the author's intentions as to capitalization and punctuation. Indeed, writers in cipher often deliberately omitted marks of punctuation or paragraph breaks to avoid assisting the efforts of enemy cryptologists who might intercept their correspondence. In such cases, the initial transcription and deciphered version should reflect the peculiarities of the original. The editor will make the necessary emendations at a later stage. The reader must be warned that all such emendations have been supplied by the editor, and in the substance of deciphered texts, as in those based on a clear source text, the editor must identify occasions when editorial guesswork or imagination has been employed.

IV. TRANSCRIBING THE SOURCE TEXT: TYPES OF DOCUMENTARY RECORDS

The editor's transcription of his sources must also reflect the type of documentary record that each represents. The traditional literary distinction between a writer's public and private writings is of little use to the documentary editor. Unpublished letters have influenced the course of history. State papers not set in type in their author's lifetime have shaped the thinking of legislators and executives. Confidential technical reports have radically affected the history of science. Each of these is private under the literary scholar's definition, but all were composed for an audience, and all derive their historical importance from the influence that they exerted upon their contemporary readers. The documentary editor will abandon the easy distinction between public and private writings and, instead, examine the fashion in which his source texts functioned as agents of communication. Even with an audience of one, a document's words cease to be private, and any edition of such sources must strive to preserve the intended communicative effect of the original.

With documents, the editor may also have to modify his notion of what constitutes the appropriate contents of an edited text. Elements in the source that could be safely ignored by the editor of an author's published works may be an integral part of the documentary contents of a source. Such accidentals as capitalization, indentation, and spacing may perform important functions in the design of certain modes of communication. And for some documents, even nonauthorial contributions must be considered part of the source's evidentiary contents.

A. CORRESPONDENCE

The small body of literature on editing correspondence has traditionally focused upon the need to make the letters of an earlier age "readable"—even "enjoyable"—for a modern audience (see, for instance, Robert Halsband, "Editing the Letters of Letter-Writers," *Studies in Bibliography* 11 [1958]: 25–37). The move toward clear text in editions of correspondence approved by the CSE has been justified, in part, by the claim that the literary critics who form a large part of these volumes' audience will not wish to be distracted by textual symbols or numbered footnotes pointing out details of the original. Yet even exponents of silently emended expanded transcription concede that readers soon become used to archaic and idosyncratic usage in a documentary edition. And Ernest W. Sullivan has pointed out that literary critics are ill-served by standardization of texts in editions of personal correspondence ("The Problem of Text in Familiar Letters," *Papers of the Bibliographical Society of America* 75 [1981]: 115–26). The editor's compulsion to conventionalize, normalize, or otherwise emend the text of letters is under serious attack.

When letters survive in some preliminary form that reflects revision by the author, they may require the application of textual methods appropriate to such *genetic* elements (see chap. 7, below), that is, those that reflect the evolution of a text, not merely its final form. But when a letter survives in the form in which its author dispatched it to its addressee, it must be transcribed literally, and the editor must leave well enough alone. Hastily scrawled and ill proofread as that recipient's copy may be, it remains, historically, the representation of the author's final intentions. Equally important in documentary terms, it represents the form of the letter that influenced its recipient. Unnecessary emendations will make the editorial text of any letter useless as evidence either of what its author wrote *or* of what its addressee read. It is not the business of doc-

umentary editors to introduce new corruptions into a documentary
text for the sake of historically unrealized clarity.

The initial transcriptions of such sources must be as literal as
possible. Thus, any policies of emendation for letters that may be
adopted later by the editor will be as conservative as their method
of inscription allows. Even a detailed back-of-book textual record
does not give license to violate this rule. If any corrections are to
be imposed upon the author's prose, they will come from the editor
after he has established the edition's final textual policies. However,
the transcriber may be instructed to incorporate certain conventions
for standardizing formal elements of letters. Such standardization
most commonly concerns the location of datelines, greetings, and
closings. Even this degree of intervention may prove short-sighted
if the letter writer employs individual formats for different types of
correspondence. Should these variations show a significant pattern,
the original format must be maintained. If the writer has used sta-
tionary with an imprinted letterhead, there is no reason to repeat
this form at the beginning of the transcription of every letter inscribed on such paper. The editor will reproduce the letterhead's
text verbatim at some point in the edition, and he will design an
easily recognized contracted form that will be used in the printed
edition.

If the letter's envelope or address leaf survives, all authorial inscriptions must be transcribed verbatim. The editor can review these
elements at his leisure and decide upon their treatment in the edition.
Authorial notations can appear at the foot of a letter's printed text
or in the letter's source note (see chap. 9, below). At the very least,
postal markings must be noted by the transcriber. When they represent the basis for assigning a date to an undated letter, they should
be described in detail. Any notations by postal officials or others
involved in forwarding a letter to its intended recipient should also
be noted.

The transcriber must also indicate the existence of a recipient's
endorsement, that is, a notation made on the letter, its envelope, or
its address leaf at the time of its receipt or reading. Whenever such
an endorsement indicates the date of the letter's arrival, summarizes
the reader's reaction, or otherwise supplies important documentary
evidence, the endorsement should be transcribed verbatim.

For personal correspondence, a letter's documentary elements
usually end with its receipt and endorsement by its addressee (see
chap. 7, sec. II.B.1). However, correspondence with governments
or their agents may carry *dockets* (endorsements made after the

letter's receipt by someone other than its addressee) and other important documentary notations. The transcriber should record these in full.

These suggested rules apply only to sources that were truly letters, not essays or other short works written in letter form with the intention of print publication. The problem of distinguishing between the two is discussed in John A. Walker's "Editing Zola's Correspondence: When Is a Letter Not a Letter?" in Dainard, *Editing Correspondence*, 93–116.

B. BUSINESS AND FINANCIAL RECORDS

Documentary editors generally agree that such documents as business records, accounts, and all other documents recorded in a tabular manner ought to be printed in the most literally transcribed format possible. The reasons are twofold. First, such documents make sense in visual terms only if the original arrangement of columns and indentations is preserved. Within such a format, it is usually impossible to expand contracted or abbreviated forms devised by the author to make headings or entries fit into the spaces available. Second, there is no theoretical justification for emending such records in the name of recovering the author's literary intentions. Such sources have only evidentiary, documentary value, and there is no reason to improve them by emendations in a quest for easily appreciated literary value. Such aesthetic worth did not exist in the original, and no scholar will seek it in the printed text.

C. PROFESSIONAL AND TECHNICAL RECORDS

The editor who publishes professional and technical records must not only master the technical terms in the document's verbal text but also become familiar with the special formats peculiar to such professions as law, medicine, physics, or mathematics. He can assume that a large proportion of his readers will themselves be specialists in the history of these fields. Such scholars will best be served by a faithfully printed facsimile of the source's format, preserving the styled brackets of the attorney and the indentations and spacing of scientific formulas. These elements cannot be standardized in the name of readability, for they will be familiar to the edition's readers. And their normalization would destroy important aspects of the source as it was communicated to its original audience of judges, court clerks, or fellow scholars.

D. GOVERNMENT RECORDS

Official records of any government or its agents cannot bear emendations in the name of clarity, readability, or enjoyability. They are what they are what they are. Government financial records, of course, are subject to the rules for tabular documents, but special respect is due to the formats and accidentals of nonfiscal records. Legislative journals, like financial records, are often intelligible only when their original patterns of spacing and indentation are retained. State papers outside the definition of journals often reproduce the formats familiar to the lawyer-legislators and lawyer-clerks who inscribed them, and their formats often must be respected.

The nonauthorial labels and notations upon government records must also be noted, described, or printed verbatim. Such documents are remarkably long-lived in terms of their documentary significance. An unprinted legislative report or treasurer's account from the 1790s may well have been consulted by congressional committees two decades later. Often this is indicated by the notations of the clerk responsible for filing and refiling the manuscript. Unless such dockets are noted fully in the edition (either as part of the text or in the source note), the source's documentary elements have been only partially reproduced.

E. AN AUTHOR'S WORKS

An author's works—essays, stories, plays, books, or other forms written with the intention of print publication—receive different treatment from the textual and the documentary editor. Aiming for the author's intended meaning, the textual editor may emend one source text liberally or conflate authorial portions of two or more sources into one new text. The documentary editor, however, will focus upon a single source for his edition, and his noncritical editorial text will reflect that one source.

If the source is a draft version, it will be transcribed according to the edition's general rules for sources with genetic elements (see chap. 7, below). If it is a fair copy or a printed version, the transcription will be a verbatim rendering of that single source, with later emendations indicated clearly by the editor and with variants recorded later in adjacent notes rather than incorporated into the new editorial text.

F. JOURNALS AND DIARIES

Intended audience as a useful factor in determining transcriptional policies and textual method for literary works, public papers, and even letters is of little help with an author's journals or diaries. Here the intended audience is the author himself (although one wag has remarked that in the case of the Adams family, a diarist's audience was posterity). These intimate records, which can reveal so much of the inner life of a public figure, demand the most literal textual treatment their method of inscription permits.

Informal in nature and private in intent, diaries lose rather than gain by any attempt to impose excessive conventions of print publication. If a writer's punctuation or spelling is less regular and correct in his diaries than in his correspondence, so be it in the transcription and in the printed edition. The very fact that an author allows himself such lapses is significant. However, if the author employs any form of shorthand, then more liberal editorial intervention is not only permissible but necessary. As in any other instance of translation from idiosyncratic or standardized shorthand, the editor must discuss the textual problems and his methods in introducing the journal entries.

The format of a diary or journal may also require special treatment. Diary entries that are not inscribed in books whose pages carry headings with a printed date will demand additional editorial intervention in standardizing or expanding the dates of entry furnished by the author. The editor's annotational format may play a part in this decision. When numbered informational notes follow each daily entry, an arbitrarily formalized heading, free of brackets or other typographical barbed wire, may be less distracting; with bottom-of-page footnotes, the daily headings are less striking visually. Some standardization may be necessary even during transcription, and the most convenient method consists in placing each date flush to the lefthand margin. The editor will decide later whether to set the date in boldface or italic type or in large and small capital letters to give the reader easy reference. With such a run-on text of diary entries, it may be necessary to normalize the substantive elements of the date as well as its form. Expanding abbreviated forms in the dateline or even standardizing the author's arrangement of day, month, and year may be necessary to give the reader a consistently useful reference point.

The nature of bound diaries and journals requires the editor to give his readers a more complete description of the original source than is necessary with letters and other shorter manuscript sources.

If the author has paginated his journal, or if the journal carries preprinted numbers on its pages, these should be noted by the transcriber for reproduction in the new print edition with brackets reserved for such a purpose. If the diary's pages are unnumbered, the editor may need to assign numbers for easy reference (see, for example, the explanation of such a plan in the introduction to the *Irving Journals*, vol. 1).

Editions in the CSE mode tend to carry more detailed descriptions of the physical appearance of bound journals and diaries, but even historical editors recognize the need to offer more descriptive information for this category of source text (see introductory notes for the John Adams, John Quincy Adams, and Charles Francis Adams diaries). The reason for such explicit description is a practical one. The reader must be able to locate the original entry for comparison with the editorial text. Clearly, this is a greater challenge within a bound volume of diary entries than in a separately cataloged one- or two-page letter. To ensure that the challenge is met, the transcriptions themselves should indicate breaks between volumes, as well as note any special problems in arrangement of entries in the original.

G. RECORDS OF ORAL COMMUNICATIONS

The editor must transcribe records of the spoken word with special care, for any printed versions will be far removed from their archetypes. These inscribed sources present a visual record of words and thoughts intended to be communicated orally. Only with the greatest skill can the editor produce a text that is even second-best in documentary terms, and he may have to resort to the critical methods of textual editing to reconcile transcriptions of variant versions (see chap. 7, below).

The editors of the *Frederick Douglass Papers* have furnished a convenient list of the forms in which such records are likely to survive. The first is *a pretext*, the author's draft, outline, or notes for a speech. In the absence of any other record, it is impossible to determine whether the pretext bears any relationship to the lecture or oration that was actually delivered. Whenever a pretext is the sole source text, it should be transcribed and edited as conservatively as its method of inscription allows. The question of audience here is a delicate one, for the pretext itself was intended for its author in visual form—a cue to the words and phrases that he intended to utter. If such a pretext has been scribbled hastily or inscribed in some authorial shorthand, the expansion of idiosyncratic contractions and the translation of shorthand symbols should be considered. However, the editor should be exceptionally restrained in emending or standardizing such formal elements as spacing, punctuation, and the like. Each device may have served the author as stage directions in speaking, and no useful purpose is served by destroying the clues that format provides. (The forthcoming edition of Jonathan Edwards's *History of the Works of Redemption*, for instance, retains all of Edwards's unique marks of punctuation which indicate pauses for emphasis in these sermons.)

Of course, the author is not the only person likely to leave records of his spoken words. The editors of the *Douglass Papers* group records left by witnesses to a speech in the following categories: "mention," "summary," "narrative," "extract," and "stenographic" texts. The first three are likely to be paraphrases of the words actually spoken, and the distinctions among them refer to the completeness of the paraphrased record left behind. When one of these forms is the only record of an oral text, it should be transcribed and reproduced in a documentary edition as literally as possible. Editorial notes can explain the nature of the source, and the reader can judge for himself how accurately the reporter has mentioned, narrated, or summarized the speech or conversation involved.

Such fragmentary paraphrases can occur *within* a document that concerns itself with matters irrelevant to the edition. In such cases, there is no need to transcribe the document in its entirety. The editor customarily omits those portions of the letter or other document that do not concern the oral text in question, always indicating such omissions with ellipses or any other device reserved for such editorial intervention. (See, for instance, the treatment of "third-party" documents discussed in the introduction to volume 1 of the Lafayette edition.)

Through the early nineteenth century, various mentions, narrations, and summaries of the same speech or conversation are likely to survive in textually irreconcilable terms. In the absence of the use of systematic shorthand, no two reporters were likely to leave accounts of the same spoken words that can be viewed as variants of one another. They are likely to be so dissimilar that there will be no question of conflating or combining them into one master record of the spoken words. These must be transcribed literally, for any normalization of format or punctuation can obscure the meaning of the original reporter. The editor may be unable to identify one source text here. Instead, he will give his reader access to all conflicting reports. However, should one record of the speech be a ten-page narration, while the others are paragraph-long summaries of the same words, the editor may choose to transcribe and print the longest record as his editorial text, reporting transcriptions of the shorter versions in notes or as separate documents.

Verbatim extracts and stenographic reports of speeches are more common in documents inscribed after the mid-nineteenth century, when systematized methods of shorthand became increasingly common. If one verbatim extract or a single stenographic report of a speech or conversation survives, it must be transcribed literally; however, if more than one verbatim report, partial or complete, survives, the editor should consider the more sophisticated, classically textual methods discussed below in chapter 7.

Scholarly editors have not yet been forced to address the textual problem of the newest documentary records, those created by the perfection of sound-recording equipment. When tapes or phonograph discs that record an actual speech or conversation survive, the editor of the future will have at hand the archetype for his document—his transcription will be the first imperfect witness in a long series. The skill or awkwardness with which documentary editors meet this challenge will take the measure of their scholarly specialty.

An even more sophisticated textual problem arises with the results of the *oral history* movement initiated more than thirty years ago by Allan Nevins. Practitioners of oral history interview historically significant figures and then create an archive of typewritten transcriptions of these conversations. The very setting of the oral history interview introduces an intellectual challenge. As Ronald Grele has pointed out, "Unlike . . . traditional sources [written diaries and letters], oral history interviews are constructed, for better or worse, by the active intervention of the historian" ("Movement Without Aim: Methodological and Theoretical Problems in Oral History," in *Envelopes of Sound: Six Practitioners Discuss the Method, Theory, and Practice of Oral Testimony and Oral History* [Chicago, 1975], 133–34).

The editor of oral history interviews must know as much as possible about the peculiar inscriptional history of this form of document, for the practices of American oral history archives often camouflage rather than reveal pertinent facts. Customarily, both the interviewer and the subject review the typed transcriptions of such memoirs, the first correcting errors of transcription and the second making emendations for style and indicating passages that he wishes omitted from the final archival version of the transcript. Some oral history projects even destroy the original tapes, thus eliminating any chance for comparing the typed witness against its archetype.

Still other projects now employ word-processing equipment to emend transcriptions after review. This use of computer technology may ensure that only the final version of such interviews survives in the word processor's storage, with earlier and fuller versions lost forever. As American documentary editors catch up with the products of phonographic technology, this form of source text, too, may become a major focus of debate.

V. The Business of Editing Begins

Even these general rules for transcription of source texts introduce the questions central to scholarly editing—the considerations that make possible the establishment of printed texts that reflect the editor's experience and knowledge. A series of literal, verbatim transcriptions is usually the most appropriate one for any documentary edition, but the edition's textual standards as well as its organizational format may require a modification of this rule. These are only the most elementary considerations for transcription. The conventions by which American editors have presented documentary texts is analyzed in the next chapter. Even before the transcription of source texts begins, new editors must familiarize themselves with these modern textual conventions lest their working transcriptions make the business of editing an insuperable challenge.

Suggested Readings

I. The proper selection of the source text has been largely ignored in monographic literature by editors, although reviewers of documentary editions have not been so negligent. See, for instance, Ira D. Gruber's and George A. Billias's reviews of the *Naval Documents of the American Revolution* series in *William and Mary Quarterly* 22 (October 1965): 660–63 and *American Historical Review* 77 (June 1972): 831, respectively. For a useful discussion of the techniques of classical scholars in applying filiation to ancient texts see Paul Maas, *Textual Criticism*, trans. Barbara Flower (Oxford, 1958).

II. Special problems of handwritten inscription that confront American editors are discussed in Maygene Daniels, "The Ingenious Pen: American Writing Implements from the Eighteenth Century to the Twentieth Century," *American Archivist* 43 (1980): 312–24; P. W. Filby, *Calligraphy and Handwriting in America, 1710–1962* (New York, 1963); Thomas H. Johnson, "Establishing a Text: The Emily Dickinson Papers," *Studies in Bibliography* 5 (1952–53): 21–

32; E. Kay Kirkham, *How to Read the Handwriting and Records of Early America* (Salt Lake City, 1964); Leonard Rapport, "Fakes and Facsimiles: Problems of Identification," *American Archivist* 42 (1979): 13–58; and Laetitia Yeandle, "The Evolution of Handwriting in the English-Speaking Colonies of America," ibid. 43 (1980): 294–311.

Useful essays on the relationship between bibliography and editorial problems appear regularly in *Studies in Bibliography*. Vol. 3 (1950–51) includes Fredson Bowers's "Some Relations of Bibliography to Editorial Procedures." The same scholar's "The Function of Bibliography" remains an able introduction to the topic. G. Thomas Tanselle provides a good discussion of the bibliographical problems raised by nineteenth-century authors in "Bibliographical Problems in Melville," *Studies in American Fiction* 2 (Spring 1974): 57–74. Jennifer Tebbe's "Print and American Culture," *American Quarterly* 32 (1980): 259–79, is a good introduction for novices. A more sophisticated treatment of a bibliographical problem with significance for documentary editors who must use periodicals as source texts is found in Fredson Bowers's "Multiple Authority: New Problems and Concepts of Copy-Text," *Library* 27 (June 1972): 81–95, and G. Thomas Tanselle's "Editorial Apparatus for Radiating Texts," ibid. 29 (September 1974): 330–37.

III.   Ralph E. Weber surveys important elements of cryptography in *United States Diplomatic Codes and Ciphers, 1775–1938* (Chicago, 1979). Editorial notes in *Adams Family Correspondence* 4:viii–ix, 393–99, comment on the specific editorial problems raised by the cryptographs employed by one group of correspondents.

IV.   Some of the essays in Dainard, *Editing Correspondence*, touch on the special problems of transcribing letters. Good examples of editorial treatments of business and financial records can be found in the *Hamilton Papers* and the *Morris Papers*. The editions of the legal papers of Hamilton, Adams, and Webster provide examples of skillful editing of this form of professional record, while the *Henry Papers* volumes offer good examples for the treatment of scientific materials.

Although much of American historical editing has been devoted to government records, editors have contributed little to the literature in this field. The student who wishes to introduce himself to this form of diplomatic should consult Christopher N. L. Brooke, "The Teaching of Diplomatic," *Journal of the Society of Archivists*

4 (April 1970): 1–9, and Buford Rowland, "Recordkeeping Practices of the House of Representatives," *National Archives Accessions,* 53 (Washington, D.C. 1957). The state of the art of print bibliography for government records is discussed in review essays by Ted Samore and Stewart P. Schneider in *Government Publications Review* 7A (1980) and 8A (1981), respectively, and in Martin Claussen's review essay in *American Archivist* 36 (1973): 523–36. The most pointed critique is Edwin Wolf's "Evidence Indicating the Need for Some Bibliographical Analysis of American Printed Historical Works," *Papers of the Bibliographical Society of America* 63 (1969): 261–77.

The reading lists and handbooks of the CEAA and CSE, of course, must be consulted for any edition that presents the text of a published work.

In addition to the series cited in the chapter, the *Ratification of the Constitution* series, vol. 2, *Pennsylvania*, provides interesting parallel texts for accounts of speeches too discordant to be reconciled in one single emended editorial text.

CHAPTER 5

The Conventions of
Textual Treatment

In documentary editing, the patterns of characters, words, phrases, and paragraphs offered to the reader are seldom *the* text of the source on which the edition is based. Instead, they form but one text that the editor might have extrapolated from the handwritten, typed, or printed material that he presents in authoritative form. As he establishes the text to be presented in that printed version, he may have to invent new methods, as well as recur to the tools of earlier editorial traditions.

The editor of modern documents often has problems and goals different from those of the analysts of classical texts or of great literary works. The classicist's aim is usually the recension, or recovery, of a lost archetype. He must often achieve this through the careful comparison of the surviving *witnesses* to that archetype—copies made directly from it or even later transcriptions based on earlier scribal versions. Since it is impossible to hazard guesses about the formal *accidentals* (spelling, punctuation, or format) of that archetype, modern editors often standardize such elements of the text. The editor of literary works published in his author's lifetime may have something more complicated than recension as his goal. Instead of trying to reconstruct a lost archetype, he may seek to determine the author's final intentions in an idealized form that combines elements of an incomplete authorial manuscript and several printed editions of the work based on that manuscript. Frequently such an editor cannot point to a single source that represents all of the author's careful proofreading or stylistic revisions. Instead, he must painstakingly collate, or compare, manuscripts and printed editions for their variants. He must familiarize himself with the work's publishing history so that he can evaluate responsibility for such changes, and he may even have sufficient data to determine authorial patterns in the accidentals of punctuation and spelling as well as in the substantive elements of patterns of words. Thus, the editions prepared by the classicist or the literary critic can themselves be new works. Critical judgment and scholarly insight can give the reader the text of an archetype that no longer exists in a physical sense or of something that never existed, such as an edition of a novel that is more intellectually consistent and textually reliable than any published during the author's lifetime.

The noncritical editor of American documents has certain advantages over editors in other fields. In most cases, his source texts are themselves archetypes, and if they survive in transcribed form, such copies were usually made within decades, not centuries, of their original inscription. Thus recension is a comparatively rare concern. Unlike the editor of published literary works, the documentary editor seldom has to compare dozens of variant versions hundreds of pages in length. There are seldom more than two or three copies with any claim to such consideration, and many of his source texts are unarguably the final intention of the author—copies of letters dispatched to and received by their addressees or public papers that the author submitted above his signature to government bodies or other agencies.

This is not to say that the documentary editor's task is easier than other scholarly editors'—merely different. He may, for instance, have at hand a sufficiently wide selection of holograph materials left by his subject to allow him to draw conclusions about that writer's customary usage in such accidentals as paragraph indentation, punctuation, and spelling. But he does not have license to exploit this knowledge by emending the literal transcription of the source text so that the accidentals are standardized.

The printed versions of materials that have been edited as documents rather than as idealized texts must themselves be capable of use as documents—as evidence for factual research. The editorial texts must present what was written, not what might have been inscribed had the author had the luxury of revising the materials for publication. It is the responsibility of a documentary editor to translate handwritten, typescript, or printed source texts into a form that his reader can trust as an accurate representation of the specific original materials that they represent. Even when he employs traditional techniques of textual scholarship such as recension and conflation, the documentary editor must stop short of making his text too smooth, too finished in appearance. Neither the editor nor his reader can ignore occasions when editorial judgment has been at work.

If every author of documentary material obliged posterity by inscribing his letters, journals, and other papers in a regular, immaculate hand (or, better still, by leaving behind impeccably proofread typescripts), the documentary editor could discharge his duty by serving as little more than a faithful scribe. But historical figures are seldom so considerate. Their records are filled with inconsistent and confusing usages, with symbols for which no equivalent exists in any printer's font. Water, fire, insects, the ravages of time, and the scissors of autograph collectors may have defaced pages that were scarcely legible in the beginning. The array of physical details of the source texts range from authorial idiosyncrasies which are clearly pertinent to the interest of every reader to marks such as notations by a cataloger which are completely irrelevant to any conceivable use.

Thus, after collecting and cataloging materials for his edition, the documentary editor must survey his source texts and their initial transcriptions to evaluate their peculiarities. He must devise a way to present a printed version of this collection that will serve the majority of his readers almost as well as would the archive itself. And he must remember that each stage in establishing a printed editorial text of these documents will inevitably take him and his readers a step further from the source's full meaning.

If his is a collection of printed source texts, the editor's task is comparatively easy. His textual decisions are limited to the choice of a typeface that will accommodate archaic characters in the old printing. Perhaps he need do no more than devise a method of indicating his corrections of obvious typographical errors. However, the editor of unprinted sources must make one agonizing decision after another as he considers standardizing details of inscription whose nuances might serve the purpose of some researcher.

The very act of printing such source texts suppresses some of their detail, for the *contents* of an unprinted document can extend far beyond its *text* (those elements such as inscribed letters and numbers used by the writer to record ideas and facts in verbal form). The character of the handwriting or typewriting can offer clues to the author's alertness or health. Careless penmanship in one recipient's copy of a letter and painstaking inscription of a letter addressed to another can indicate varying degrees of formality between the author and the two correspondents. The nature of the paper or ink or pencil or typewriter ribbon can provide important clues to the time and place of the preparation of an undated letter or journal entry. Many of these important factors in the source's documentary contents cannot be reproduced; they can only be described.

Even elements of the document added by persons other than the author must be considered part of the source text's documentary contents. Postal markings can indicate the date of receipt of a letter whose recipient has not endorsed it. That date, in turn, can shed light on the letter's influence on its addressee. The recipient's endorsement of a letter can be an exposition of his reaction to that communication, making the endorsement, in its turn, a separate document that is physically a part of the first. Words, numbers, and codes entered by a clerk in his docket of a public document, or similar notations made by a compositor on a manuscript that was printer's copy for a published essay or poem—these, too, are important parts of a source's evidentiary, documentary contents.

In short, the special problem of the modern documentary editor is more often an embarrassment of textual riches than the absence of an archetype or of some single manuscript that represents final authorial intentions. The question that faces the documentary editor is how to share as much of this wealth as possible without making the printed pages of his edition an incomprehensible mass.

This chapter begins an examination of the methods used by modern American editors to produce documentary texts for the sources of the nation's political, intellectual, and social history. The examination opens with a discussion of the mechanical aspect of the process, the broad categories of textual approach adopted by American editors and the technical systems of symbols and descriptive annotation with which these general methods are put into action. This chapter and the one that follows are those least loved of creatures, a reference book's glossary.

I. Standardizing, Recording, and Emending

Documentary editors have urged that editorial intervention be limited to standardizing certain elements of the texts, recording or describing certain physical details of the source that cannot readily be reproduced in print, and emending the source's transcriptions to meet a few clearly defined standards. The boundaries between these categories are not well defined, and one editor's standardization may be another's emendation.

In general, standardization concerns elements in the source's physical format. An edition of correspondence may arbitrarily place all datelines for letters at the beginning of their texts, no matter where the date appears in the source text. Similarly, it is customary to standardize an author's paragraph indentation in handwritten

a new page in the middle of a sentence) or in the margin (when the new page represents a new section of the document).

Examples of a *pure* printed facsimile, without the use of any textual symbols or other editorial conventions, are rare in modern editions. An approximation of facsimile technique can be found in Julian Boyd's "literal presentation" of Jefferson's drafts of the Declaration of Independence (*Jefferson Papers*, 1:417–27), in the texts of letters in *Shelley in His Circle*, and in Cornell University's Wordsworth edition.

Because of the expense of setting such a format, printed facsimiles generally are used for nonprinted source texts only when textual symbols will not adequately communicate the nuances necessary for understanding the source text, and when readers have an uncommon interest in these subtleties. The editor of a series of colonial laws, for instance, would realize that his readers would be more concerned with the final versions of statutes—the words or phrases that were promulgated by the provincial government—than with a clerk's corrections of his copy of that law. For such an editor, a printed facsimile would be a needless luxury. However, the editor of documents relating to the legislative history of a colonial assembly would have good reason to consider a printed facsimile of a draft of an important legislative report, where the placement of interlineations and marginal additions indicates the evolution of the final version of laws and is essential to understanding their history.

Certain elements of printed-facsimile techniques may be employed for certain documents in editions that otherwise modify this editorial technique. One legal historian has remarked, for instance, that the reproduction of the format of Hamilton's draft legal papers in the *Hamilton Law Practice* volumes "allows the reader to see Hamilton's mind at work." This edition uses conservative expansion of some archaic abbreviations and contractions and thus cannot be described as a true printed facsimile. But its editors recognized those special documents whose full meaning could be conveyed only by retaining Hamilton's positioning of headings, subheadings, spacing, and line breaks.

Some form of typographical facsimile is, of course, the method of choice for reproducing printed documentary source texts. Even within editions where substantial liberties are taken with manuscript source texts, editors do their best to reproduce as exactly as possible the appearance of such printed sources as pamphlets and newspapers (see, for example, the treatment of "A Representation of Facts" in volume 5 of the *Laurens Papers*). This rule of thumb for the treatment of printed source texts is consistent among editions of eighteenth-century materials, but editors of more modern documents have departed from the mode. In the *Woodrow Wilson Papers*, for example, the same rules for emending spelling and punctuation are applied to both manuscript source texts and Wilson's published works. And the editors of the *Harold Frederic Correspondence* have allowed themselves far greater latitude in emending printed, and even typewritten, source texts of letters than in treating handwritten sources.

Although printed facsimiles of unprinted source texts traditionally have been viewed as extravagantly expensive, modern technology may make this textual approach economically practical for many more editions. The first volume of the *Documentary History of the Supreme Court* offers its readers page after page of documents in which superscript letters, marginal additions, interlineations, and archaic symbols are reproduced literally in type. The series publisher, Columbia University Press, was able to offer the editors this option because the Supreme Court project encoded editorial copy for both documents and notes with computerized equipment. This equipment enabled them to reproduce the special features needed in the published version. In turn, the press retained the services of a compositor who employed the most sophisticated computer composition methods available. Thus the press and the compositor could take full advantage of the savings in labor costs that computer-assisted editing makes possible. It is estimated that the cost of producing each page of the *Supreme Court* volumes in printed facsimiles in 1985 was a bit less in real terms than the cost at which the press produced the more standardized texts of a final volume of the *Hamilton Papers* in 1978.

B. DIPLOMATIC TRANSCRIPTIONS

In modern American editions, a diplomatic transcription is one step removed from the printed facsimile. The editor employs carefully chosen critical symbols or abbreviations to indicate details of inscription such as interlineations and cancellations instead of reproducing their physical appearance in the original. Editors of diplomatic transcriptions often standardize the placement of such routine elements of the source text as datelines, greetings, salutations, titles, and the indentation of paragraphs, and they may also supply missing punctuation, expand ambiguous or archaic abbreviations and contractions, or even supply words unintentionally omitted by the author or destroyed by mutilation of the original source text. However, none of these corrections or emendations is made silently: each is given within a form of brackets that indicates such editorial activities. If some emendation or detail of original inscription cannot be described conveniently with symbols or a bracketed interpolation, a footnote immediately adjacent to the text explains the problem at hand.

Examples of exhaustive diplomatic transcriptions are almost as rare as printed facsimiles among editions of modern American materials. Perhaps the best-known are Fredson Bowers's annotated diplomatic transcription of the surviving manuscripts of Whitman's *Leaves of Grass* and the Hayford-Sealts genetic text of Melville's *Billy Budd*. In both, the reader has immediate and convenient access to the details of the original manuscript source text.

It should be noted that in both of these editions the reader also has access to a critically edited *reading text*, which represents the author's apparent final intentions for the work in question. In *Leaves of Grass*, the reading text and the diplomatic transcription are presented as parallel texts on facing pages. The Hayford-Sealts reading text of *Billy Budd* precedes the genetic text of the author's manuscript. For materials whose diplomatic transcriptions rival these in complexity, providing a reading text is not only a kindness to the reader but a necessity.

C. THE MIDDLE GROUND: INCLUSIVE AND EXPANDED TEXTS

Most editors compromise to one degree or another between a detailed diplomatic text and a clear reading text. Among editors in the CEAA/CSE tradition such methods are described as *inclusive*. For historian-editors the practice has come to be known as *expanded* transcription. The difference between the inclusive and expanded methods is not so much the editor's basic conservatism or liberalism in emending and standardizing his text as it is the degree to which such editorial tinkering is reported to the reader. In inclusive editions, some of the emendations (although by no means all) are reported individually in accompanying textual notes that meet CEAA or CSE standards. Expanded texts in historical editions offer no supplementary record of emendations or suppressed details beyond what appears in the text and in footnotes immediately adjacent to the documentary text.

In both techniques, some of the details of inscription are reported overtly in the editorial text, that is, through the use of textual symbols or numbered footnotes adjacent to the text. And both breeds of editors may standardize certain elements of the format of the source text silently. Datelines and placelines in letters are usually printed above the greetings and text, no matter where they appear in the original. Headings for diary and journal entries are standardized for easy reference. Paragraph indentations of varying length are made uniform, as are dashes of whimsically varying dimensions.

Beyond such standardization of the format, inclusive and expansive editors often emend the text's accidentals and substantives without giving any overt indication. Superscript characters are commonly lowered to form a one-line abbreviation or contraction, with a mark of punctuation placed after the resulting form. Archaic holographic symbols are generally rendered in their closest equivalent in print (as *th* or *y* for the thorn, or *per* or *pro* for the tailed *p*). Abbreviations or contractions that the editor judges to be archaic or unfamiliar to his readers are not reproduced exactly—they may be expanded silently or overtly, with brackets to indicate that the editorial hand has been at work. Erratic punctuation is standardized—silently or overtly—and missing marks of punctuation are supplied.

1. Inclusive Texts

The most cogent description of requirements for an inclusive text appears in the CEAA's revised *Statement of Editorial Principles* of 1972. First, inclusive methods should be employed for a source text whose audience is "limited mostly to scholars and specialists," and they are specifically recommended to editors whose source texts are "manuscript letters or journals or notebooks" for which no authoritative published version exists. The *Statement* also points out that this method is preferred whenever "reporting the author's process of composition directly is important."

Once an editor has established his text, the *Statement* continues, he may report deletions and revisions on the same page as the editorial text, as he would with a diplomatic transcription. However, he may also supplement that text with accompanying textual footnotes that appear at the bottom of the page or are placed between such "separable" items as letters and entries in a journal. These textual notes are to explain the use of symbols in the text and to record details of inscription that the editor has been forced to omit from the text itself.

In addition to such notes, the CEAA inclusive editor is required to furnish "in some form" a record of editorial emendations of the source text that are not clearly indicated in that text or its adjacent notes. Thus, an inclusive text may be followed by a back-of-book record of emendations similar to the ones that appear in CEAA/ CSE editions of literary works, with their references keyed to the line and page of the edited volume where they occur. An inclusive text of documentary materials, like any CEAA/CSE edition, must also be accompanied by a report of "editorial decisions in the handling of possible compounds hyphenated at the ends of lines in the copy-text, along with an indication of which end-of-line hyphenations in the newly edited text should be retained in quotations from the text."

In practice, only one multivolume CEAA/CSE edition—the Washington Irving edition—has consistently followed these rules for documentary materials. The Irving *Journals* and *Letters* employ editorial symbols in their texts for most details of inscription. Numbered footnotes at the bottom of the page (*Journals*) or at the close of individual items (*Letters*) report emendations and details suppressed in the reading text.

The various modern editions of Emerson's writings have used varying textual methods for documentary source texts. The *Emerson Journals* provide an example of inclusive methods, with editorial sigla within the journal entries for major details of inscription and a further back-of-book record of editorial emendations not apparent in the reading text itself. The *Emerson Lectures*, on the other hand, appear in clear text. A third series, bearing the CSE seal, the *Harold Frederic Correspondence*, imposes different editorial methods on different groups of source texts in the same volume. The 203 letters whose source texts are holographs are offered as inclusive texts, while the 163 letters in the volume that survive as typescript letters, transcriptions, and earlier published versions appear in clear text.

Still another CEAA/CSE series has adopted inclusive methods midstream in its progress. The first volumes of documentary material in the Mark Twain Papers—Twain's *Letters to His Publishers* and his *Letters to H. H. Rogers*—were heavily emended by the editors, and these volumes contain neither a report of canceled passages nor a record of other details suppressed in the reading text. However, ensuing volumes of documentary materials have adopted inclusive methods. The volumes of Twain's *Notebooks & Journals* are a superb example of inclusive textual editing at its best. The reading texts employ conventional editorial symbols to indicate such items as legible canceled passages, revisions, and other significant details of the source texts. A back-of-book record conveniently divides textual notes between "Editorial Emendations and Doubtful Readings" and "Details of Inscription in the Manuscript." The first alerts the reader to elements of the reading text that result from editorial judgment, while the second records elements of Clemens's accidentals and substantives in the source texts that either did not warrant inclusion in the reading text or could not be reproduced symbolically on the printed page.

2. *Textual Records*

None of the above-mentioned inclusive editions pretends to report all of the details of the source texts. Two forms of emendations are made silently within the text, with no record in the textual apparatus. One comprises standardization of the manuscript's format, including the placement of such elements as a letter's dateline, salutation, and complimentary close; the uniformity of spacing between lines; and uniform indentation of paragraphs. The other consists of standardization of irregularly formed letters of the alphabet and marks of punctuation. Inclusive editors seeking CSE approval may expand upon this list of silent emendations, but they are required to list such categories in statements of textual method in their volumes.

As for editorial activities reported in the edition, certain generalizations are possible. In the case of details of inscription, the following are customarily reported overtly, either through the use of symbols or facsimile printing in the text or in footnotes adjacent to the text: (1) legible canceled passages, especially those that reflect a change in the substance of the author's thought; and (2) legible additions to the original passage, such as interlineations, on-line additions, and marginal insertions. (An interlined spelling correction, for instance, would not fall into this category.)

On the other hand, details of inscription in the following categories are usually omitted from the inclusive text and are recorded only in back-of-book textual notes: (1) false starts so brief that they give no sense of the author's preliminary intention; (2) slips of the pen such as words repeated unintentionally or minor errors of spelling or punctuation that the author has not corrected; (3) authorial corrections of spelling and punctuation (whether as writeovers, interlineations, added characters, or marginal insertions) that do not indicate a change in the desired sense of the passage; (4) illegible canceled passages; (5) catchwords at the bottom of a page that are repeated at the top of the following page; (6) a change in the media used in the original manuscript: variations in paper, ink, or pencil within the same document; (7) symbols that cannot be reproduced in set type in any readable form and must be described rather than represented by visual symbols; (8) authorial revisions so complicated that not even diplomatic transcription or facsimile printing could represent them clearly.

Similarly, there are specific categories of editorial emendation that are usually presented overtly within the text rather than in the back-of-book record of an inclusive edition. The following editorial contributions are signaled by a symbol in the text (usually a square bracket) that warns the reader that the reading may be ambiguous: (1) supplying a word, phrase, or a single mark of punctuation omitted by the author; (2) supplying mutilated or obliterated material; (3) any change in the identity of the source text, when two or more sources are conflated to produce the complete text of an item; (4) any editorial expansion of authorial shorthand necessary for the passage's sense (completion of incomplete dates, expansion of ambiguous contractions and abbreviations or of a set of initials to a full name); (5) any editorial interpolations of factual material; (6) any editorial omissions of material that the author clearly intended as part of his final letter, diary entry, essay (e.g., standardized headings).

While the reader is alerted immediately to these forms of emendation, others are made silently within the text, with some note of their existence in the back-of-book record: (1) expansion of unambiguous but obsolete contractions or abbreviations; (2) the supply of missing punctuation that is part of a set (half of a pair of quotation marks, or one or more commas in a series); (3) the supply of terminal punctuation when the author has begun a new sentence with a capital letter but has omitted the period, question mark, or exclamation point that should have preceded that character; (4) correction of an author's lapse from his usual patterns of punctuation or spelling; (5) the supply of breaks for paragraphs in a lengthy passage.

3. Expanded Text

The term *expanded transcription* for the textual practices of historical editors gained currency in the 1954 edition of the *Harvard Guide to American History*. In his discussion of documentary publication, Samuel Eliot Morison categorized the methods used for American historical materials in three groups: "the *Literal*, the *Expanded*, and the *Modernized*." As an aside, he pointed out, "[I]n addition there is one that we might call the *Garbled* or *Bowdlerized*, which should be avoided." Morison's rules for all three of the recommended methods included providing clues to the provenance of the source text; standardizing the address, dateline, and greeting of letters; marking all editorial interpolations by square brackets ([ ]); indicating editorial omissions by suspension points (. . .); bringing interlineations down to the line; and rendering words underscored once in italics and those underscored twice in small capitals. A final instruction to all editors advised them "to prepare a fresh text from the manuscript or photostat" instead of relying on an earlier printed version.

Morison's specific rules for each method make it clear that even his "literal" method of transcription was many degrees removed from a printed facsimile or diplomatic transcription. He advised "modernized" methods only for English translations from other tongues and for "an early document, chronicle, or narrative [whose] average reader [might be] put off by obsolete spelling and erratic punctuation."

Most of Morison's time and attention were directed to describing the expanded method of textual presentation that had been used in the first volumes of Boyd's Jefferson edition, then a new and exciting addition to any historian's library. Unfortunately, Morison confined himself to describing his preferences for expanded transcription and noting his minor differences with Boyd. At no point did he explain the goals or rationale of the method, and his six rules for expanded transcription were hardly helpful:

(a) Retain the spelling, capitalization, and punctuation of the source text, "but always capitalize the first word and put a period at the end of the sentence no matter what the writer does."

(b) Spell out any abbreviations not in current usage.

(c) Standardize abbreviations for units of money and weight and measure.

(d) Modernize the writer's archaic use of the interchangeable *v* and *u*.

(e) Retain the writer's erratic usage of capital letters for the initials of proper names.

(f) Exercise caution in imposing punctuation and capitalization that herald the beginning of a new sentence. "Punctuation in all manuscripts before the nineteenth century is highly irregular," Morison reminded his readers, "and if you once start replacing dashes by commas, semicolons, or periods, . . . you are asking for trouble."

Morison's exposition of expansion transcription has two flaws. First, it addresses only the problems of pre-nineteenth-century documents and ignores the special problems of later materials. Second, and more important, it provides no explanation for the rules that it lays down. Studying Morison's precepts for expanded texts is less useful than examining the reasons for the adoption of the methods by Julian Boyd or the modifications of the technique by later historical editors.

The patterns of silent emendation cited by Morison were worked out by Boyd and Lyman Butterfield during their fruitful partnership at the Jefferson project in the late 1940s. Acutely aware of the loss suffered by the transfer of any eighteenth-century source text to a twentieth-century printed page, they cast about for some device that would preserve the flavor of the original materials. They hit upon the idea of printing manuscript materials more or less as they would have been printed at the time of their inscription. Consulting products of Benjamin Franklin's press, the two scholars compiled what could be termed a style sheet for compositors of the late eighteenth century. The conventions used in the *Jefferson*, *Rush*, and *Adams* volumes edited by Boyd and Butterfield were largely those employed by the printers who were contemporaries of their statesmen-subjects. In printing houses of that day, for instance, the ampersand was used only when it was part of the name of a business firm or part of the abbreviation *&c* or *&ca* for *etc*. This usage was transferred to the printed texts published in the 1950s and 1960s. Since by the late eighteenth century the thorn was no longer employed in printing, its use in a manuscript was silently translated to *th*.

Unfortunately, Boyd and Butterfield assumed that their readers and fellow editors would recognize the patterns of silent emendation for what they were—the printing conventions of America in the Revolutionary era. They believed that they were justified in imposing these conventions upon the materials at hand, because Jefferson, Rush, and Adams were literate men who would have expected to see such conventions imposed on any holograph materials that they submitted to a compositor. In effect, Boyd and Butterfield sought to publish volumes of documents edited as Jefferson, Rush, and Adams themselves would have edited them.

But other scholars missed this central point. They assumed that Boyd and Butterfield's patterns of emendation were designed to serve *any* documentary edition (a misconception popularized by Morison). Some attempted to transfer these methods to manuscript source texts of later periods, where the Boyd-Butterfield printing conventions had no validity. Worse still, some experimented in their use with documents composed by semiliterate men and women, thus obscuring almost every bit of the texture and flavor of the source texts that Boyd and Butterfield had hoped to preserve.

Morison neglected to furnish what would have been an invaluable corollary to his general rule for documentary editors: that they must not only state a method but also explain its rationale and point to its implications for the documents at hand. In addition, in focusing solely on patterns of emendation, Morison neglected to discuss the second element of expanded methods. Not only did editors following this tradition expand certain forms abbreviated in the original but they also included within the text or its accompanying footnotes elements in the source text that were not part of the final version of the document's form. Thus, Boyd and Butterfield and their followers, like inclusive editors in the CEAA mold, reported cancellations and insertions whose existence seemed of primary importance to their readers. Textual symbols were employed by some editors, while others preferred to explain these details of inscription in footnotes adjacent to the text. But expansionist editors did not pretend to record every detail of inscription, nor did they provide a back-of-book record of such suppressed details or of their emendations of the source text.

Expanded textual techniques can be exploited conservatively or liberally. The text of letters in the *Ulysses S. Grant Papers*, for instance, is close to a diplomatic transcript of the sources. If the editors provided a back-of-book record of minor emendations, their volumes would easily qualify for the CSE seal. However, volumes in the Adams and Jefferson series continue the practices of traditional expansionist emendation. In part, this diversity comes from the traditions of the editions in question, but another factor plays a part. Ulysses S. Grant's letters require fewer silent emendations under the definitions of expanded text because they are not eighteenth-century materials. Grant and his correspondents did not use the thorn or the tailed *p*. Their style was already a century closer to modern conventions. The editors of the *Grant Papers* did not need to violate the rules of expanded methods to create their near-diplomatic transcriptions, for the rules laid down by Julian Boyd and summarized by Samuel Eliot Morison did not apply to the textual problems that they faced.

The fathers of expanded transcription made another assumption that Morison and their followers ignored. Although Boyd and Butterfield were selective in their inclusion of details of the source text in their volumes, they did not ignore the requirements of readers who needed access to the contents of the originals. They assumed that microfilm editions of their projects' archives would make facsimiles of these source texts available to a wide audience.

The lessons to be drawn from experience with expanded methods are clear. The editor can never assume that the reader will understand the reasons for the editorial policies he has adopted. The reader requires and deserves an explanation of such methods as well as a description of them. And no editor is justified in automatically adopting conventions or policies of emendation employed by a colleague. The textual methods of an edition must be designed to suit the manuscript or printed materials that provide source texts for the volumes at hand. "Generally accepted," "traditional," and "time-honored" are adjectives that should not be used to justify the adoption of any editorial practice. In choosing his textual methods, each editor must start afresh, making decisions based on the needs of his audience and on the peculiarities of his source texts.

D. CLEAR TEXT

The term *clear text* traditionally describes the preferred method for presenting the critically edited texts of published works. The texts themselves contain neither critical symbols nor footnote numbers to indicate that an emendation has been made or that some detail has been omitted. All such emendations and alterations are reported in back-of-book tables whose citations are keyed to the pages and lines of the new printed edition.

With the publication of the *Hawthorne Notebooks* in the early 1970s, however, clear text was applied to CEAA-approved volumes of writings not intended for publication—the private writings that had hitherto received more conservative textual treatment. The method has since been used in the *Howells Letters*, the *Thoreau Journals*, and portions of the *Harold Frederic Correspondence*. Each of these series, of course, bears the CEAA or CSE seal, even though the CEAA *Statement* for editors urges the adoption of more inclusive methods for source texts of this kind. While there is no official standard for the adoption of clear text in documentary editing, the experience of editors who have employed the technique furnishes some useful guidelines.

A note of caution has been provided by Elizabeth Witherell, editor of the Thoreau Edition. She recommends that clear text for manuscript source texts of private writings be used "only when a great deal of editorial emendation is required, or when almost none at all is necessary." This apparent contradiction is easily explained. Thoreau revised many journal passages for use in lectures, essays, and books, so a manuscript page may contain two distinct versions of the same passage: Thoreau's original jottings in pen, along with his later revisions of these entries in pen and pencil. Although an ingenious book designer might have improvised a method to present a single printed facsimile, diplomatic transcription, or inclusive text giving simultaneous access to both stages of composition, the reader would be hard-pressed to make sense of the results. The Thoreau editors chose to present a clear text of the earliest version of the journal entries, and each volume is complemented by tables of emendations (applying only to that first version), as well as by tables of significant variants between the earlier and later stages of the journals' physical contents. The editors do not pretend that their reading text conveys all that can be learned from the manuscript journals; they have simply provided a legible and reliable text of one of the two versions in the same document.

At the other extreme, Witherell feels that clear text is a practical option for documents that are themselves close to final versions of the documents that they represent. Neatly inscribed recipients' copies of letters, fair copies of literary manuscripts or of political treatises—each of these is clean enough to serve for clear text. In each instance the extent of editorial intervention is so slight and of so little substantive importance that the editor can responsibly assign the record of such emendations to a back-of-book table.

The editor who considers clear text as an option must be sure that this treatment will not suppress important inscriptional details or distort the documentary value of the resulting editorial text. If a writer customarily sent his correspondents copies of letters containing canceled passages, a clear text of such letters, which would omit all such cancellations from the reading text, would seriously distort the document. The edition's readers would be denied immediate access to words, phrases, and paragraphs that could be easily read by the letters' recipients. Similarly, if a writer consistently sent his correspondents carelessly proofread letters where words were inadvertently omitted, a clear text of these letters, with many missing words supplied silently by the editor, would be a disservice. In both cases, the editor would have gone too far to make clear text a practical and honest solution.

The editor considering clear text should first analyze the emerging patterns of emendation and details of transcription that would have to be relegated to back-of-book records in a clear-text edition of his source. If these fall into the categories that the inclusive editor would ordinarily report within his text (legible canceled passages with substantive implications, editorially supplied material for a mutilated document, and so on), then the source is not an appropriate candidate for clear text. On the other hand, if the evolving

patterns fall into the categories that inclusive editors normally con-
sign to the back-of-book record or emend silently, the source is
clearly a perfect object of clear-text methods.

And clear text is justifiable in a scholarly edition only when that
reading text will be accompanied by a full record of editorial emendations and suppressed inscriptional details. Editorial intervention
of any degree can be justified only when the reader is provided with
a complete report of what he has been denied by the editor's decision
to be exclusive rather than inclusive.

III. CONCLUSION

The summary description of the five general textual methodologies
in documentary editions only hints at the different results that each
approach can produce. This chapter is only preparation for the one
that follows: a review of the weapons of documentary editing in
the form of textual symbols and descriptive textual notes and a
sample of the results of applying different contrasting textual strategies to the same source. The possible variations are as startlingly
different as the scholarly traditions and personal preferences that
gave birth to the textual methods now in use.

SUGGESTED READINGS

The most valuable discussions of editors' choices of one textual
method over another appear in the introductions to the editions
themselves. The only attempt to survey a wide variety of methods
is G. Thomas Tanselle's "The Editing of Historical Documents,"
an essay that should be read in conjunction with his more recent
"Textual Scholarship." An interesting summary of the arguments
concerning the responsibility of editors of private source texts appears in *CEAA Newsletter*, no. 3 (June 1970): 16–21. And Hilary
Jenkinson's "The Representation of Manuscripts in Print," *London
Mercury* 30 (September 1934), is worth rereading if only for its
reminder to editors, "It is possible to make the path too smooth."

CHAPTER 6

The Practical Application of Editorial Conventions

In putting their general theories of textual method into practice, American editors have employed a broad, sometimes bewildering, variety of mechanical devices. The results differ as widely as the methods that produced them. The pages that follow examine the technical aspects of establishing the printed editorial text. An introduction to the use of textual symbols (or *sigla*) is followed by a survey of the use and evolution of descriptive editorial notes, which range from the carefully thought-out to the hastily improvised. To make clear the application of differing textual methods, theories, and editorial devices, the chapter closes with a demonstration of these methods at work. A sample holograph document appears in photoreproduction (fig. 1), followed by the printed editorial texts that would result from applying different textual procedures to the same source (figs. 2–5).

I. TEXTUAL SYMBOLS

Except for printed facsimiles, all of the general methods of documentary editing described in the previous chapter may make use of editorial devices that supply those details of inscription in the original that cannot be readily duplicated in a typeset version. In a diplomatic transcription, such symbols or abbreviations appear in the documentary text itself. In inclusive or expanded texts, the symbols may appear both in the text and in supplementary notes. In clear text, such symbols are used in the back-of-book record of editorial emendations and details of inscription.

The use of such symbols goes back to the work of classical scholars in their editions of ancient works. The first systematic use of textual symbols for materials later than the classical era appeared in the early 1920s in the Malone Society's *Reprints* series, edited by W. W. Greg. The society's editions of British literary works of the Renaissance and the early modern period employed two sets of characters to indicate details in manuscript sources: angle brackets (⟨ ⟩) to enclose passages lost through mutilation or other damage and restored by the editors; and square brackets ([ ]) to enclose passages deleted in the original manuscript.

After World War II, these and other symbols were applied to American documents and literary works. The first system of textual symbols for American materials was the one devised by Julian Boyd and Lyman Butterfield for their Jefferson and Rush editions. They confined their sigla to the same two pairs employed by the Malone Society, but they modified the meaning of each set of brackets. Because common American usage had already assigned to square brackets the function of setting off interpolated material, these symbols were given a related meaning in the text of American documentary editions. Instead of denoting authorial deletions, the square brackets in the Jefferson and Rush editions indicated some form of editorial intrusion in the text—the insertion of characters or words not physically a part of the original, whether these were added to restore mutilated passages or interjected to explain some aspect of the text. Angle brackets, which had no generally accepted function in American usage of the time, were a "neutral" symbol to the eyes of readers of the Jefferson and Rush editions. They bore no preexisting connotations, and the editors arbitrarily assigned them to enclose restored canceled material in their source texts.

In the thirty years following publication of the first volume of the *Jefferson Papers*, scholarly editors here and abroad have devised symbols and abbreviations for almost every detail of inscription of which the human mind, hand, and pen could be guilty. Indeed, the use of symbolic description of textual detail won popularity so quickly that many of its adopters were unaware of the novelty of their methods. In the statement of textual method for the first volume of the *Emerson Journals*, published in 1961, the use of angle brackets to enclose restored authorial deletions was described as traditional, although that tradition was only a decade old. The symbol has proved so convenient that some editors no longer bother to define its meaning in prefaces to their volumes of documentary texts.

Other sigla have won less universal acceptance and acclaim. The tables below record only some of the devices that modern editors have devised to represent textual details—what Lewis Mumford dubbed the "barbed wire" of modern American scholarly texts:

A. PASSAGES DELETED BY THE AUTHOR

⟨*italic*⟩	*Jefferson Papers*
⟨roman⟩	Emerson, Howells, Irving, and Frederic editions; most historical editions
⟨⟨*italic* or roman⟩⟩	A deletion within a deletion in an edition that employs single angle (or "broken") brackets for a primary deletion
~~canceled type~~	Grant and Hamilton papers; most editions of literary works
⟨	A crossed-out deletion, *Billy Budd*
⟨⃥	An erasure, *Billy Budd*

B. UNRECOVERABLE GAPS IN THE SOURCE TEXT

[. . .]	The number of suspension points within the square brackets usually offers a clue to the length of the lacuna, or unrecoverable material. In the Jefferson and Adams papers, "[. . .], [. . . .]" indicates one or two missing words; if a footnote number follows the brackets, the lacuna is longer, and a note estimates the number of missing words. The Cooper edition employs a similar technique. In the *Grant Papers*, the number of points represents the approximate number of missing letters, not words.
[ ]	A missing portion of a number, *Jefferson Papers*
‖ . . . ‖	The number of suspension points approximates the number of missing words in the *Emerson Journals*, with three dots representing one to five words; four dots, six to ten words; and five dots, sixteen to thirty words. The abbreviation *msm* within the vertical lines stands for "manuscript accidentally mutilated."
xxx	Missing letters in the *Emerson Journals*, with the number of x's approximating the number of lost characters
[- - -]	Missing words in the Grant and Wilson papers, with the spaced hyphens indicating the

	number of words lost. The editors of the *Ratification* series employ the same symbol, but three hyphens are used regardless of the length of the lacuna.
. . .	Lacunae in the *Hamilton Papers*, with the suspension points representing the approximate number of unrecoverable characters
// . . . //	Illegible words in *Mark Twain's Satires*
[***]	Unrecoverable shorthand characters, *Wilson Papers*

Countless variations upon this theme are possible. The Irving edition, which employs angle brackets (⟨ ⟩) to enclose deleted passages, combines that symbol with italicized descriptive words or phrases to indicate unrecoverable canceled passages, as with "⟨*illegible*⟩" for a hopelessly obliterated section.

C. ADDITIONS TO THE ORIGINAL INSCRIPTION

)	An insertion with Melville's caret, *Billy Budd*
⚬	An interlinear insertion without a caret, *Billy Budd*
∧ roman ∧	All insertions (interlinear and marginal), *Mark Twain's Satires*; interlineations only, *Frederic Correspondence*; interlineations made with author's symbol for an interlined addition, *Emerson Journals*
↑ roman ↓	"Substitutions for a deletion," *Mark Twain's Satires*; interlineations in *Emerson Journals*, Irving edition, and most other "literary" series
/ roman /	*Marcus Garvey Papers*
I roman I	Marginal additions, *Emerson Journals*
w.o.	Superimposed addition ("written over"), *Billy Budd*

D. UNDERLINING IN THE SOURCE TEXT

| *italic* | Single underlining (universal) |
| small capitals | Double underlining (universal) |

E. AUTHORIAL SYMBOLS

thorn

The handwritten thorn, which had been formalized to *y* by the mid-eighteenth century, is customarily printed as a *y* or as *th* for materials in American history and literature.

~

Many eighteenth- and early nineteenth-century authors employ the curved tilde or a simple straight line at the point in a word where characters have been omitted to form a contraction. The tilde is reproduced in type by the Laurens, *Ratification*, and Burr editors. Many editions, following the lead of the *Jefferson Papers*, ignore the tilde and silently expand the resulting contraction where it is employed.

℘

The "tailed *p*" is either rendered by the character for this symbol in print (*Jefferson Papers*) or expanded to the intended form of *per*, *pre*, or *pro* (*Hamilton Papers, Letters of Delegates*). If the meaning of the symbol is unclear, an edition that ordinarily expands it must indicate an ambiguous usage by "p[er?]" or some other method reserved by the edition for conjectural readings. Changes in modern day typesetting are rapidly eliminating the option of using the symbol.

✳

The asterisk is the most commonly employed rendition of an idiosyncratic symbol used by an author to indicate his own footnote numbers (*Emerson Journals*). However, when the author uses a standardized (even if rather archaic) form of citation, it is preferable to retain those forms that have equivalents in modern type fonts, such as a dagger (†).

☞

A "fist" or "index" drawn by the author in the margin to call attention to a passage in his text can be translated to the printed "fist" that survives in many typefaces.

{ }

Bracket used in the *Emerson Journals* to enclose page numbers supplied by Emerson himself

¶   Author's marking for a new paragraph

no ¶   Author's marking for the consolidation of paragraphs

F. LINE BREAKS IN THE SOURCE TEXT

/   Most historical editions; *Howells Letters*

| Hawthorne, Whitman, and James editions

G. EDITORIAL SUPPLY

[roman]   The most common device for both literary and historical series; if doubt exists concerning the supplied material, a question mark precedes the closing bracket ("[reading?]").

⟨roman⟩   *Hamilton Papers*

‖ roman ‖   *Emerson Journals*

| roman | *Howells Letters*

{roman}   *Frederic Correspondence*

⊦roman⊦   *Wilson Papers* device for "word or words in the original text which Wilson omitted in copying"

H. EDITORIAL EXPANSION OF ABBREVIATIONS OR CONTRACTIONS

[roman]   Universally accepted symbol in those editions that expand such forms within the text

I. EDITORIAL OMISSIONS

[. . .]   *Emerson Journals*

. . . .   *Booker T. Washington Papers*

J. ALTERNATIVE READINGS

/   Introduces alternative readings in *Mark Twain's Satires*

/roman/   The virgules enclose alternative readings in the *Emerson Journals*.

When variant copies provide alternative readings in documentary materials, it is far more common to describe the variations in notes than to represent them symbolically within the text.

K. EDITORIAL INTERPOLATIONS

[*italic*]   This is the most commonly used device, although both the *Emerson* and *Ratification* volumes employ "[roman]." If the documents in the edition contain a substantial amount of material that must be represented within square brackets for other reasons (lacunae in the text; expanded abbreviations; supplies of mutilated passages), then the editorial apparatus must distinguish clearly between bracketed material that can at least be inferred from the source text and bracketed contributions that do not stem from the source (corrections of outrageously misspelled words; catchwords such as *illegible*, and so on). The reader must not be left to wonder to which category the bracketed material belongs. If brackets are used sparingly in the text, and there is no possibility of confusion, then all bracketed letters, words, and phrases can be in roman type.

italic   *Frederic Correspondence*

L. SOME RULES FOR EDITORIAL SIGLA

The variety of symbols employed by different editions to represent the same textual problem is so great that it is impossible to escape the conclusion that some symbols were adopted because editors were unaware of the conventions already in use. Some other editors may have tried to prove their inventiveness by adopting a new form of bracket or a new arrangement of virgules (or "slash") instead of imitating another edition's practices. Nothing short of an editorial Council of Trent could impose order on the symbolic chaos in existing documentary editions. Still, a few of the lessons to be learned by the novice editor who is beginning his work from scratch are provided in the following brief review.

A careless choice of symbols can make the reader's task more difficult. If two symbols are to represent related details in the manuscript, then the symbols themselves should have a visual relationship. The reader's memory will be burdened sufficiently without the addition of sets of characters that contradict each other in appearance and meaning. Following this rule, the editors of Melville's *Billy Budd* used variations on the opening half of a pair of angle brackets (⟨) to indicate different kinds of authorial cancellation and employed variants on the closing half of that same pair of symbols (⟩) to represent two methods of interlineation in the source text.

If the edition requires a lengthy series of textual symbols, the editor should use as many devices as possible that mirror the physical appearance of the original. If an author cancels material both by lining out phrases and by erasing them, the lined-out deletions should appear in canceled type, whose meaning is easily grasped. Should the author interline material both with and without a caret, the editor should consider enclosing the careted interlineations with a pair of printed carets (∧interlineation∧). Uncareted interlineations (whose desired location is ambiguous) can be set off by one of the other common symbols for this detail, either a pair of arrows (↑ interlineation ↓) or a pair of virgules (/interlineation/).

Advances in computerized publishing technology may make it possible to eliminate a good many symbols altogether. Symbols were frequently adopted because of the expense of producing a typeset facsimile of the source text's details. An editorial project with access to a word processor and with a cooperative and imaginative publisher may find that it is economically feasible to expand its use of facsimile techniques and to eliminate all but a few of the arbitrary sigla of documentary editing.

II. DESCRIPTIVE TEXTUAL NOTES

In diplomatic, inclusive, and expanded texts, many details of inscription defy symbolic representation, and some editors prefer to avoid the use of textual symbols or sigla altogether. Instead of symbols, their textual notes use verbal descriptions of textual problems whenever possible.

Such textual descriptions can be provided in three ways: (1) in the documentary text within square brackets (*Calhoun Papers*); (2) in footnotes whose numbers are keyed to the location of the cancellation, interlineation, marginal addition, or other detail in the printed editorial text of the document (*Franklin Papers*); and (3) in a back-of-book textual record. The reasons for choosing each variation on the method are instructive.

The format of the *Calhoun Papers* allows for no footnotes. Textual explanations must be presented within square brackets in the text, and this design hardly lends itself to arrows and other sigla within the initial brackets. For the *Franklin Papers*, William Willcox explains that he finds the use of sigla within the texts of printed documents to be "disfiguring," and his choice of descriptive methods rests on an aesthetic preference.

Editions in the literary tradition must carry a complete textual record, and here the use of descriptive rather than symbolic methods may rest on very different and more complicated grounds. Some of the details and patterns that these editors are obliged to report simply do not lend themselves to symbolic treatment. And the number of textual notes would make it impossible for such editors to consider reporting these details within the text of a document or even in numbered footnotes, whose profusion would make the text a field of numerals rather than words and phrases. The textual record must be presented in unnumbered notes keyed to the line and page of the printed edition. It appears either in a section of notes following the text or in a back-of-book section. In either case, the textual note is at some distance, physically, from the section of edited text to which it refers. The complicated nature of many of the textual problems explained in such notes requires that the editor offer his reader adequate cues for understanding the significance of emendations or omissions that have occurred, and brief verbal descriptions frequently serve this purpose better than a reliance on symbols.

Fredson Bowers is the leading exponent of descriptive rather than symbolic textual annotation, and his edition of *Leaves of Grass* is the best example of a diplomatic transcription employing this technique. The notes follow each poem and can easily be consulted. However, Bowers has since argued persuasively for the use of descriptive textual annotation for inclusive and clear texts as well, and the practical effect of the method was first seen in the *Hawthorne Notebooks*, for which Bowers served as textual consultant. The system has become more highly refined in Bowers's textual notes for the William James edition, and Bowers's exposition of the method appears in his "Transcription of Manuscripts: The Record of Variants" (*Studies in Bibliography* 29 [1976]: 212–64).

The back-of-book record of emendations and inscriptional details in these series follows the traditional format for literary works. Each line-page reference is followed by the *lemma* (a word or phrase in the editorial text that indicates the site of editorial activity), followed by a left-opening bracket (]), which divides the lemma from the reading in the source text. At its simplest, the method can be seen in the record of the first editorial emendation in Hawthorne's *French and Italian Notebooks*:

$$\text{"6.3 a little more or less] } \overset{a}{\wedge} \text{ little more less"}$$

This merely indicates that in line 3 on page 6, the editors have supplied the word *or*, which Hawthorne omitted from this entry in his notebook.

Usually, only three sigla are needed in such textual tables in addition to the left-opening bracket that follows the lemma: / indicates a line break in the source text; the mathematical symbol ~ represents a repetition of the same word after the bracket; and a caret (∧) can indicate the absence of punctuation in the source text. Thus, in the same Hawthorne volume, "of] of/ of" shows that the editors have omitted the *of* that Hawthorne repeated when he began a new line. And "Liverpool,]~∧" shows that the editors have added the comma after *Liverpool*.

The words and phrases that describe more complicated emendations and details in the source can be written out or abbreviated. The *Thoreau Journals* contain descriptive textual notes without abbreviations, for the best and most practical of reasons: brevity. The notes seldom run to more than one line with unabbreviated descriptive forms, and using contracted forms would not have saved space. The editors spared their readers a table of abbreviations to be mastered before consulting the notes. However, many editions require abbreviations to prevent their descriptive textual notes from becoming unmanageable. The most common abbreviations used in such notes represent the most frequently seen details of manuscript source texts: *del.* for *deleted*; *ab.* for *above* the line; *interl.* for *interlined*, and so forth. A descriptive textual record is offered for the clear-text version of the sample document that concludes this chapter, and Bowers's essay in the 1976 *Studies in Bibliography* offers a detailed analysis of the method in practice. The following examples, drawn from Bowers's essay, make clear the effectiveness of the technique:

would] *interl.* (for which read " 'would' interlined")
is not] *after del.* 'may' (for which read " 'is not' after deleted 'may' "
on occasion] *interl. aft. del.* 'often' (for which read " 'on occasion' interlined after deleted 'often' ")

A scheme of descriptive textual annotation must be designed as carefully as one of symbolic representation of emendations and inscriptional detail. Privately, Bowers cautions novices to consult "established procedures that have been shown to work" before creating a system of their own. As Bowers has been considerate enough to provide an easily available printed analysis of the method and its rationale, the new editor is well-advised to take that hint and to investigate the method thoroughly before trying to imitate it in a new edition.

III. Contrasting Textual Methods at Work

The reader who has survived this chapter's discussion of textual methods may well ask, What difference does it make? This can be answered by a demonstration of the results of applying the five broad editorial approaches to the same source text. The sample offered here is the draft of a note from the author of this book to Richard K. Showman, chairman of the committee that supervised her work. The letter was written in April 1982, when the author was engaged in arranging the date for a meeting in Bloomington, Indiana, where she was to discuss the final details of this volume with an executive subcommittee composed of David Chesnutt of the University of South Carolina, David Nordloh of Indiana University, and Paul Smith of the Library of Congress. It was expected that another person might attend these meetings—Don Cook, then president of the ADE and a member of the Indiana University Department of English.

Figure 1 is a photoreproduction of the holograph. (The reader should remember that the letter's author was a historian specializing in the eighteenth century, and she had incorporated many of this era's inscriptional forms into her personal shorthand.) Figure 2 shows a typographical facsimile. Figure 3 shows a diplomatic transcription. Figure 4 represents an expanded transcription of the document, as well as a possible reading text for an inclusive text that would meet CSE standards. Finally, figure 5 shows a clear text reflecting the author's final intentions. In figures 4 and 5, the lines are numbered for the reader's convenience in consulting the textual records for these editorial texts. The textual record for figure 5 is presented twice, once using symbolic methods and once using descriptive techniques of annotation.

The following symbols are used in the figures and in their textual records:

⟨ ⟩	Deleted passages
↑ ↓	Interlined material
∧ ∧	Material interlined with a caret
[roman]	Editorial expansion of abbreviated forms
[. . .]	Unrecoverable canceled matter, with each suspension point representing one illegible character

Dear Dick,

I've begun ~~nagging~~ to nag members of ye Executive Sub-Comm. to make up their minds about the date ~~of~~ for our planning meeting in Bloomington. Chairman Dane N. has his summer school teaching schedule to consider. Dane C. may be going to Italy. Paul S. doubtless has vacation plans.

Another week in the life of the author of the ADE "guide's: one blizzard (Tuesday) and one lunch with a member of the "Comm^e on ye Manual" (Wednesday).

I'll state once again that editing documents is a lot more fun than writing about editing them. There are only so many ways to say "the responsible editor should...." Moved more frequently I must restrain myself from typing, "Look fellow editors, this is the way to do it! " and don't give me any arguments. I realize that this isn't the tone we should strive for.

I'll let you know when the date for our Bl'ton meeting is set — I hope that D.C. can be one of our party, but that must be left to chance. I so can hardly blame him for finding an excuse to miss two days' worth of arguments about the history of the angle bracket as a symbol for authorial cancellations.

More seriously, there could be disagreement among members of the Sub-Comm. ~~Chestnutt~~ One member will argue that the entire book should be written in FORSAN. ~~Noodlok~~ another may insist that the book is written too simplistically — that it isn't intended for those ~~too~~ ignorant that they confuse stemma with a lemma. I wish that you could be there to play peacemaker.

I'll keep you advised of all developments. Any advice in-advance ~~you~~ ain't will be welcomed and, perhaps, heeded!

Yours in a quandary --
Mary Jo

9 April

Figure 2.   Typographical Facsimile

Dear Dick

           to nag

I've begun ~~nagging~~ members of ye Executive
Sub-Comm. to make up their minds about the
     for
date ~~of~~ our planning meeting in Bloomington.
Chairman Dave N. has his summer school teaching
schedule to consider. Dave C. may be going to
Italy. Paul S. doubtless has vacation plans.

Another week in the life of the author of
the ADE "Guide⟨,⟩": one blizzard (Tuesday) and
one lunch with a member of the "Comm^ee^ on ye Manual"
(Wednesday).

I'll state once again that *editing* documents is a ~~h~~
lot more fun than *writing* about editing them. There
are only so many ways to say "the responsible editor should. . . ."
More and more frequently I must restrain myself from
typing, "Look fellow editors, this is the way to do it!" ⟩ , and
        this   don't give
I realize that isn't the tone we should strive for.   me any

I'll let you know when the date for our   [. . .]
Bl'ton meeting is set—I hope that D.C. can be one of arguments
our party, but that must be left to chance. I ~~eo~~ can
hardly blame him for finding an excuse to miss two days'
worth of arguments about the history of the angle bracket
as a symbol for authorial cancellations.

More seriously, there could be disagreement among
               One member
members of the Sub-Comm. ~~Chesnutt~~ will argue that
                    Another
the entire book should be written in FORSAN. ~~Nordloh~~
may insist that the book is written too simplistically—that
          ~~too~~   that they
it isn't intended for those ~~so~~ ignorant to confuse a
stemma with a lemma. ¶I wish that you could be there
to play peacemaker.
I'll keep you advised of all developments. Any advice-
        give
in-advance you ∧ will be welcomed ∧
and, perhaps, heeded.

                    Yours in a quandary—
                    Mary-Jo

9 April

Figure 3.   Diplomatic Transcription

Dear Dick   9 April [1982]
I've begun ⟨nagging⟩ ↑ to nag ↓ members of ye Executive Sub-
Comm. to make up their minds about the date ⟨of⟩ ↑ for ↓ our
planning meeting in Bloomington. Chairman Dave N. has his
summer school teaching schedule to consider. Dave C. may be going
to Italy. Paul S. doubtless has vacation plans.

Another week in the life of the author of the ADE "Guide ⟨,⟩":
one blizzard (Tuesday) and one lunch with a member of the
"Commee. on ye Manual" (Wednesday).[1]

I'll state once again that *editing* documents is a ⟨h⟩ lot more fun
than *writing* about editing them. There are only so many ways to say
"the responsible editor should. . . ." More and more frequently I
must restrain myself from typing, "Look fellow editors, this is the
way to do it ↑, and don't give me any [. . .] arguments ↓ !"[2] I realize
that ↑ this ↓ isn't the tone we should strive for.

I'll let you know when the date for our Bl'ton meeting is set—I
hope that D.C. can be one of our party, but that must be left to
chance. I ⟨co⟩ can hardly blame him for finding an excuse to miss two
days' worth of arguments about the history of the angle bracket as a
symbol for authorial cancellations.

More seriously, there could be disagreement among members of the
Sub-Comm. ⟨Chesnutt⟩ ↑ One member ↓ will argue that the entire
book should be written in FORSAN. ⟨Nordloh⟩ ↑ Another ↓ may
insist that the book is written too simplistically—that it isn't intended
for those ⟨so⟩ ↑ ⟨too⟩ ↓ ignorant to ↑ that they ↓ confuse a stemma
with a lemma. I wish that you could be there to play peacemaker.[3]

I'll keep you advised of all developments. Any advice-in-advance
you ∧give∧ will be welcomed ∧—∧ and, perhaps, heeded.
                                            Yours in a quandary—
                                                Mary-Jo

[1]The author has marked this paragraph for insertion at the opening
of the letter's text.

[2]The phrase ", and don't . . . arguments" added in the margin,
with a guideline for its insertion at this point.

[3]The author has marked the beginning of this sentence to open a
new paragraph. The following sentence ("I'll keep you advised. . . .")
is marked to "run on" as the second sentence of the new closing
paragraph.

Figure 4. Inclusive Text or Expanded Transcription

---

1   9 April [1982]
2   Dear Dick
3   Another week in the life of the author of the ADE
4   "Guide": one blizzard (Tuesday) and one lunch with a
5   member of the "Comm[itt]ee. on the Manual" (Wednesday).[1]
6   I've begun ⟨nagging⟩ to nag members of the Executive Sub-
7   Comm[ittee]. to make up their minds about the date for our
8   planning meeting in Bloomington. Chairman Dave N. has his
9   summer school teaching schedule to consider. Dave C. may be
10   going to Italy. Paul S. doubtless has vacation plans.
11   I'll state once again that *editing* documents is a lot more fun
12   than *writing* about editing them. There are only so many ways
13   to say "the responsible editor should. . . ." More and more
14   frequently I must restrain myself from typing, "Look, fellow
15   editors, this is the way to do it, and don't give me any [. . .]
16   arguments!"[2] I realize that this isn't the tone we should strive
17   for.
18   I'll let you know when the date for our Bl'ton meeting is
19   set—I hope that D[on]. C[ook]. can be one of our party, but
20   that must be left to chance. I can hardly blame him for finding
21   an excuse to miss two days' worth of arguments about the
22   history of the angle bracket as a symbol for authorial
23   cancellations.
24   More seriously, there could be disagreement among
25   members of the Sub-Comm[ittee]. ⟨Chesnutt⟩ One member
26   will argue that the entire book should be written in
27   FORSAN. ⟨Nordloh⟩ Another may insist that the book is
28   written too simplistically—that it isn't intended for those ⟨too⟩
29   so ignorant that they confuse a stemma with a lemma.
30   I wish that you could be there to play peacemaker. I'll keep
31   you advised of all developments. Any advice-in-advance you
32   give will be welcomed—and, perhaps, heeded.

                                  Yours in a quandary—
                                     Mary-Jo

  [1]This paragraph was initially the second paragraph in the body of
the letter. The author has marked it for insertion at the text's
beginning.
  [2]The phrase ", and . . . arguments" entered in the margin, with a
guideline for its insertion at this point.

Figure 5.   Clear Text

---

1   9 April 1982
2   Dear Dick
3   Another week in the life of the author of the ADE "Guide":
4   one blizzard (Tuesday) and one lunch with a member of the
5   "Committee on the Manual" (Wednesday).
6   I've begun to nag members of the Executive Sub-Committee to
7   make up their minds about the date for our planning meeting in
8   Bloomington. Chairman Dave Nordloh has his summer school
9   teaching schedule to consider. Dave Chesnutt may be going to
10   Italy. Paul Smith doubtless has vacation plans.
11   I'll state once again that *editing* documents is a lot more fun
12   than *writing* about editing them. There are only so many ways to
13   say "the responsible editor should. . . ." More and more
14   frequently I must restrain myself from typing, "Look, fellow
15   editors, this is the way to do it, and don't give me any
16   arguments!" I realize that this isn't the tone we should strive for.
17   I'll let you know when the date for our Bloomington meeting
18   is set. I hope that Don Cook can be one of our party, but that
19   must be left to chance. I can hardly blame him for finding an
20   excuse to miss two days' worth of arguments about the history of
21   the angle bracket as a symbol for authorial cancellations.
22   More seriously, there could be disagreement among members
23   of the Sub-Committee. One member will argue that the entire
24   book should be written in FORSAN. Another may insist that the
25   book is written too simplistically: that it isn't intended for those
26   so ignorant that they confuse a stemma with a lemma.
27   I wish that you could be there to play peacemaker. I'll keep
28   you advised of all developments. Any advice-in-advance you give
29   will be welcomed—and, perhaps, heeded.
                                        Yours in a quandary—
                                        Mary-Jo

A. TEXTUAL RECORDS

1. Inclusive Text

The textual record for the inclusive text (see fig. 4) uses the traditional "lemma]" form for locating alterations in the reading text.
Line numbers precede the first lemma in each line.

1   9 April] entered at the foot of the letter in the MS
3   "Guide"] ~ ⟨,⟩
5   Comm[itt]ee.] Comm^{ee}; the] ye
6   the] ye
7   for] ⟨of⟩ ↑ for ↓
11   a lot] a ⟨h⟩ lot
14   Look,] ~ ∧
15–16   lemma. and don't] "and . . . arguments" added in margin,
            with a guideline directing its insertion after *it*.
16   that this] that ↑ this ↓
20   can] ⟨co⟩ can
28   those so ignorant] those ⟨so⟩ ↑ ⟨too⟩ ↓ ignorant
29   that they confuse] to ↑ that they ↓ confuse
30–31   lemma. I wish] "I wish . . . peacemaker" originally part of
            the preceding paragraph, with authorial markings for a new
            paragraph. "I'll keep. . . ." was originally the beginning of
            a new paragraph, with authorial markings for a "run-on."
31–32   you give] you ↑ give ↓   welcomed—] welcomed ↑ — ↓

2. Clear Text, Symbolic Method

The textual record for the clear text (see fig. 5) is presented in the
symbolic format used by the *Howells Letters*. Editorial emendations
are reported in the "lemma] manuscript reading" style, with heavy
reliance on traditional textual symbols. Suppressed details of inscription are indicated without the citation of the lemma unless
confusion might result from abbreviated treatment.

1   9 April 1982] "9 April" entered at the foot of the letter in
            the MS; "1982" added by the editors.
3   Guide] ~ ⟨,⟩
3–5   This was initially the second paragraph of the body of the
            letter. The author marked it for insertion at this point.
5   Comm^{ee}
6   ⟨nagging⟩ ↑ to nag ↓   the]ye; Sub-Comm.
7   date ⟨of⟩ ↑ for ↓
8   Nordloh] N.
9   Chesnutt] C.
10   Smith] S.
11   a ⟨h⟩ lot
14   Look,] ~ ∧

15–16 "and don't give me any [. . .] arguments" added in the margin, with a guideline for its insertion after "*it*"

17 Bloomington] Bl'ton

18 Don Cook] D.C.

19 I ⟨co⟩ can

23 Sub-Comm. ⟨Chesnutt⟩ ↑ One member ↓

24 ⟨Nordloh⟩ ↑ Another ↓

26 ⟨so⟩ ↑ ⟨too⟩ ↓ ignorant to ↑ ⟨that they⟩ ↓ confuse

27–28 "I wish. . . peacemaker. I'll keep. . . of all developments." Originally, "I wish . . . peacemaker" was the concluding sentence of the preceding paragraph. The author marked it to begin the letter's last paragraph and marked the following sentence to "run on" as part of that paragraph.

28 ↑ give ↓

29 ↑ — ↓

3. Clear Text, Descriptive Method

This alternative textual record for the clear text (see fig. 5) employs Bowers's descriptive method of details of inscription (see above, pp. 142-43), which employs the following abbreviations:

ab. = above   *del.* = deleted   *interl.* = interlined
aft. = after   *insertd.* = inserted

1 9 April, 1982] "9 April" entered at the foot of the letter

3 "Guide"] comma *del. aft.* Guide

3–5 This was initially the second paragraph of the body of the letter. The author has marked it for insertion at this point.

5 Committee] Comm^ee

6 to nag] *interl. ab. del.* "nagging"; the Executive Sub-Committee] ye Executive Sub. Comm.

7 for] *interl. ab. del.* "of"

8 Nordloh] N.

9 Chesnutt] C.

10 Smith] S.

11 lot] *aft. del.* "h"

14 Look,] ~ ∧

15–16 and . . . any arguments] *insertd.* in margin with illegible cancellation *aft.* "any"

17 Bloomington] Bl'ton

18 Don Cook] D.C.

19 can] *aft. del.* "co"

23   Sub-Committee] Sub-Comm.; One member] *interl. ab. del.*
        "Chesnutt"
24   Another] *interl. ab. del.* "Nordloh"
26   so . . . confuse] *del.* "too" *ab. del.* "so"; "that they" *interl.*
        ab. "to"
27–28   I wish . . . . of all developments.] Originally, "I wish . . .
        peacemaker" was the concluding sentence of the preceding
        paragraph. The author marked it to begin the letter's last
        paragraph and marked the following sentence to "run on"
        as part of that paragraph.
28   give] *interl. aft.* "you"
29   —] *interl.* with caret

IV. CONCLUSION

As the sample texts in section III reveal, some of the variations
produced by applying different textual methods are of comparatively little importance. The fact that the letter's author used the
thorn as shorthand in drafting correspondence is of some interest,
but it could easily be reported in a general statement on her style,
without the need to reproduce every such symbol as "ye" or "[th]e"
or to supply a textual note on each occasion when the thorn appears.
However, the treatment of revisions and substitutions in the clear
text (fig. 5) conceals not only changes in wording and tone but also
factual information, such as the identities of the committeemen to
whom she refers. In each text, the conventions peculiar to the editorial method employed show their own virtues and limitations.
The reader must weigh the clarity and efficiency of each approach
for himself.

SUGGESTED READINGS

Documentary editors have confined their remarks on the use of
symbols or descriptive notes for textual problems in unpublished
writings largely to the introductions to volumes where such sigla
or notes are employed. Nothing in this field, for instance, compares
to G. Thomas Tanselle's analysis of methods for published literary
works in "Some Principles for Editorial Apparatus," *Studies in Bibliography* 25 (1972): 41–88.

I. The sigla of classical scholarship were standardized at a conference in Leiden in 1929, and their forms are summarized in the
pamphlet *Emploi des signes critiques; disposition dans les editions*

savantes de textes grecs et latins: Conseils et recommandations, by J. Bidez and A. B. Drachmann (Paris, 1932; rev. ed. by A. Delatte and A. Severyns, Brussels, 1938). For examples of textual symbols in the Malone Society's *Reprints* series see *John A Kent and John A Cumber* (London, 1923) and *Believe as You List* (London, 1927).

II. In addition to the essays cited in the text, the student of descriptive textual annotation should see Joel Myerson's review essay on *The Autobiography of Benjamin Franklin: A Genetic Text* in *ADE Newsletter* 4 (May 1982); and Fredson Bowers's comments on Myerson's remarks in a letter to the editor of the *Newsletter,* September 1982.

III. An interesting example of the modern application of different methods to the same source text can be seen in the Franklin Papers edition of *The Autobiography of Benjamin Franklin* (New Haven, 1964) and in J. A. Leo LeMay and P. M. Zal's genetic text of the same work (Knoxville, Tenn., 1981).

CHAPTER 7

General Rules and Their Exceptions

In recent years American editors have established guidelines designed to meet the challenges inherent in nearly every type of document. After designing an editorial technique appropriate to the bulk of these sources, they follow that technique until they encounter a situation in which the standard documentary formula of "one source equals one editorial text" cannot apply. Whenever the equation proves invalid, documentary editors turn to other traditions for appropriate solutions. Yet they tend to apply such borrowed techniques in a conservative fashion, choosing to remind their readers when editorial judgment or guesswork has occurred rather than to conceal that fact in the name of elegance or readability.

I. CONSERVATIVE PATTERNS OF EMENDATION

There is a distinct pattern in the choice of a general method for any group of documentary texts. As a practical matter, that method must be the one that best serves the majority of the sources being edited so that announcements of exceptions to the editorial rule are no more frequent than necessary. And in the past thirty years, American editors have found that a general policy of conservative emendation is more effective than a liberal one.

Indeed, a recent survey of veteran editors revealed that nearly all had adopted less intrusive editorial policies than the ones announced in their original statements of editorial methods. It is no longer possible to find editors who endorse without question the practices sanctioning liberal editorial intervention commonly accepted a decade or two ago. To a degree, this is the product of the probing analysis of editorial practices published by G. Thomas Tanselle in 1978, but however much editors' views of their responsibilities have been shaped by critiques found in scholarly literature, their day-to-day experience has been the chief influence determining their policies. This underscores the point that no statement of principles is likely to cover all the issues and problems that one will encounter in any documentary edition and that the fledgling editor is well advised to examine in detail the practices of a wide range of editions before launching a new documentary project. In particular, the lessons of some editors who have modified their method in mid-stream are instructive.

Among literary series, the first volume of the *Howells Letters* is emended far more heavily than any other number in the series. In part, this is because Howells himself standardized his own letter-writing style as he approached middle age. The later source texts need less emendation by any standards. However, the frequency of emendation also decreased as the editors themselves grew more accustomed to Howells's usage. Patterns of punctuation or spelling that appeared odd or ambiguous in the early years of the project no longer seemed to need correction or explanation, because they had become familiar to the project's staff.

Historical editions, too, are not without their noticeably modified editorial methods. From its inception, the *Ratification* series gave conservative, almost diplomatic treatment to certain documents, generally those that could be regarded as government records. Such texts were labeled "LT" to indicate a literal transcription of the source, while others, such as private correspondence, diary entries, and the like, were heavily emended in one of the most liberal applications of expanded transcription on record. As the project continued, this dual standard of textual treatment became increasingly unsatisfactory. At last the method was abandoned in favor of a single general policy described in volume 13 of the series (the fourth volume to appear): "With only a few exceptions all documents are transcribed literally."

A. RECORDS OF THE INARTICULATE

From the beginning, one group of editors has ignored the temptation to emend or "improve" their source texts—those who deal with the records of the illiterate and the inarticulate. (Such problems have not, of course, confronted editors in the CEAA/CSE tradition, for their attention has been confined to the writings of the verbally skilled.) In recent years historians and historian-editors have become sensitive to the significance of the evidence available in the writings and records of the poorly educated. Political, social, and economic historians now focus on the inarticulate as well as on the literate elite in our society, and the documentary records of such groups and individuals are now the subject of scholarly editing as well as the general scholarly interest.

It should be no surprise that the methods employed in editions such as the papers of black Abolitionists and the Southern freedmen differ from those designed to serve the correspondence of Adams and Jefferson. Editors of the traditional "statesmen's papers" series were concerned with documents that fell within the realm of conventional scholarly research. Source texts that stand outside that tradition demand different methods. The patterns of emendation and conventionalization employed in the earliest historical papers projects were selected with an eye to illuminating the writings of individuals who were not merely literate but exceptionally well-educated. As newer editorial projects confronted the texts of documents that recorded the words and thoughts of ill-educated, even wholly illiterate men and women, they discovered that these old conventions were unsatisfactory.

The imposition of normalized punctuation, for instance, presupposes that a source text's author would understand the functions of such marks and that he or she would approve such repunctuation if given the chance to be his or her own editor. This assumption was articulated by Julian Boyd when he explained, "This expanded text represents the kind of clear and readable form that Jefferson himself would have used for a document intended for formal presentation in print" (*Jefferson Papers*, 1:xxxi). Similarly, correction of spelling errors in the writings of an ill-educated writer imposes a false sense of authorial intentions. Worse still, it can destroy much of the special value inherent in documents inscribed by the semi-literate—the phonetic rendering of colloquial language and dialect that make such documents a treasure for philologists.

In many instances, the records of the inarticulate had already suffered nonauthorial conventionalization before they became subjects of a scholarly edition. Illiterate "authors" had no choice but to dictate letters or memoirs to second parties, who imposed their own notions of correct spelling and punctuation and even syntax upon them. The only way to emend such a dictated source text to bring it closer to authorial intent would be to make it less correct syntactically and to introduce phonetic misspellings to match the author's dialect. Luckily, no editor has been tempted to follow such a course. Documents dictated by the illiterate, like documents inscribed laboriously, if incorrectly, by the semiliterate, must be allowed to stand, even though they may reflect a degree of elegance superimposed by the amanuensis and completely foreign to the author himself.

II. DOCUMENTARY PROBLEMS WITH TEXTUAL SOLUTIONS

Even the editor following the most conservative general policies on emendation will encounter situations when one source text will not provide one editorial text. The summary of methods of inscription and forms of documentary records in chapter 4, above, hints at some of the occasions when the documentary editor must borrow the methods of specialists in related fields. Any editor of orally communicated texts, for instance, may have to deal with the theoretical implications of dissonant witnesses to a lost archetype, the central problem of the classicist. But even editors spared this special form of documentary record must recognize the possibility that the best method for editing a specific source text may be one from the tradition of critical and not documentary publication.

A. GENETIC ELEMENTS IN SOURCE TEXTS

Any document—letter, state paper, literary work, scientific essay— can survive in forms that reflect the development of an author's intentions, preserving not only a final text but also the false starts, preliminary wording, and stylistic evolution of that text. Few editors can escape confronting source texts that carry intrinsic clues to their genesis. These are encountered most commonly when an editor's source text is a manuscript obviously revised during composition. An edition of a draft letter or an author's holograph corrections and additions to galley proofs or the pages of an early edition used to prepare a revised edition will demand identification of original, intermediate, and final versions of the same document.

In editing Melville's successive draft versions of *Billy Budd*, his editors coined the term *genetic text* to describe their diplomatic transcription of the manuscripts of this work, left unpublished at Melville's death. The genetic elements of the transcription were their painstaking efforts to devise a system of symbols and descriptive abbreviations that would allow the reader to understand the order in which the changes were made by the author. In a single set of pages, densely packed with symbolic barbed wire, they allowed the reader to follow Melville through two, three, sometimes four versions of the same passage.

The genetic text of *Billy Budd* is one of the most complicated and sophisticated products of modern American scholarly editing. Simpler genetic texts have been with us since the first editor presented an inclusive or conservatively expanded text of a handwritten draft. Any editorial method that includes the use of symbols for deletions, insertions, and interlineations holds out the prospect of a genetic text for individual documents. Editors who eschew the use of textual symbols can instead give their readers clear texts of the final version and supply notes that permit the reader to construct a genetic version of his own.

1. *Collaborative Source Texts*

Source texts that represent collaboration between two or more persons are as challenging as genetic documents by a single author. The identity of each reviser, as well as his specific contributions, must be recorded. With modern authors, editors often deal with writers who worked closely with publishers' editors. The evaluation of authorial intention in such cases has provided critics of copy-text application to modern writings with some of their most telling attacks upon the CSE. The problem of editing such collaborative documents is often encountered, too, in legislative and professional records, documents that frequently represent action by committee. A manuscript report or public paper may contain passages in the hands of two or more legislators assigned to prepare that document. The rough draft of a state paper may reflect the fact that an executive assigned its preparation to one aide, circulated the draft to other advisers, and then approved or vetoed their suggestions—leaving the record of all these actions on the same scribbled, dog-eared set of pages.

The collaborative aspects of a document's composition can be represented quite easily if one contributor had primary responsibility for its drafting. This fact can be stated in the document's source note, and the editor can focus on additions, revisions, or deletions in other hands. Such records may be provided by using a special form of symbol enclosing such additions (e.g., "The document was originally inscribed by AB. All revisions by CD appear in the text within square brackets"). However, if the collaborators' contributions are fairly equal or if a third or fourth writer is involved, the editor must consider descriptive notes that supplement the text. Each addition, deletion, or revision might be keyed to a footnote explaining that the words or phrases in question were "added above the line by CD" or "entered by EF in space left in the MS" or "deleted and revised by GH."

Clearly, the choice between a truly genetic text, an inclusive text supplemented by textual notes, and a clear text is both a theoretical and a practical one. The editor must choose the device that enables the reader to reconstruct inscriptions in the source text with the finest distinctions possible. The use of numbered footnotes with a clear text can serve this purpose, although the multiplication of superscripts necessary to record numerous significant revisions will run counter to the purposes of the editor who has chosen this method to avoid "disfiguring" the documentary text. Obviously, clear text with a back-of-book record cannot serve the reader when the genetic aspects of the source are central.

Documents may defy the editor's attempts to reproduce their genetic values if the proliferation of symbols or footnote numbers would make their texts useless. In such cases, it has been traditional to offer the reader *parallel texts* of the same material. In the classic form, the two texts were truly parallel, printed in two columns on the same page or on facing pages (as in Bowers's edition of *Leaves of Grass*). However, modern editors use the term and technique more broadly. The Yale University Press edition of Jonathan Edwards's *History of the Works of Redemption* will print a reading version of the manuscript draft of these sermons in a fairly conservative expanded transcription. The book will be accompanied by a microform of the original manuscripts, and the volume's editor freely refers to the printed version as a "pony" that will guide the reader in the use of the microform.

B. MULTIPLE-TEXT DOCUMENTS

Similar treatment can be accorded *multiple-text documents*, a term coined by David Nordloh to describe sources inscribed in such a way that the reader could reasonably extract the texts of two or more distinct documentary communications from the characters that appear on the same page or set of pages. In multiple-text documents, the entries on the same page are so widely separated in time, intention, and even authority that they must be viewed as separate examples of one author's writing or as examples of the writing of two or more authors. Their textual problems are distinct from those in ordinary drafts, in which the author has left records of his evolving intentions for a work prior to its completion.

Notebooks used as literary commonplace books are an obvious example of this practice. Thoreau first inscribed entries in his journals in ink. Months or even years later, he reworked many of these passages for publication, considerately making his revisions and emendations in pencil and ink that could be distinguished from the original inscriptions. After weighing many alternatives, the Thoreau editors chose to provide a clear reading text of Thoreau's original

entries. Textual notes in the *Thoreau Journals* reproduce only those
revised passages that never achieved print publication. The same
notes can refer the reader to other volumes in the Thoreau edition
for emended journal entries that served as the basis for works actually published in Thoreau's lifetime.

A somewhat similar problem is created by the writer who uses
his years of leisure and retirement to rewrite diary entries and other
portions of his personal papers for a contemplated memoir of some
kind but never executes plans for such a publication. Here the editor
cannot refer his reader to an authoritative text of the final version
of the material in another section of the edition or in any printed
source. The problem of providing access to such revised variant
passages becomes a time-consuming and serious consideration.

The challenge has already been dealt with by the editors of the
Madison and Lafayette editions. When Madison set out to compile
autobiographical material, he rewrote his own retained copies of
correspondence (or recovered addressees' versions from his correspondents or their heirs), revising the pages to suit his matured
notions of style and discretion and adding marginal comments to
the documents. Fortunately, Madison's later emendations are easily
distinguishable from his original inscriptions. When one of these
"corrected" manuscripts must be used as a source text, the Madison
editors can easily recover the original words and marks of punctuation, and the later revisions are discussed in footnotes. Thus the
reader has immediate access to the texts of letters and state papers
in the form that gives them validity as documents of American
political history, while the notes allow the reader to evaluate the
areas in which Madison felt correction or suppression was necessary
to make these materials ready for publication to the world.

The marquis de Lafayette was a more systematic memoirist. In
the early nineteenth century he revised not only personal letters but
also his 1779 manuscript "Memoir." These revisions were incorporated into transcribed copies which Lafayette then sent to Jared
Sparks, and most of the emendations were reflected in the published
version, *Mémoires*. The Lafayette editors collated all printed versions of the *Mémoires* against the emended manuscripts to establish
the pattern of the author's revisions. In their edition, the editors
simply disregard later revisions of the letters and manuscript "Memoir" that were "purely stylistic." When they encounter a "significant
passage" deleted in the manuscripts or omitted from the printed
Mémoires, it appears in the new edition within angle brackets. Any
other changes deemed significant by the modern editors are treated
in footnotes.

Other instances of multiple-text documents create mechanical problems in transcribing the source but do not pose deep theoretical questions. For example, a writer may use an existing inscribed document as scratch paper for drafting another letter or report.

A sheet of paper may carry a letter received by John Smith on one side and Smith's draft of his reply on the other. Some frugal eighteenth-century figures carried this practice to the extreme of drafting replies to a letter over that letter's own lines, inscribing the new draft at right angles to the old lines. Such practices make the texts of two documents part of the same physical whole. Although the textual notes that describe the provenance of each item must indicate that it is physically a part of the other, no special textual problems will arise.

1. Nonauthorial Emendations and Additions

In many cases, additions to a manuscript made by someone other than the author or the document's recipient can be ignored. These include dealers' notations, symbols entered by archivists who have cataloged the materials, and notes by collectors through whose hands the manuscripts have passed. These are no more an intellectual part of the document's text than is an owner's signature on the flyleaf of a rare book or pamphlet. With unprinted documents, just as with rare printed materials, such entries can be helpful in determining the item's provenance, and they should not be ignored in determining and describing the source text's history, but they need not be reproduced verbatim in an authoritative edition.

Still other categories of nonauthorial inscription require more careful notice and on occasion warrant reproduction in the edition itself. Few members of an author's family have resisted the temptation to edit literary memorabilia with pen, pencil, or scissors. Perhaps the worst offender in this category was Sophia Peabody Hawthorne, whose contributions to her husband's posthumous literary image are immortalized in the defaced notebooks and other manuscripts that she prepared for publication in her years of widowhood. Mrs. Hawthorne's activities as editor and censor had such a pervasive influence on her husband's reputation that they could not be ignored by the editors of the Centenary Edition of his works. No physical description of the notebooks would be complete without reference to Sophia's emendations and mutilations. And students of American cultural history would be ill-served by an edition that did not report these instances. Thus the textual notes to the clear texts of Hawthorne's writings include detailed descriptions of

Sophia's handiwork, as well as notes recording similar revisions by the Hawthornes' son Julian.

It is the historical significance of any nonauthorial additions—their independent documentary value—that determines how fully they should be recorded in a scholarly edition and, indeed, whether they should be recorded at all. If a writer's spouse marked the deceased's letters and papers for a print edition that did not, in fact, take place, the nonauthorial emendations clearly have less importance than they would had bowdlerized texts appeared and influenced a wide reading public.

Some examples of posthumous editing by friends, relatives, and publishers can be ignored because the edited or bowdlerized printed texts that resulted have not been as influential as Sophia Hawthorne's. The editors of the *George Washington Papers*, for instance, ignore Jared Sparks's "styling" of punctuation and spelling on the pages of the Washington manuscripts entrusted temporarily to his care while he prepared his selected edition of Washington's writings. Had Sparks's *Washington* volumes been the only ones available to scholars and laymen in the century and a half before the inauguration of the new George Washington project, an argument could have been made for recording his emendations in the new edition. However, in those intervening decades, scholars had access to the original Washington manuscripts on which Sparks had based his texts. The source texts were used for several other, and better, editions of Washington's letters and papers, and the public was not left at the mercy of Sparks's version of the documentary record. If the editors of the *George Washington Papers* listed every one of Jared Sparks's "improvements" to Washington's writings, they would have to list, as well, variants in hundreds of other printed transcriptions that followed Sparks's. No useful purpose would be served.

In some ways, the treatment of such nonauthorial revisions in manuscripts is comparable to a critical editor's approach to the works of an author whose editor demanded or imposed changes upon a manuscript for the sake of literary style or public acceptance. In such instances, the editor must offer his readers both the text that the author originally considered final *and* the revised version that was actually read by his public. If the author accepted such revisions, they bear directly upon his sense of craftsmanship and the courage of his aesthetic convictions. Even if they were imposed over his objections, it was they, and not his original words, that were circulated to the world and became known as "his" text. The author's original intentions form one historically significant document, and so does the revised and published version that became a part of literary history through its influence on those who read it.

C. CONFLATION

Just as a single manuscript can contain many versions of the same document or, indeed, the texts of distinct documents, so two or more sources may produce a single editorial text. Few documentary editors will entirely escape the task of *conflating*, or combining, the elements of two or more sources into one reading text, although their methods will differ from those traditional to critical textual editing.

1. Fragmentary Source Texts

Conflation occurs most frequently when the best source text survives in fragmentary form, while less authoritative versions exist with a more complete text. It is no novelty to catalog a manuscript letter whose last page has been lost but for which a contemporary copy, later transcription, or even printed text will furnish the missing material.

The problem of conflating fragmentary sources was the subject of an exchange between David Nordloh and Wayne Cutler in the *ADE Newsletter* in 1980 and 1982, when Nordloh took Cutler to task for the Polk edition's treatment of a letter from Andrew Jackson to Polk for which two manuscript sources survived. The first was a draft in the hand of Jackson's secretary, revised and signed by Jackson. The second was a copy of the letter made by James Polk from the version that he had actually received. Polk's copy contained a postscript added when the fair copy was made from the draft.

In this situation, three editorial choices were available. Nordloh argued for the clear-text format, in which the postscript would have been printed as part of the letter, with the change in authority indicated in a back-of-book note. An inclusive- or expanded-text editor might have printed the postscript as part of the editorial text, noting the change in authority in a footnote indicating the change in source texts. Cutler chose the most conservative solution to the problem, printing only the contents of the draft as the letter's reading text, while printing the postscript verbatim in a note adjacent to the text. Nordloh defended his position with a discussion of the primacy of authorial "final intentions." Cutler explained his own decision by analyzing the special attitudes of documentary editors toward their source texts.

In any documentary edition, conservative methods of conflation better suit the reader. Even if the conflated passages appear in one reading text, notes adjacent to the letter provide the reader with easy and convenient access to the information that he needs. In a clear text, without a superscript number to indicate that annotation is necessary, the reader would be ignorant of the crucial textual and evidentiary problem at hand.

When overlapping fragments of the text of the same document survive, and when each version can be considered reliable in terms of substantives if not in terms of accidentals, overt conflation of the sources into one editorial text is preferable. The fact and location of such conflation can be indicated using numbered notes or other devices. Even here, documentary editors should resist the temptation to impose a single pattern of accidentals upon resulting conflated text, even though this can produce a text in which three paragraphs represent the author's usage in a surviving eighteenth-century manuscript, while another three paragraphs show the style imposed upon the text by a late nineteenth-century transcriber.

If all the pages of a manuscript source text survive in mutilated form (as with documents damaged by fire or water or defaced by descendants or collectors), the editor may have to supply missing words or phrases at regular intervals throughout the editorial text rather than perform conflation at a single point where one source text ends and another continues. If this is a consistent problem in the edition, the editor should devise a symbolic system that indicates such routine conflation. Dozens of footnote numbers within the document to indicate the source of words or phrases from the supplementary source text would be needlessly intrusive.

Regular conflation may also be required when the author's drafts are routinely copied for transmittal as letters or other communications by a scribe who is less than conscientious. Some editors have met this problem by adopting a special bracket to enclose words in final versions of letters and state papers that were supplied from the more authoritative draft versions. Such simple devices give the reader simultaneous knowledge of authorial intentions *and* the text of the document as it was read by its intended recipient.

2. *Synoptic Texts*

More sophisticated problems of conflation arise when the editor discovers that the genetic stages of a document are recorded in not one but several source texts. If the variants between these preliminary versions are wide, the editor may print each document separately in parallel texts or treat each one as a variant of the other, indicating substantial differences in editorial notes. However, it may be that these separately inscribed evolutionary stages of the text are so directly related that they represent a direct intellectual line of revision. In this case, the editor has the option of creating a *synoptic text*, a technique closely related to the critical editing of a literary work.

This form of editing is as old as the synoptic editions of the Gospel, but the term *synoptic text* was coined for modern works by the editors of the James Joyce edition when they described their methods in editing Joyce's *Ulysses*. Joyce's revisions of the novel survived, not in a single draft manuscript, but in manuscript fragments, corrected galleys, and authorially emended copies of early editions of the book. The Joyce editors combined the information contained in these separate documents to create a synthetic genetic text, a synoptic text that summarized the information in several source texts in one new editorial text.

The process of textual synopsis is not confined to Biblical scholarship and editions of great literary works. The first volume of the *Ratification of the Constitution* series includes (on pages 271–96) two synoptic texts that allow the reader to trace the evolution of the articles of the American Constitution through the debates of the Philadelphia Convention of 1787. The editors did not have at hand separate copies of the Constitution reflecting its wording at every stage of its consideration. Instead, they worked from four source texts: the draft constitution submitted to the Convention on 6 August; the text of the Constitution as recorded in the Convention journals on 10 September; a printed copy of the report of the Committee on Style, which revised the articles between 10 and 12 September; and the text of the Constitution as adopted on 17 September. To supplement these sources, the editors analyzed James Madison's notes of debates in the Convention, records that indicated the date and nature of each revision of the frame of government.

The successive surviving versions of the Constitution qualified as source texts for a synopsis because they were similar enough to allow the editors to draw valid conclusions about the sequence of revisions at each point. The editors supplied a reading text of the final state of the evolution to parallel their synoptic texts by reprinting the articles of the Constitution as adopted by the Convention.

3. Reconciling Accounts of Independent Witnesses

In classical scholarship, the witnesses that survive for a lost archetype are usually in the form of scribal copies. Each must be collated with the others to determine patterns of transcriptional descent so that the editor can determine whether one or more was a copy made from an earlier and thus more reliable copy. Once this process of textual filiation is complete, variants among the witnesses are recorded and analyzed so that the editorial text can represent the best readings provided by the imperfect witnesses.

For editors of modern documentary materials, the problem of reconciling discordant witnesses is most likely to appear when verbatim, even shorthand, accounts survive to record words communicated orally in the form of a speech or conversation. Editors who may confront this challenge should consult the treatments of such records in the _Woodrow Wilson Papers_, 24:vii–xiii, and the _Douglass Speeches_, 1:lxxv ff.

In these two series, the verbatim account that is the longest is chosen as the basic text when the editors need to conflate variant accounts. (If nothing else, the longest report was usually made by the reporter who stayed alert after his rival scribes had lost interest.) Collating each variant version against this basic text may show that some of these versions were based upon another. The editors then establish patterns of textual filiation and ignore those reports that were obviously the scribal descendants of another stenographic version.

Once the editor has identified those verbatim accounts that have claims to authenticity, he must isolate and analyze every _crux_, or substantive disagreement between the texts. This task is easier if an expert in shorthand methods is available to determine when one reporter simply misread his own shorthand. Wilson himself helped his later editors, for the president often reviewed transcriptions of shorthand reports of his speeches prepared by his personal secretary and corrected his aide's inaccurate reporting.

The pattern of variants and cruxes will determine final editorial treatment of the _oral_ text. Variants are often comparatively minor in length, and many cruxes are easily explained in terms of the mishearing of similar spoken words or the misreading of the reporter's shorthand notes. In such cases, the editor may silently conflate or combine the accurate words and phrases from two or more reports into one text. Only when variants are substantial and inexplicable need editors intervene with brackets or numbered footnotes.

While the editors of American documents based on oral communications of the late nineteenth and early twentieth centuries have turned to the techniques of classical and literary scholarship to meet this problem, it should be noted that these documentary editors are likely to perform conflation more *overtly* than their classical and literary colleagues. In the *Douglass Speeches*, for instance, the editors could not afford the luxury of conflation and emendation, even with the use of a textual record. Shorthand-based newspaper reports of Douglass's speeches contained variants that were not only *cruxes* (in orally transmitted documents, anomalies in reporting the same words) but also reflections of inconsistent reporting of the same passages in Douglass's speeches. Such inconsistencies resulted in one newspaper's publishing long passages from a speech, which must have taken twenty or thirty minutes to deliver, while another paper ignored this section of the oration completely.

The Douglass editors could not conflate such variant texts as gracefully as editors whose cruxes were largely confined to minor, easily explained anomalies. Whenever it was necessary to add passages to the basic text from another version that had reported one section more fully, the conflated material was added to the basic text in angle brackets, and its source was indicated immediately in a note. If the basic text contained a summary of the sentences or paragraphs reported more completely in the second text, a dagger in the editorial text leads the reader to a note where the basic text's summary version is reported verbatim.

III. BASIC RULES FOR DOCUMENTARY EDITING

The format of these texts in the Douglass edition highlights the basic rule for transferring critical textual techniques to documentary source texts. Even when borrowing such methods, the documentary editor will let the seams of editorial tinkering show rather than mislead the reader into assuming that the editorial text is more *documentary*, more unique and integral, than it is.

By and large, any documentary source text will tend to dictate conservative treatment, and the important elements of such sources are more likely to survive the flexible application of a conservative editorial approach than those of a source that entails more liberal editorial intervention. The reader with a taste for watchwords may be reminded of A. E. Housman's comments on the "science" and the "art" of textual criticism:

A textual critic engaged upon his business is not at all like Newton investigating the motions of the planets: he is much more like a dog hunting for fleas. If a dog hunted for fleas on mathematical principles, basing his researches on statistics of area and population, he would never catch a flea except by accident. They require to be treated as individuals; and every problem which presents itself to the textual critic must be regarded as possibly unique. . . . If a dog is to hunt for fleas successfully he must be quick and he must be sensitive. It is no good for a rhinoceros to hunt for fleas: he does not know where they are, and could not catch them if he did. ("The Application of Thought to Textual Criticism" [1921], reprinted in *A. E. Housman: Selected Prose*, ed. John Carter [Cambridge, 1961], 132–33)

The documentary editor, like the critical editor, must be a knowing and sensitive fleahound. The fact that his editorial product will be used as documentary evidence imposes a special responsibility, for his imagination must be directed toward reconstructing inscribed truth, not offering fanciful guesses. Liberal policies of editorial emendation and intervention represent the "rhinoceros" approach to documentary editing, for they miss the fleas and crush the source texts under their own weight.

Suggested Readings

I.   For arguments in favor of conservative methods in emending source texts with documentary elements see Hershel Parker's review of two *Hawthorne* volumes in *Nineteenth Century Fiction* 33 (1978): 489–92; Sullivan, "The Problem of Text in Familiar Letters"; and G. Thomas Tanselle's "The Editing of Historical Documents," as well as his remarks on the overrated virtues of readability in his essay "Literary Editing" in Vogt and Jones, *Literary and Historical Editing*.

Excellent discussions of the many facets of the documentary records of the ill-educated can be found in John W. Blassingame's introduction to *Slave Testimony: Two Centuries of Letters, Interviews, and Autobiographies* (Baton Rouge, 1977) and in C. Vann Woodward's review essay in *American Historical Review* 79 (April 1974): 470–81.

II.   Examples of clear reading texts without the use of textual symbols can be found in such editions as the *Howells Letters* and the *Franklin Papers*. For remarks on the editorial challenges raised by authorial collaboration with contemporary editors see Davis, "The CEAA and Modern Textual Editing."

A useful summary of the methods of the Joyce editors is found in Michael Groden, "Editing Joyce's 'Ulysses': An International Effort," *Scholarly Publishing* 12 (October 1980): 37–54.

CHAPTER 8

The Mechanics of
Establishing a Text

This chapter examines the mundane but all-important practical aspects of documentary editing. A sound theoretical plan for transcribing and emending documentary sources is but one side of the process by which an editor *establishes* the proper editorial text to be offered to his public. The mechanical side of that process requires just as much care, and it demands relentless attention to detail at every step.

The theoretical basis and practical execution of any editorial plan must be equally sound. The most elegantly designed scheme for evaluating textual problems will fail if the editor is unable or unwilling to maintain proper control over his transcriptions or to proofread those transcriptions accurately. And the best-designed office procedures for transcribing source texts and verifying those transcriptions are useless unless they implement a theoretically valid editorial approach to the source's accidentals and substantives.

I. Transcription Procedures

In the literature of documentary editing there is often confusion over the meaning of *transcription*. It is sometimes assumed that an editor's transcription practices—his standards for rendering the source text's words, phrases, and other symbols into a typed copy that can be used in editing—are reflected precisely in the editorial text that is finally printed. This is seldom the case. The transcription described here is merely the initial conversion of the document's contents to an editorial working typescript. This may bear little resemblance to the editorial text that finally appears in print.

In CEAA/CSE editions, the source text is always transcribed as literally as possible, even when the editorial text will be a heavily emended clear text. Unless that original transcription is literal, the edited transcript will not provide a clear record of the changes made by the editors—changes that CSE guidelines demand be recorded in the edition's editorial apparatus. There are, however, forceful arguments for literal transcription even for editors with no desire to achieve CSE approval. These arguments are both practical and philosophical. At the most pedestrian level, literal transcription is far easier and more efficient for the transcriber. Translating handwritten or typed pages to typescript is a sufficient challenge to the transcriber without the additional burden of mastering lists of preferred editorial emendations and corrections.

If the editor does wish the typed transcripts to reflect some of his policies of emendation, he must prepare written instructions that make perfectly clear what forms are to be expanded, which types of misspellings are to be corrected, and so on. At projects where a permanent staff of trained transcribers is available, a considerable amount of emendation can be incorporated into initial transcription. But this is possible only if the editors prepare a carefully planned transcription guide—treating matters such as capitalization, punctuation, and the expansion or retention of contractions and abbreviations. The editor who does not have the time or inclination to prepare such a manual should order his transcribers to type what they see in the pages of the source text.

Beyond this practical consideration, there is the more important one of editorial responsibility. Emendation of the source text is the role of senior editors, not of the junior members of the staff, who usually bear the brunt of transcriptional typing. If the editor himself is willing to assume the burden of transcription, he has greater latitude in making emendations while transcribing, but even then he will find it easier to make his initial transcription a literal one.

There is a special practical advantage for literal transcription when the source text contains substantial canceled matter. If the transcriber is instructed to reproduce all legible canceled passages and to leave ample space for any that cannot be read, the editor's task will be immeasurably easier. The editor may well choose to delete many of these insignificant canceled passages. With a literal transcription, a simple mark of deletion will suffice, and a clean copy remains. However, if the transcriber is given latitude in deciding which canceled passages to reproduce, the editor will frequently have to add significant words or phrases that have been omitted. If manual methods are used, this may require unnecessary retyping of the transcription. Even if word-processing equipment is used, the addition of material is slightly more time-consuming than its deletion.

Further, the availability of word-processing devices eliminates most of the arguments for an emended transcription. If manual methods are used, an editor's markings on a literal transcript often render that typescript unusable as printer's copy, and retyping all or most of the transcriptions becomes necessary. Word processors allow the editor to enter such changes when editing is complete and to obtain a new copy that can be handed to any compositor without hesitation.

There are, of course, certain conventions of documentary publishing that can and should be reflected in the initial transcription. Before transcribing begins, the editor should make decisions on retaining or suppressing such details as the position of the date and place lines in letters; the treatment of salutations, closings, signatures, and paragraph indentations; the standardization of formal headings in public papers; and the treatment of addresses and endorsements.

If the project's publisher is amenable, many printed sources need not be transcribed at all. Editors of previously published works have frequently given their printers copy that is merely an editorially marked photocopy of the edition that they have chosen as their preferred text. These photocopies, with the addition of corrections of typographical errors and of numbers for editorial annotation, can be given to the printer with confidence, and because the printed materials are not retranscribed, the chance of introducing new errors is minimized. Projects using computers, of course, need not concern themselves with what goes to the printer, since their own staff will produce the final editorial text. Even with a sophisticated computerized system, a photocopy of a printed source text will furnish the best working copy for the editor. When textual emendations and annotation are completed on this photocopy, the results can be keyboarded.

Many printed source texts will not lend themselves to the convenience of editing on photocopy. The original of a unique printing may be so discolored or faded that its photoreproduction is nearly illegible. And if photoenlargements are not available, the copies of newspaper columns or other materials set in a small typeface may be an inconvenient basis for working editorial copy and completely useless as printer's copy. When printed source texts are to be transcribed, literal methods are essential. The editor should remember that most accepted patterns of emendation and correction are merely conventions to make readable to print what was intelligible in an unprinted original. The printed source text already reflects many of these conventions, and any further corrections should be made with the greatest caution; their choice is a serious subject for editorial judgment, not a transcriber's whim.

A. RULES FOR TRANSCRIPTION

"Exact copying," Edith Firth reminded her fellow editors, "involves a fair amount of hack work." There is no way to make transcribing fun, but there are some simple rules that can make the process less painful and will avoid duplication of effort and unnecessary retyping.

Whenever possible, the editor should consult his publisher before transcribing begins. If certain details of inscription in the original such as raised letters or archaic symbols will not bear reproduction in the printed volumes, there is no point in attempting to reproduce them in the typed transcription. However, if the publisher shows any willingness to preserve such details on the printed page, so much the better. The editor can then tailor his instructions to transcribers to fit the outline of design in the final printed edition, and unnecessary corrections can be avoided.

The editor using computer equipment must train his staff of transcribers (as well as himself) in the special needs of the equipment at hand. If a project using a conventional word processor may eventually have access to more sophisticated methods, the editor must plan ahead. The processor's transcription files can be converted to a file capable of being processed by a computer-driven typesetter. And even the editor without computerized equipment must think ahead to the day when he might be able to afford such a luxury. At its most basic level, this will affect the choice of typewriters for the project. Not all typewriters produce script that can be read by an optical character scanner, a device capable of creating machine-readable files which can be transferred to a computer or word processor. Whenever possible, the editor should obtain typewriters compatible with such scanners.

Some editors have ignored commonsense rules and suffered the painful consequences. At the risk of insulting the reader's intelligence, documentary editors offer these guidelines:

1. It is conventional to produce at least two copies of every transcript. The *first copy* will remain a pristine version that will receive no emendations or corrections until it is sent to the printer. The second will serve as the editor's working copy. For the project with

only a typewriter at hand, the first copy will be the ribbon typescript, while a carbon copy will become the editor's working material. If the project has access to a photocopying machine, it is preferable simply to duplicate the ribbon copy rather than to require typists to correct easily smudged carbons. With computer equipment, the information stored on disk or tape can be regarded as the transcription's first copy.

In practice, editors must consider the fact that some word-processor storage disks have not been tested for longevity and that even mainframe computers have been known to "lose" stored materials. For the editor's peace of mind, it may be wise to print out two copies of each computer-created transcript, one for editorial use and the second as insurance should the computerized storage facility falter. As editorial work progresses, a project with computer access should immediately create backup files in machine-readable form for each level of revision.

2. Transcribers should be instructed to leave spaces in the transcript for material that they cannot read. Whether manual or computerized methods are used, it will be easier for the editor to fill in such blanks than to write or type the recovered material between the lines or in the margins.

3. Transcribers will, of course, give their work a preliminary review before filing the copy. If manual methods are employed, any corrections made at this time—like all preliminary corrections or emendations—should be made only on the working copy and only in pencil, never in uneradicable ink. With a computerized system, the transcriber will make corrections with appropriate keystrokes before giving the final "print" command to the terminal. If the project uses photocopies as working copies, the transcript should be corrected before it is photocopied so that errors will not be immortalized in the master xerographic impression.

4. The physical format of the transcription must reflect its intended use not only as working copy for an editor but as copy to be submitted to a compositor. Like any such manuscript, it should be double-spaced, with generous margins on all four sides.

5. The transcription should introduce no new punctuation in the form of end-of-line hyphenation. Transcribers must never break a word at the end of the line. Ragged righthand margins on the typescript are a small price to pay for accuracy.

6. If transcription can wait until the editorial collection is complete, it is often more efficient to assign each transcriber a chronological sequence of source texts or a group of topically related

sources. Thus the transcriber can become expert in the problems peculiar to the time period or theme in question.

B. SPECIAL TRANSCRIPTION METHODS

The editor who aspires to the CSE emblem must adopt methods to facilitate the preparation of records of editorial emendations required by that agency. Literal transcription, of course, is a prerequisite, but the transcriber must also transcribe documents in facsimile fashion in certain areas:

1. The transcriber should preserve the end-of-line breaks of the original document. This will allow the editor to create an accurate record of the author's end-of-line hyphenation.

2. In transcribing paginated source materials such as notebooks or journals, it is also useful to transcribe not only line for line but also page for page. A new page in the document will call for a new transcription sheet so that the editor will have a convenient record of such breaks.

The editors of Thoreau's writings found that oversized sheets of typing paper accommodated the transcription of any page from Thoreau's journals, and these sheets were employed so that new page breaks were not introduced.

3. The lines of transcription, as well as their pages, must be numbered so that the editor can prepare textual notes without the use of footnote numbers.

C. TRANSCRIPTION FORMS AND CONTROL

Clearly, for any CSE project, specially designed transcription sheets are almost a necessity. Those sheets would carry line numbers along one margin, and their standardized headings would include spaces in which to record the completion of special procedures demanded by the CSE: verification or *perfection* of the transcript against the original document; completion of requisite proofreadings; and so on. Computer-assisted systems are a special boon here, for such details of format can be entered automatically. As with any documentary transcripts, of course, such sheets must allow for double-spaced lines, and the first copy of the transcription should be stored carefully in its unemended state.

Even a project without CSE aspirations may have to establish some forms for its transcriptions, and these may demand a standardized sheet. The transcription's heading should indicate the document's title, preferably in the form that will appear in the printed edition. The transcription should also bear the project's code for the location of the original of the source text, as well as the identifying number assigned to that version. Each succeeding page of the transcription should repeat the document's date and some part of the source information, as well as the new page number. If computerized equipment is used for transcribing, the heading might also include a code indicating the location of the transcribed material in the word processor's or the computer's storage device.

If computer methods are used, it is essential to assign sequential transcription numbers if transcription begins before the editorial search is completed. In such cases the arrangement of transcriptions on the disk or tape will not reflect the order in which the documents are arranged in the final volume, the sequence of the office's control files, or any other rationally established system. A coded reference is necessary to retrieve the original text. Sequentially assigned transcription numbers may be demanded in other cases as well. They are useful for the archival or semiarchival project, where identifying accession numbers obviously should be placed on the manuscript source texts, and the transcription number may be the only identifying code that such manuscripts receive. The same consideration dictates transcription numbers when source texts are transcribed from microfilm reels. And a project of large scope may find transcription numbers a useful device for estimating the project's scheduling, since they will provide a running record of the number of materials that have been transcribed.

If transcription numbers are used, a running record must be established to show which number represents which variant among possible source texts. The editor may create a special log of transcribed documents, which can be maintained in a ring binder or a card file. The sequential list of transcription numbers will be keyed to the date, title, and location of their source texts. If several transcribers are at work simultaneously, a card file is obviously more practical than a looseleaf binder because of the need to interfile records from each transcriber.

Beyond such a log of the progress of transcription, the simplicity or elaborateness of office procedures for control of transcribed materials and their processing depends on the size both of the project's collection and of its staff. At its simplest level, the process might require the transcriber to mark a transcribed document's file folder with a *T* and the transcriber's initials. Later reviews of the transcription could be indicated by the initials of the editors, along with other codes to indicate verification, annotation, final proofreading, retyping, and so on.

Projects that have collected thousands of documents and that employ large, rotating staffs may require more complicated records of responsibility and processing. The file folder for a transcribed source text can often hold such a record, and the editor may wish to design a special stamp for the folders that will leave a legend such as the following:

transcribed by＿＿＿ date＿＿＿ proofread by＿＿＿ date＿＿＿
verified [or "perfected"] by＿＿＿ date＿＿＿ annotated＿＿＿
date＿＿＿

Obviously the design of the transcription log can also be modified to include such information. The entries for each transcribed source text could contain columns to record the various steps through which the transcription passes. However, the transcription log can do such double duty only when transcription progresses in the same order in which the documents will appear in the print edition or when the transcription log is stored in the computer, where the data can be rearranged in appropriate order. It is more likely that the editor will have to create an independent control system for the transcripts. Many projects in which a number of editors work on the same volume prefer to create such a control system only after all transcriptions for a unit of the edition are completed. At such projects, the format for this system is often a chart posted on the wall for convenient reference by all concerned.

If the project's budget allows, and its needs demand, the record of transcription control can even be incorporated into headings on specially prepared transcription sheets that will serve as the first page of each typescript. These transcription logs tend to be more elaborate for projects that must meet the special requirements of the CSE. Computerized methods make inclusion of the transcription record on the first page of the typescript an easy and inexpensive matter. The form can be designed in advance and stored in the system so that its entire text can be summoned up by signaling with one or two keystrokes.

D. FILING TRANSCRIPTIONS

The master copy of the transcription should be filed immediately in boxes or file drawers where it will remain undisturbed until the editorial day of reckoning when it is to be marked for the printer. In a project where a number of transcribers are able to work far in advance of the editors, the second, or *working*, copy may also have to be stored. Many projects simply place the working copy in the file folder with the original or photocopied source text until it is time for it to receive editorial attention. This is impossible, of course, when the source texts are original manuscripts that could be damaged by the chemical reactions to the transcriptions' paper or inks or when the source texts are on microfilm. Such projects have to devise separate storage for the working transcriptions, and if many months or years will pass before some of these transcriptions are needed, it will be convenient to place both master and working copies in boxes or file drawers.

If the transcriptions will be called for by the editor in fairly short order, it is more practical to file the working copies immediately in the form that will be used by the editor. Normally well-mannered editors have lost their temper in arguing the relative merits of placing working transcriptions unbound in labeled boxes, in looseleaf binders, or in other varieties of notebooks. In truth, the best method is the one that suits the editor involved.

However the typescripts are stored, their containers must be given labels showing the inclusive dates for chronologically arranged materials or titles for items arranged topically. Once it is complete, each box or binder should receive a rough table of contents. For correspondence and papers, such a table need list only the date and an abbreviated form of the title (e.g., "13 April 1781   To John Jones"). Such a table is especially useful to a selective edition, for it serves as a convenient guide to items from a given time period or subject division that have been chosen for publication. With computerized equipment the preparation of such tables can be almost automatic. If transcriptions are made in the sequence in which they will be filed and published, a computer program can be used to retrieve and print out a sequential list of the dates and titles periodically. When transcription is complete, these printouts will provide an accurate master list of all transcriptions.

Once transcriptions are placed in their working order, it is convenient to separate each transcript from its neighbors by a sheet of whatever type of paper will be used by the editor in drafting his annotation. Many projects use colored paper for such annotation sheets, and interleaved blank sheets of yellow, pink, blue, or green between the white transcriptions serve as a helpful guide in leafing through the boxes or binders. Even before editorial work begins, such annotation sheets serve as convenient places for special queries or cautions concerning the source texts to which they refer. Here the transcriber can remind the editor that the source text was an enclosure in another item or indicate special reasons for any apparent novelties in treatment.

II. Establishing the Editorial Texts

The initial transcriptions must be reviewed and reviewed again to ensure that they meet the exacting standards of a documentary series. Anyone engaged in documentary editing must become familiar with the methods editors use to make their editions as reliable as possible. Mastery of the following terms and techniques is essential:

1. *Proofreading* indicates oral, tandem proofreading, in which one member of the editorial staff "holds" the newer version of the text while the second member of the team reads aloud, word for word, punctuation mark for punctuation mark, from the earlier textual version on which the later transcription, galley proof, or page proof is based. Thus, when proofreading a source text's initial typed transcription, one editor reads aloud from the source text while the second follows the characters on the typescript.

2. *Visual collation* occurs when a single editor compares two versions of the text visually. To increase accuracy, it is customary to place a ruler or other straight-edged device under each line in both versions so that one's eye will not carelessly skip an inscribed, typed, or printed line in either copy.

3. *Machine collation* requires the use of a mechanical collating device that can detect variants between two printed texts presumed to be identical. The earliest such device, the Hinman Collator, made possible the convenient collation of sample copies from each printing of a published work. CSE editors have since expanded the use of machine collation to check corrected page proof against unbound gatherings for their editions.

4. *Perfection* is the term used by some editors to describe checking editorial transcriptions made from photocopied source texts against the originals for each text. Perfection may have to consist of a visual collation, although team proofreading is preferable.

5. *Verification* is the task of checking the accuracy of the contents of informational annotation. Verification of quotations in such notes follows the edition's general policies for proofreading or visual collation of documents printed in their entirety. The verification of other elements in the notes should always be performed by someone other than the original annotator.

A. EVALUATION OF PROCEDURES

Some of the terms and practices described above refer to processes demanded of editors who aspire to CSE endorsement. The editor without such aspirations can ignore some of the stipulations attached to that center's guidelines, but he cannot ignore the reasons for their existence, nor can he ignore the experience of editors outside the CSE tradition who have employed other methods.

1. No one denies that team proofreading is a more effective insurance against error than visual collation. It is especially useful in the transcription of nonprinted source texts, for oral proofreading ensures that the person who reads aloud (preferably the senior editor, who bears the responsibility for the edition's consistency) will not be influenced by the interpretation of the person who has prepared that transcription. Whenever the oral reading produces a character, word, or phrase at variance with the transcription, the editor must naturally pause to reevaluate his own interpretation. But he must make his reassessment with a fresh eye, uninfluenced by what someone else has seen in the source text.

For printed source texts, the differing levels of accuracy between proofreading and visual collation may be less marked, for fewer instances of subjective interpretation will arise. However, any veteran of the process can attest that the visual collation of printed sources easily leads to skipping lines in either the source or its transcription. And those who have experimented with both methods report that proofreading is far less tiring to the eye (although not, obviously, to the voice) than visual collation, where the editor must continuously switch his field of vision from primary to secondary textual version while remembering what he has just seen.

Still, considerations of time and staff size will often make it impossible to apply the number of independent proofreadings set down by the CSE guidelines. Many editorial projects cannot muster the number of people required for multiple independent proofreadings by the CSE. And many more cannot expend the time necessary to perform these readings. For projects that must compromise on the matter of independent, team proofreadings, the use of cassette tape recorders offers useful supplements. The *reader* can record his part of the proofreading process at his own convenience, while the second member of the team can check those recorded, spoken words against the version he holds at his convenience. Two or more staff members may hold against the same tape, thus producing semi-independent proofreading sessions. Tape-recorded proofreading has an advantage beyond that of easing scheduling problems. Either member of the team can cease proofreading when his voice or his eyes begin to falter, and he can return to his task later without inconveniencing other members of the staff.

2. If it is not possible to give the editorial text the number of multiple formal proofreadings demanded by the CSE, the editor must perform at least one proofreading against the source text. This should be done as late as possible in the editorial process, preferably immediately before copy is to be sent to the printer. This rule merely recognizes the fact that the editor will become progressively more familiar with the peculiarities of his source texts, and in many cases the preparation of informational annotation will make the source more intelligible. If proofreading against the source text is performed only immediately after that source's transcription, it will be less accurate than proofreading performed weeks or months later.

3. Whenever possible, transcriptions should be perfected against the originals of their source texts, not merely against photocopied versions. When this is not feasible, the edition's introduction should make this omission clear. Whenever perfection of a given document or group of documents is performed by someone other than one of the editors, this fact should also be noted.

4. Some editors prefer to proofread or collate galley proofs of documentary texts against the source texts instead of against printer's copy. This offers the editor a last chance to catch errors of interpretation or mistranscription, but publishers do not look kindly upon long lists of *author's alterations* in galley proofs that arise from such a technique. If the editor plans to proofread or collate galleys against the source texts, he should do so only if the same exacting process was applied to the printer's copy before its submission to the compositor.

5. Proofreading must be supplemented by visual collation and simple "reading for sense" of both documentary texts and annotation. Transcriptions, printer's copy, galleys, and page proof must be read (not merely proofread) by as many people as possible. If a project's staff is a small one, it is wise to enlist professional colleagues as reviewers of the edition.

III. BACK-OF-BOOK TEXTUAL NOTES

For many editors, textual responsibility does not end with proofreading or perfecting the editorial reading text. Whenever an edition will relegate all or part of its record of emendations or details of inscription to the back of the book, the editor must establish an accurate reporting system for that apparatus as early as possible.

Even though these records will be checked again and again, the possibility of error is reduced substantially if their format is established in advance.

The process of such reporting may begin with the transcriber. If instructed to type only final authorial intentions in letters, journals, or draft works, the transcriber must also initiate a record of what is omitted—authorial deletions or interlineations or nonauthorial contributions in the source text. This is done most easily on a series of file cards carrying the individual document's title or identifying number, as well as the page and line of the typescript where the suppression of detail occurs. If the editor has already established the method by which such details will be reported (that is, through symbols, narrative description, descriptive abbreviations, or a combination of these methods), the transcriber can enter remarks in the proper form. Even in an inclusive text, there are likely to be some details that cannot be reported fully in the editorial text through symbols. Here, too, the transcriber should prepare a card describing the textual problem that will require further explanation in the back of the book.

When the editor reviews the transcriptions, he will begin the process of emending, or correcting, minor authorial errors or slips of the pen. Emendations, like suppressed inscriptional details, should be recorded on index cards with references to the transcription's page and line number. Editions that plan to provide separate records of inscriptional details and editorial emendations must distinguish between the two groups from the moment that record keeping begins. The easiest device is the use of cards of different colors. The two sets of cards can be interfiled, so that editors and proofreaders can consult a single sequence of textual notes when proofreading or perfecting the same document and its textual apparatus. When the time comes to prepare copy for the printer, the cards' distinctive colors will simplify the accurate separation of the two sets of textual notes.

No matter what their policies in reporting emendations and inscriptional details, all CSE editors are required to supply one kind of textual record in the back of the book—the report of ambiguous line-end hyphenations. The CSE demands not only a complete record of all such ambiguous authorial hyphenations (possible compound words whose line-end division coincides with the position of the hyphen) but also a list of any new ambiguous hyphenations introduced in the modern printed edition. Such a record allows scholars to give accurate quotations from the new text. To identify such ambiguities in the source text, the editor must refer both to dictionaries contemporary to the document's inscription and to the author's customary usage. Most projects create an in-house record of their author's preferences in hyphenating specific compounds. Complete consistency is too much to expect, but useful patterns will soon emerge.

Once the editor has established that line-end hyphenation occurs at a point where the author would ordinarily have hyphenated a compound, that hyphen must be marked in the transcription for retention in the print edition should typesetting place the word in the middle of the line. (Any project contemplating such a record will have transcribed source texts line for line, and no new hyphenations will be introduced until the copy is set in type.) The Thoreau Edition has been able to streamline the scope of its hyphenations by forgoing a *justified*, or consistently even, righthand margin in printed volumes of Thoreau's private writings. Thus typesetters cannot add new hyphens, and the Thoreau editors need report only their retention or omission of ambiguous line-end hyphens that appeared in the source texts. Editors who cling to justified righthand margins in their editions must check galley proofs and page proofs for new and potentially misleading hyphens.

Since all such back-of-book textual records will be keyed to typeset lines, not to footnote numbers within the texts, the final preparation of their contents must await proofs from the compositor. However, work on these lists can begin far earlier. Records of emendations and inscriptional details can be typed and proofread well ahead of time. The first column for each entry in these lists will bear a penciled reference to the line and page of the transcription or printer's copy. After page proofs are reviewed, new page-line references to the print editions can be substituted. The Thoreau Edition is now experimenting with computer-recorded reports of inscriptional details, emendations, and hyphenations. The data are entered on a terminal with each reference keyed to page and line references in the computer-stored transcription records. When page proofs are available, the editor need only substitute the typeset page-line reference, and the coded tape can be submitted to the compositor.

Complicated as such records may seem, there are ways to simplify their preparation. Some projects can choose to adopt the format of the *Howells Letters*, where line references in textual notes refer to the line of each document, not to the line of the printed page where an emendation or suppression has occurred. Thus this part of their textual record can be prepared from galley proofs.

The editor should also remember that there are ways to make the textual record easier for his reader to use. Instead of asking their readers to consult a separate section for records of ambiguous hyphenations, the editors of *Mark Twain's Notebooks & Journals* categorized these problems as a special form of editorial emendation and included them in the general emendations lists for each section of the *Notebooks*. In the *Howells Letters*, where textual issues are far simpler than in the Twain texts, a combined record of both emendations and "details" serves the reader well.

IV. COMPUTERS AND TEXTS

The overwhelming majority of the rules, suggestions, and guidelines discussed above for the preparation of printer's copy of texts and textual notes draw on the experience of editors with access to nothing more technically sophisticated than an electric typewriter. Word-processing equipment and sophisticated mainframe computers can simplify the process of checking the evolving versions of both texts and notes. With such tools, many documentary transcriptions and sections of annotation that would otherwise have to be completely retyped will require only minor changes entered in the system. This may produce fewer physically distinct versions to be proofread or collated.

If a project has established general rules for checking copy before acquiring computerized equipment, modifications may be necessary to ensure that the same standards of accuracy prevail. Projects using word processors have generally found that it is more effective to proofread against hard copy (pages of the machine's printout) than to proofread with one member of the team looking at the image projected on the word processor's viewing screen. Thus a new step must be introduced—that of ensuring an accurate transfer of corrections from the printout to the electronic system's memory. Projects that have relied on visual collation of copy may have to convert to team proofreading: collation against a word processor's screen for any length of time is physically impossible.

Each word-processing system or mainframe computer terminal will present its own problems. The editor who acquires such equipment must make sure that the methods he uses with the new technology produce the same standards of accuracy that he attained while using manual methods.

SUGGESTED READINGS

For a discussion of the nature of an established text see Fredson Bowers, "Established Texts and Definitive Editions," *Philological*

Quarterly 41 (1962): 1–17. Anecdotal, but useful, accounts of the lessons to be learned in establishing texts are found in Ronald Gottesman and David Nordloh, "The Quest for Perfection: or Surprises in the Consummation of Their Wedding Journey," and Frederick Anderson, "Hazards of Photographic Sources," both in the first number of the *CEAA Newsletter*, March 1968. As for the textual record required in an edition of private writings, see Nordloh's comments in ibid., no. 3 (June 1970). G. Thomas Tanselle addresses the problems of editorial records for literary works in "Some Principles for Editorial Apparatus," but there are no comparable studies of the special problems arising in creating such an apparatus for documentary sources.

CHAPTER 9

Preparing a Documentary Edition for the Printer

Even while establishing the documentary texts that form the core of any edition, editors must consider the documents' needs in the form of editorial explanation—informational annotation, glossaries and gazetteers, back-of-book records, and even an index that will give the reader access to the texts' contents. While struggling to maintain the integrity of the editorial texts, they must weigh the advantages of adding editorial comments on context, fact, and allusions to elucidate those texts.

I. Contextual or Informational Annotation

Most modern documentary editions go beyond offering accurate texts to supply editorial notes that make clear words, phrases, and sentences whose meaning might otherwise elude the reader. Editors seldom agree on how much annotation documents require, but they all strive to keep in mind the needs of two audiences: (1) the group or individual to whom the document was originally directed and (2) the readers who will use the new annotated edition. Ideally, the modern reader will be given sufficient information to understand the document as it was grasped by its initial reader. The editor's annotational responsibility generally ends with making clear what the document meant when it became part of the historical record. Documentary editions are seldom the place for a lengthy analysis of later misconceptions of a document's meaning. In 1963, Lester Cappon claimed that proper informational annotation was part of the very "rationale" of modern documentary editions, but editors have done little to refine this rationale.

Among literary scholars, Arthur Freedman suggested useful "Principles of Historical Annotation in Critical Editions of Modern

Texts" four decades ago (*English Institute Annual*, 1941, 115–28), but Freedman focused on the needs of editions of published works, not of the private writings of literary figures. His essay concentrated on standards for what Freedman called "notes of explanation" that "attempt to make a work more intelligible by showing its relationship to earlier works." He paid scant attention to the other category of annotation that he recognized, those "notes of recovery" that would "supply information that would presumably have been known to the author's contemporaries, but that has been lost by the passage of time."

A more recent literary scholar has raised points relevant to all editions. In "A Rationale of Literary Annotation: The Examples of Fielding's Novels" (Vogt and Jones, *Literary and Historical Editing*, 57–79), Martin Battestin admits that "there can be no single rationale of literary annotation that will prove universally practicable and appropriate." But he goes on to suggest three variables that will affect the extent and methods of annotation: first, "the character of the audience which the annotator supposes he is addressing"; second, "the nature of the text he is annotating"; and third, and admittedly the most unpredictable, "the peculiar interests, competences, and assumptions of the annotator himself."

If Battestin's definition of the nature of the text can be expanded to include not only the text's contents but also the form of communication that it represents (letter, journal, state paper), then his formulation can serve all documentary editors. The specific problems of historical documentary editing are addressed by Charles Cullen in his "Principles of Annotation in Editing Historical Documents" (ibid., 81–95). Cullen reminds his readers that the "proper scope" for annotation is determined "first, last, and always [by] the subject of the volume or series." By *subject*, of course, Cullen means both the form of the source text and the identity of the person or group that provides the focus for the series. Annotation to a group of diaries can be confined to supplying information that would have been known to their author—no other contemporary audience need be considered. Considerably more information on public events might have to be provided for an edition of correspondence between political leaders, for the reader would need the facts that would enable him to gauge the response of each letter's recipient, as well as the motives of its author. The correspondence between a writer and contemporary readers with expert knowledge in a given field demands fairly technical annotation to present accurately the facts and data that would have influenced both.

The editor must also estimate the needs and the abilities of his own audience. Military historians are far more likely to read the *Papers of Nathanael Greene* than the *William Dean Howells Letters*. Such scholars will need few reminders of the significance of major battles or minor skirmishes, whereas literary critics reading the *Howells Letters* might well appreciate an additional sentence or two from the editor pointing out the date and outcome of a military engagement mentioned by Howells.

The danger that threatens all editor-annotators is interpreting rather than explaining. Battestin sums up the problem when he says that the editor's "aim is to make the act of criticism possible, not to perform it." Excessive annotation is expensive as well as unnecessary. Documentary editions should be the beginning of research, not its culmination. "The editor can frequently discharge his duty," Cullen says, "by pointing out where they [his readers] can do more research on a given point. It is not necessary for the editor to pursue every lead, merely to point out the direction that others' research might take." And there is no shame in resorting to what Battestin terms "those most pitiable of adverbs, 'probably,' and 'possibly'; or declaring his utter helplessness in that still more humiliating phrase—'Not identified.' "

All of this does not mean that the editor is excused from trying to explain every element of the document to himself, if not to his reader, for as Cullen points out, "the adoption of a casual attitude toward annotation inevitably results in a casual questioning of the documents." The editor must understand the texts he publishes before he can decide which elements require annotation. Cullen's motto here will serve all editors, whatever their discipline: "The editor is under no obligation to explain every subject or identify every person mentioned in a document he is printing. He is, however, obliged to consider doing so."

II. MODELS

It is impossible to tell someone how to annotate documents. It is somewhat easier to show interested scholars through examples of first-rate annotation. Thirty years after the publication of Lyman Butterfield's *Letters of Benjamin Rush*, editors such as Harold Syrett still pointed to the volumes as a model for others to imitate, and readers of the edition second this view. In 1952, J. H. Powell remarked of the *Rush* volumes that their "notes are an essential part of presenting a manuscript" (*Mississippi Valley Historical Review* 39 [September 1952]: 325–27). And Henry Graff, who reviewed the edition for another periodical that year, recalled that on picking up the volumes three decades later, "I still found that the texts and their notes took me into Benjamin Rush's world."

The best-planned and best-executed annotational schemes accomplish this journey in time for readers, but they achieve these ends only when they rival the elegance and intelligence with which Butterfield put his own plan to work. Unfortunately, the student cannot read Butterfield on annotation, for he never published guidelines to documentary explication. The only clues to his methods survive in the massive "Directive" on annotation that still serves editors of the Adams papers. Still, Butterfield's methods, by implication, offer lessons to other editors. He achieved his ends through consistency and clarity. That consistency entailed establishing a recognizable pattern of annotation that the reader could grasp quickly. Other editors need not imitate those patterns, but they must strive for the same level of consistency. If the editor's introduction promises his readers that persons mentioned in the text will be identified at their first appearance, that promise must be kept. The reader can then reasonably assume that if he finds no footnote identification for an unfamiliar personal name, he need only refer to the index to find the earlier page where such a note occurs.

Many editorial rules need not be stated in the volume's introductory sections. Readers are remarkably adaptable creatures who can soon detect annotational patterns for themselves. After a few pages, for instance, the reader will sense that the editor has chosen to identify names mentioned in a series in a single footnote following that series rather than in several footnotes keyed to each item in the group. If this pattern is maintained throughout the edition, the reader will adjust his rhythm of reading accordingly. If the pattern changes without warning or reason, the reader will be distracted from the text while he vainly attempts to figure out just what has happened to the scheme to which he had become accustomed.

Clarity is an even more elusive goal than consistency, since it cannot be ensured by the most detailed style sheets or the most explicit statement of editorial method. In Butterfield's *Letters of Benjamin Rush*, annotation is light compared with that of many editions that have followed. The notes not only appear in logical places but also do their work efficiently, occupying no more space than necessary and allowing the reader to return quickly to the text. Informational annotation should be as brief and as clear as possible. Many scholars have discovered to their chagrin and surprise that drafting such notes places the greatest strain imaginable on their talents as literary craftsmen. And the ordeal has few rewards, for if notes are well written, they do not impress readers with their brilliance or wit; they merely remind them of a name or fact or date so that they can get on with the business of mastering the documentary texts.

A. OVERANNOTATION

Excessive informational annotation is the "occupational disease of editors" (James Thorpe, *Principles of Textual Criticism* [San Marino, Calif., 1972], 201). Martin Battestin warns editors to fight "the impulse to tell all that they have learned rather than what readers need to know." The disease usually appears in one of two forms. The editor can simply furnish too many footnotes, explaining matters that require no clarification or whose explication goes beyond the needs of any reader or any documentary text. Such practices drew criticism for the *Jefferson Davis Papers* and early numbers in the *Madison Papers* series. Another form of the plague has been charged to Julian Boyd, the father of the modern tradition of historical editing. In the later volumes of the *Jefferson Papers*, readers detected a tendency to publish as editorial headnotes monographs that had little to do with the texts at hand. Valuable as these essays were, some critics suggested that they might better have been published as separate works unrelated to the Jefferson edition.

III. ANNOTATIONAL FORMS

The choices of references to be annotated and the length of such explanations are not the only factors that the editor must consider. The format of such notes on the printed page can impose interpretation upon the documents or can subject the reader to mystification rather than lead him to enlightenment. The wide choice of footnote designs available for inspection and comparison in American documentary editions sometimes seems a testimonial to their editors' and designers' artistic impulses.

A. THE SOURCE NOTE

A *source note* or *provenance note* is one form of annotation required of every documentary editor. If he uses textual symbols, he may omit notes that describe details in the manuscript. If he forgoes explanations of allusions in the source, he may eliminate the need for historical (or informational) footnotes. But the editor of every documentary edition, scholarly or "general," must provide his readers with both the location of the originals of the sources he has used and a description of the physical form represented by those sources.

An edition of diaries or letterbooks may be drawn from comparatively few physically distinct sources. If he chooses, the editor of such an edition may describe the location and physical details of his sources in an introductory note to the volume or in the back-of-book textual apparatus. Additional notes within the text will cue the reader when the editorial text progresses from one source to the next.

The editor whose source texts are many and varied (such as letters recovered from a hundred manuscript repositories) must devote more time to designing his source notes, for each document will require separate notice. Customarily, such notes first state the physical form of the source. For letters, this means that the editor must indicate both the means of inscription (the author's autograph, handwritten copy, typewriting, printing) and the version of the letter inscribed in this manner (recipient's copy, retained copy, draft, transcription). Usually the editor will discover that it is unnecessary to give both sets of facts explicitly for each item. His introductory statement of editorial method can explain that all source texts for letters are addressees' copies unless otherwise indicated, or he may announce that all letters described as recipients' copies are in their authors' hand unless otherwise noted.

It may be necessary to adopt a series of codes indicating methods of inscription. In such systems, "A," usually represents *autograph inscription;* "L" is *letter;* and "S" *signed.* Thus, "ALS" stands for a letter written and signed by its author. Items inscribed after the mid-nineteenth century will demand a new series of symbols for *typewritten, carbon copy,* and even *telegram.* Variations on these symbols are countless. The would-be editor is best advised to consult the lists of such codes in editions whose sources resemble his own in both their time of inscription and their archival nature.

The descriptive symbol for the source's documentary version is usually followed immediately by the name of the owner-institution of the original source text or by an alphabetical symbol for the repository. Most projects rely on modifications of the Library of Congress's *National Union Catalog* symbols for repositories, the same ones used in cataloging materials for the project. In the case of many documents, it will be helpful to give the source text's collection, not merely the name of the repository. Not only does this aid the reader in locating the original for comparison but it can furnish valuable information as to the document's provenance. When the collection is arranged in a single consistent order (either chronologically or alphabetically by author), no further details are needed. However, if the collection's arrangement is in various series or is erratic, it may be necessary to provide numbers for the documents' volumes, boxes, folios, or record group.

The source's version and location are usually followed by certain details of inscription that are not part of the body of the document. These should be described or printed verbatim in the order of their inscription. Thus, for a letter, the editor first indicates its address, then its postal markings, then an endorsement by its recipient, and finally any significant dockets by clerks or later owners of the original manuscript.

Some editors find the source note a convenient place for listing enclosures in the original document when these are not printed in the edition. Other editors prefer to describe these enclosures in footnotes keyed to references to the items in the body of the documentary text. The latter method fails, however, if the edition's central figure or his associates are given to enclosing newspaper clippings, promissory notes, or the like, without commenting on their transmittal in the covering letter or report. In such cases, the editor has no choice but to expand his source note to list these items. When the enclosures in a given document can be identified but have not survived with their covering letter or report, the editor should refer his readers to a convenient and reliable source for another copy of these vanished enclosures and summarize their contents when pertinent. The editorial comment "enclosure not identified" is a perfectly honorable form that will spare the reader the trouble of hunting for information that the edition does not give.

Some series also employ the source note for any historical annotation that refers to the document as a whole. For instance, if an individual's name first appears in the edition as the author or recipient of a letter, the source note for that letter may be a convenient place to identify him. Similarly, the source note is also used to explain any editorial decisions that affect the document as a whole. If the editor has assigned a date to an undated source, the source note can justify this decision. When the editor has attributed authorship to an unsigned document, the source note can explain this attribution. Some editors prefer to keep their source note clear of such editorial comment. In their editions, a footnote "dropped" from the date explains the editor's reasons for assigning a day, month, or year to the document. And a footnote dropped from the document's title may explain the methods used to determine the item's author or recipient.

Whatever the form of the source note or its location in the volume, its function must be consistent throughout the edition. The reader must know that he will always find information on the source's manuscript version and location in (*a*) an unnumbered source note preceding the document or its historical annotation, (*b*) the first numbered footnote appended to the document, or (*c*) the first element of information in a back-of-book textual apparatus for the item. The information in these notes must be presented uniformly, using the same codes and the same sequence of information. There is no room for creativity in this part of the edition's scheme of annotation.

B. FOOTNOTES

American editors have managed to produce a number of footnote formats. The most common methods for editorial annotation that appear immediately adjacent to the documentary texts (as opposed to in-back-of-book records) are described below.

1. A format that distinguishes between textual and informational notes. Julian Boyd introduced this convention in the *Jefferson Papers*, but the example has not been widely imitated. In the *Jefferson* volumes, each documentary text is followed by an unnumbered source note that indicates the source's provenance, variant versions, and so on. This note is set in a typeface that distinguishes it from the double-columned notes that follow. The only numbered footnotes whose superscript symbols appear are those related to textual details. Informational annotation appears in the single, unnumbered note. For the reader's convenience, the key words and phrases to which portions of this note refer are printed in small capitals.

This device works well only for short documents that require little editorial explanation; it is less satisfactory for longer ones that demand lengthy explication. As a purely practical matter, the reader of a fifteen-page printed text will be hard put to find references to specific words or phrases in five pages of double-columned notes at the close of that document. There are also philosophical objections to this method, for by combining information that might have appeared in a dozen separate notes, the editor risks imposing interpretation upon the document's contents. Such notes, arranged in one note printed in the form of paragraphs with topic sentences, will inevitably impose an interpretive order on the information, and they can easily go too far in telling the reader what the editor believes the document means. Arranging the information in this neatly organized fashion can also lead to inconsistent annotational habits. If the editor promises to identify significant individuals in numbered footnotes, his readers will soon detect instances in which this engagement has been broken. When all the information is collected into one massive note, it is tempting to omit time-consuming identifications or explanations of "inconsequential" allusions, and it is all but impossible for the reader to catch such slips.

2. A combination of an unnumbered source note with bottom-of-page numbered notes covering both textual and contextual details. This format can be seen in the John Marshall and Franklin editions. In the *Marshall* volumes, the unnumbered source note follows the document's text; in the *Franklin* volumes, it precedes the text. Although the source note may contain comments on general textual problems in the source, such as the existence of mutilated passages, specific textual matters appear in the numbered notes keyed to the text.

The editor who chooses this option must find a footnote-numbering sequence long enough to ensure that he will never run out of numbers on the same printed page and risk two footnotes numbered 1, 2, or 3 at the foot of the same page. Both the Franklin and the Marshall editors use the sequence 1–9. Such a system demands the most scrupulous care on the part of the editors, for footnotes will be prepared by document, not by the final sequence of their numbers in the edition. The final superscript numbers in the text and at the beginning of each note can be entered only when editing of the entire volume is complete. Any modifications in annotation that change the number of notes will demand a complete revision of footnote numbers throughout the volume. The use of computer equipment can reduce the manual labor involved in such revisions, but a high degree of editorial caution must still prevail.

Bottom-of-page footnotes are generally more expensive in terms of production costs than end-of-item methods, but they are the format of choice for any edition in which the individual documentary texts consistently run more than ten or twelve pages and require frequent annotation. Clearly, it is inconvenient for a reader to flip back and forth across several pages of text to locate an end-of-item note.

3. End-of-item numbered footnotes. This is the most common convention among historical editions, and it also appears in the Cooper edition and the *Irving Letters*. The source note or provenance note appears first, either as footnote number 1 or as an unnumbered note preceding the numbered footnotes. The source note provides general textual information, but explanations of specific textual problems appear with the informational footnotes in one sequence of notes for each document. In such editions, it is customary to break the end-of-item rule for footnote location when annotating the text of an exceptionally long source. In such cases,

bottom-of-page footnotes are provided, although the sequence of such numbered notes still begins and ends with each document.

4. Headnotes for provenance. Such formats provide information on provenance in an unnumbered source note that precedes the documentary text. Numbered footnotes provide further textual details, as well as historical explication. This format was modified in the eighth volume of the Madison edition, where the source note was moved to the end of each documentary text as an unnumbered note preceding the numbered series. This modification was required by the nature of the source texts, which frequently appeared in several variant versions, required discussions of complicated patterns of transmittal or referral, or demanded lengthy lists of enclosures, which could inflate the unnumbered headnote from a few lines to several paragraphs. The Henry and Franklin editions employ the headnote device and have thus far avoided such textual problems, and the format continues to serve their projects well. In instances where special considerations demand a detailed editorial explanation of some detail in the source, a footnote numbered 1 is dropped from the unnumbered headnote.

C. BACK-OF-BOOK ANNOTATION

Literary editors whose tradition includes extensive back-of-book records have sometimes applied this method to both source information and nontextual annotation, as well as to the conventional reports of editorial emendations and hyphenation lists. In the *Howells Letters* and the *Frederic Correspondence*, the source note is defined as part of the textual apparatus to be consigned to the back of the book, although informational footnotes follow each document. In the *Hawthorne Notebooks* and the *Emerson Works*, even informational notes appear in the back of the book, with line-page references instead of footnote numbers keyed to superscripts in the texts.

The relegation of any of this information to the back of the book can have serious consequences. Whenever the editorial texts' primary function is to provide historical evidence, the provenance of the original must be readily available to every reader. It cannot be argued that placing the source note in an appendix is part of a plan to make the textual apparatus detachable from the text in a projected general edition, for even the general reader must be told the location of the original of each editorial text.

Back-of-book records of informational annotation serve the reader only when such notes are infrequent and inconsequential to grasping the meaning of most of the source text's contents. This distinction has been recognized by the Thoreau editors. Thoreau's manuscript journals, for instance, are literary daybooks, not diaries of the author's life. Thus the informational notes in the printed edition of that source are few in number and supply little but the sources of scattered literary allusions. But Thoreau's letters are filled with references to friends, casual acquaintances, and the events of his daily life. Volumes of his letters will furnish informational notes immediately after each letter.

D. INTRODUCTORY EDITORIAL NOTES

Any format for footnotes or back-of-book notes can be supplemented by editorial introductory passages or *headnotes*. In near comprehensive editions, such notes customarily refer to the specific document or group of documents that they introduce. However, compilers of volumes arranged topically and editors of highly selective editions will have to ignore this rule.

Whenever all or part of a series is organized by topics, each group of documents must be preceded by an editorial introduction. This note explains the criteria for selection, as well as the scheme of organization of the texts that follow, and it must provide the information the reader will need to understand the texts included in the section that it introduces.

In selective editions organized in one chronological series, the editor may find it necessary to insert paragraphs of editorial comment as transitional bridges between two sections of documents. Such notes may summarize the events not documented by the texts, as well as offer the reader the information required for the texts that follow. In the *Webster Correspondence*, such notes are printed at regular intervals between the texts of letters. In the *Jay Papers*, whose volumes are organized by chapters, such notes open each unit.

Such introductory notes should be terse. Even in a selective edition, it should be the documents that tell the story. If the texts and their footnotes do not present a coherent narrative, the editor may need to reconsider the justification for publishing these sources in printed volumes as a documentary edition.

IV. CITATION OF SOURCES

The length of footnotes and introductory notes can be determined not only by the editor's skill in writing clearly and concisely but also by the devices employed to give sources for these statements.

All documentary editors concede that sources must be given for any direct quotations that appear in their historical notes. And scholarly editors in general omit sources for information that can be verified in any conventional reference book or textbook. On other points there is little agreement. The care with which citations are offered in editorial notes seems to depend upon (1) the editor's assumption as to whether his source is obvious or obscure; and (2) the degree to which footnote length would be inflated by offering a full list of citations for a given sequence of facts.

The more recent the date of the documents involved, the more likely the editor is to leave his readers to their own devices in retrieving sources for historical annotation. Editions of late nineteenth- and early twentieth-century materials, no matter how light or heavy their annotation, are less likely to give detailed citations for the sources of these notes. An exception to this rule is editions of documents dealing with the history of inarticulate groups. Here, editors are acutely aware that they are part of a new historiographical movement and that the sources of their notes will not be obvious even to fellow specialists. As an example, the *Marcus Garvey Papers* provide not only more informational annotation than the *Woodrow Wilson Papers* but also more detailed citation of sources for each fact.

At times, the cumbersome nature of the research process required to produce a given set of notes makes specific source citation impractical. The biographies of delegates to federal and state ratifying conventions in the *Ratification* series carry no source citations. For many of these men, the editors had to function as primary biographers, drawing on dozens of original sources for even the briefest sketches. A list of all these sources, complete with full details of publication, would have been five times as long as the note produced by the books, manuscripts, and newspapers involved. A similar problem confronted the editors of the *Booker T. Washington Papers*. The voluminous records of the Tuskegee Institute provided invaluable data on students, faculty, and supporting personnel at the school. A biographical sketch for an individual who figured prominently and consistently in Washington's life provides full citation of its source references. But when a person is mentioned only in passing, the note gives little beyond his full name and the dates of his association with the institute. Here, the identifying information provided in the note implies its own source. The interested reader will know whether he should check the records of matriculated students, tenured faculty, or nonteaching Tuskegee staff for a specific period of time to glean more information.

The editor's introduction to a volume can inform the reader of categories of information in notes for which the source is somehow implied and will not be mentioned specifically. However, the editor must be sure that the nature of the note will, in truth, imply that source. When the contents of a note will indicate its source, the volume's introduction should make this clear. The editor of the papers of a Revolutionary general can responsibly inform his readers that all casualty figures for battles come from *Boatner's Encyclopedia of the American Revolution* unless otherwise indicated. The editor of a volume of political correspondence can remind his readers that sketches of persons identified as members of the U.S. House or Senate are based on their entries in the *Biographical Directory of the American Congress* unless another source is cited.

The editor should confine himself to no more than three or four categories of such implied sources, and he should use the device only for sources whose omission from footnote citations will save considerable space in the edition. The reader may be asked to remember the meaning of angle brackets, Library of Congress symbols for manuscript repositories, and lists of short titles, but he should not be expected to master an array of implied citations unless some useful purpose is served.

A. THE FORM OF CITATIONS IN EDITORIAL NOTES

The length and kind of information supplied in editorial notes can determine the format of the source citations. The longer and more complicated the note, the more pains the editor must take to make clear which facts come from which source.

In the lightly annotated *Andrew Johnson Papers*, all sources that have contributed to a given footnote follow the note's text, separated only by a period. However, in selective editions or any other series whose notes will frequently carry several direct quotations, it may be necessary to insert source citations within the body of the note, enclosed in parentheses following each quoted passage. Parenthetical citation of sources is also more effective for lengthy footnotes dealing with two or more topics. The use of parentheses enables the editor to insert the source for each factual category as it arises, without confusing the reader with a list of a dozen sources preceded only by a period.

New problems of citation arise in editions that employ introductory editorial notes as well as footnotes. Since these headnotes may be several pages in length, it will be more convenient for the reader to have the source citations immediately available to him as he reads the text. The source citations can be supplied periodically within parentheses or in numbered footnotes at the bottom of each page.

The editorial staff must keep a running bibliographical record of every printed work or manuscript collection cited in the notes. These sources should be presented as clearly and concisely as possible, and the editor may wish to place an arbitrary limit upon the number of times that a source will be cited before it warrants short-title treatment in his notes. Once a book or article meets this standard, the editor must choose an appropriate abbreviated form to use throughout the edition. All earlier references should be changed to reflect the new short title, and all later references should employ this form.

The editorial staff must maintain a separate file of short titles for the edition. If manual methods are used, slips in the file will be arranged in alphabetical order reflecting the short form, and they will carry the work's full title as well as a list of the notes in which the form has been used. These short titles, with complete bibliographical data for the works that they represent, will form part of the editorial apparatus in the published volume. Computerized equipment gives the editor a special advantage in maintaining bibliographical and short-title files. Even a comparatively modest word processor can be used to recall instances in which a specific author or title has been cited. The editor can check these for consistency, and if he wishes to convert any of these full citations to a shortened form, the system can be instructed to make this *global* conversion automatically.

Whether he uses manual or computerized methods, the editor is denied one method of citation available to conventional authors. His footnotes may not carry the formula "This book will henceforth be cited as . . ." when a title first appears if there is no short-title list in the volume. Any abbreviated form of citation that will be used consistently throughout the edition must be listed in the short-titles compilation, not disposed of in a footnote explanation. Annotation in such series is so complicated that the reader must have a separate list of such titles at hand rather than be expected to leaf back through hundreds of pages to discover the meaning of a short title in an earlier footnote.

The project's bibliographical file should have a separate section for repositories cited in notes. If the edition uses Library of Congress symbols or some other system of abbreviated forms to indicate the location of the originals of its source texts, the same system can be used for manuscripts cited or quoted in editorial notes. Maintaining a bibliographical file for manuscripts as well as printed works will, of course, ensure consistency of citation. It will also serve as the basis for any list of such symbols that forms part of the editorial apparatus in the printed volume.

V. PREPARATION OF FOOTNOTES

The annotation in any edition must reflect the documentary texts involved, but even veteran editors have difficulty explaining to others exactly how or when to insert footnotes. Still, their experience offers some helpful practical advice for any scheme of annotation, be it light or heavy.

1. As the editor prepares notes, he should begin a rough running index of the contents of those notes and the documents they explain. This annotation index will facilitate cross references to related notes and texts. At the Franklin papers project, where several editors work on a single volume, each editor's annotation index is periodically entered on the project's computer terminal, so that a cumulative index is available to the staff as a whole.

2. The editor must establish and maintain a record of broad editorial decisions on matters of informational annotation as well as textual treatment. During the volume's preparation, this will help the editor himself remain consistent in his methods, and it will be invaluable in training any new members of the editorial staff. Such a record will also be the basis of that section of the edition's introduction that explains any idiosyncrasies of annotation or source citations.

In preparing such a statement, however, the editor should remember the advice of Wilmarth Lewis: "Resist the temptation to invent ingenious devices for presenting your notes. . . . Do not on any account be clever. References should be made in as concise a manner as possible, but compression can be carried too far; the edition should not be turned into a private language intelligible only to those initiated into it" ("Editing Familiar Letters," 32–33).

3. In the past, many projects have found it useful to distinguish between documentary transcriptions and typescript footnotes by using different colors of paper for each category. If the color-coding system is continued throughout the editorial process, it gives the compositor a useful visual cue for the points at which new typefaces must be used.

4. No one who has prepared a footnote or introductory note should verify his own handiwork. If he has once misread a source, he is likely to do so a second time. And independent verification

ensures that the footnote's wording makes sense not only to its author but also to the first of many readers. Even editors working without a project staff should consider retaining a temporary assistant for this task.

5. Before copy is submitted to the printer, the editor should enlist colleagues to read over the documentary texts and their notes. The unbiased reaction of potential members of the edition's audience is the best insurance against the unintelligible edition against which Lewis warned his peers.

6. When the editor suspects that a footnote is unnecessary, it should be omitted. In imposing annotation upon a documentary text, the best rule is "When in doubt, leave it out." Many readers share Fredson Bowers's reaction to superscript footnote numbers in a text: Bowers explains that he "responds like one of Pavlov's dogs" to such signals and obediently moves his eye from the text to the note. Any such interruptions should be essential to comprehension of that text, not mere diversions from the proper business at hand.

VI. Supplements to Informational Annotation

Numbered or unnumbered editorial notes are only one device that makes documentary volumes useful for nontextual research. American editors have experimented with several supplements to these notes, and some of these are so commonplace that their informational function has been forgotten.

A well-designed table of contents, for instance, assists the reader who must follow cross references that give a document's date or number in the series but not its page in the volume. The Woodrow Wilson project reports success with an *analytical* table of contents which does not list documents in their page order or chronological sequence but is, instead, a quasi index that locates specific documents through subject listings. However, this method can be used only in a near comprehensive edition. When editorial selection has been at work, the reader must have a convenient list of documents in chronological order so that he can determine quickly whether the item in which he is interested has been chosen for publication. In a select book edition not accompanied by a microform supplement, the editor should consider a checklist of documents in the larger collection that are not published in his volumes. Such formal checklists are common in CSE series.

Other editors have streamlined documentary annotation by providing a special section of biographical sketches of prominent individuals who figure in their volumes. This section may appear either in the front or the back of the book. If the editor chooses such a device, he must include these sketches in the material covered by his index. Otherwise, the reader will continually have to check two alphabetically arranged units (the biographical sketches and the index entries) to locate the information that he needs.

Whenever documents in an edition consistently use unfamiliar foreign words or technical phrases, the editor should consider providing a glossary for these terms rather than (1) translating them each time they appear or (2) translating them only once and leaving the reader to flip back through hundreds of pages in search of the initial explanation. Any group of documents that continually presents unfamiliar place names may require a gazetteer that provides appropriate geographical or topographical information. Specially designed maps can supplement or replace such a gazetteer in many instances.

Editions of a public figure's papers often provide a chronology of the significant events in his career for the period covered by each volume. Such a chronology must be part of the volume's introductory section so that the reader can master its contents before reading the documentary texts.

VII. THE INDEX

The most important supplement to informational annotation in any edition is the index. Editors know that no volume of documents is any better than the index that follows those texts—and no reader trying to make sense of a badly indexed or unindexed volume will quarrel with this statement. Because the design of the index is central to the edition's success, the editor may need to begin planning that finding aid long before the documentary texts and their notes are ready for submission to the printer.

The editor who has never before indexed a book should not try to pick up the skill on the job. Reliable introductory books on the mechanics of indexing abound. After mastering these elementary rules, the novice should compare the indexes in documentary editions whose contents resemble those of his own projected volumes. He must then think carefully about the materials that he must index and the audience that will have to rely upon that guide. Many editors regard the indexing system of the *Adams Papers* as a model for others. In preparing the index to the edition's first unit, *The Diary and Autobiography of John Adams*, Lyman Butterfield established a pattern of entries and subentries that proved adaptable to the succeeding twenty volumes of Adams diaries, letters, and public papers. Butterfield believed in the serendipitous value of documentary editions, and his indexes testify to his determination to make the unexpected in the *Adams Papers* volumes available to readers. The specific subject entries in the Adams series will not, of course, meet the needs of other editions, but the intelligent planning and anticipation of readers' needs in that index are the standard against which others can measure their own efforts.

A properly designed index can reduce the number and length of editorial notes. *See above* references to earlier identifications of individuals can be eliminated when the index provides a key to such sketches. (Most commonly, the index entry for such a note will carry a key word such as *sketch*, or it will be introduced by an asterisk or printed in boldface or italic type.) The index can also give the reader access to pertinent information to other numbers in a continuing series, thus eliminating the need for another category of cross references in the notes. (The *Madison Papers*, for instance, print such cross references to earlier volumes in the edition within parentheses in the index entries.)

Whether an index is prepared manually or with a computer, there are basic rules to be followed by any documentary editor. Even though the rules for indexing one series cannot be transferred wholesale to any other edition, a few guidelines can be drawn from the experience of American editors.

1. The index should cover all the materials that precede it in the volume. If a selective edition of correspondence includes a checklist of letters omitted from the printed volume, entries in this list should be picked up by the index. If the editor uses devices such as a separate biographical section or gazetteer to streamline his annotation, these supplements should be indexed. The volume's introduction and its appendixes deserve index entries, as do any lengthy descriptive notes on illustrations. There is no excuse for a partial index of a volume of annotated documents. Even if some of its elements, such as biographies, are already in alphabetical order, the reader deserves an index that presents a guide to every page in the volume with the exception of its title page and table of contents.

2. The editor should generally provide one index and one index only for each volume or for each set of volumes published simultaneously. The reader is seldom served well by multiple indexes.

3. Index entries must reflect the nature of the documents in the edition. The editor of correspondence must provide entries for personal names that pinpoint the pages where each individual's correspondence appears. A string of undifferentiated page numbers will

not suffice. A volume of legislative papers requires an index that breaks entries down into subentries that allow the reader to trace the evolution of specific pieces of legislation or of committee action upon bills or resolutions.

4. Index entries should be phrased so that they will serve the needs of the readers of the specific edition in question. A volume of legal papers, for example, can use technical phrases drawn from the law in its index, although such subject entries would be pretentious and baffling in the index to the personal correspondence of a poet.

5. Whenever a documentary edition focuses on a central figure or organization, index entries under that name must be broken down into intelligible subentries, and these should be kept to a minimum. The reader can assume that every entry in the index is in some way related to that central figure. However, certain topics can be located only if considered part of the entry for the edition's subject. Efforts to avoid this approach have been embarrassingly unsuccessful, as have experiments in limiting index entries for the central figure to "mentions," which results in columns of undifferentiated page numbers of no use to the reader.

6. Even though the final form of the index may not be prepared until page proof is available, the editor must keep its design in mind as he prepares the volume itself. Unnecessary cross references can be eliminated from the notes if the editor knows that his index will provide easy access to such material. And the indexer's work will be eased if editorial copy bears marginal notes indicating that "J. Smyth" should appear in the index as "Smith, John." If maintained properly, the project's running index of annotation should answer most of the indexer's questions.

VIII. STATEMENTS OF METHOD

Once documentary texts and annotation have been proofread, collated, perfected, and verified, the editor must prepare editorial statements that meet the standards of full disclosure demanded by modern editing. Here textual policies, methods of factual annotation, and indexing are explained. The editor must then ensure that the product of his editorial labors emerges as an accurately printed work. In all of this, he must check and check again. Copy supplied to the printer will return as galley proofs and then as page proofs. Each must be examined scrupulously to guard against the introduction of new corruptions in the texts that he has established so painstakingly and to ensure that his editorial notes remain models of clarity, not thickets of typographical errors.

SUGGESTED READINGS

I.   For the justification of annotation as part of the editorial process, Lester Cappon's "A Rationale for Historical Editing Past and Present" should be consulted, along with George C. Rogers, Jr.'s "The Sacred Text: An Impossible Dream," in Vogt and Jones, *Literary and Historical Editing*, 23–33. An excellent example of a scholar's amplification of the raw material provided by a documentary edition is Bernhard Fabian, "Jefferson's *Notes on Virginia*: The Genesis of Query xvii, The different religions received into that State," *William and Mary Quarterly* 12 (January 1955): 124–38.

II.   The scholar in search of model style sheets for annotation procedures should consult the Adams Papers's "Directive" on annotation and the Thoreau Edition's "Guidelines for Annotating Thoreau's *Journal*," both, unfortunately, unpublished in-house memoranda. Attempts to define the proper model for annotation in correspondence can be found in Wilmarth S. Lewis's "Editing Familiar Letters" and Robert Halsband's "Editing the Letters of Letter-Writers."

Perhaps the most widely criticized edition in terms of overannotation is the *Jefferson Papers*, particularly in respect to the lengthy editorial notes provided in vols. 17 and 18. Editors have offered some of the critiques of their colleagues' annotation procedures. See, for instance, Lyman Butterfield's "New Light on the North Atlantic Triangle in the 1780's," *William and Mary Quarterly* 21 (October 1964): 596–606, and George C. Rogers's review of the *Mason Papers*, ibid. 28 (October 1971): 676–79. Other worthwhile reviews take to task the *Adams Legal Papers* in *Journal of American History* 53 (December 1966): 590–91; the *Calhoun Papers* in the *American Historical Review* 73 (December 1968): 1637; the *Jefferson Davis Papers* in ibid. 82 (December 1977): 1329–30, *Journal of American History* 62 (1976): 950–52, and *American Archivist* 39 (1976): 210–11; the *Franklin Papers* in *Journal of American History* 60 (March 1974): 1071–73; the *Hamilton Papers* in ibid. 60 (September 1973): 409–11; the *Henry Papers* in *American Historical Review* 84 (April 1979): 547–48; the Lafayette series in *William and Mary Quarterly* 36 (July 1979): 484–86; the *Madison Papers* in *Mississippi Valley Historical Review* 49 (December 1962): 504–6,

Journal of American History 51 (September 1964): 299–300 and 59 (June 1972): 115–17, *William and Mary Quarterly* 20 (1963): 146–50 and 35 (April 1978): 147–55, and *Papers of the Bibliographical Society of America* 62 (1968): 149–50; the *Morris Papers* in *American Historical Review* 83 (December 1978): 340–41; the *Letters of Benjamin Rush* in *Mississippi Valley Historical Review* 39 (September 1952): 325–27; and the *Woodrow Wilson Papers* in *American Historical Review* 83 (December 1978): 1356–57.

III.   Differing forms for source notes can be compared in the Adams and Henry papers. The Jefferson and Adams papers use introductory editorial notes in a traditional fashion, while the *Freedom* and *Ratification* series employ the technique in a different way for volumes that are selective and topically organized.

VI.   For examples of special biographical supplements to annotation see the *Howells Letters* and the Livingston, Mason, and *Ratification* series. Introductory chronologies are furnished in volumes of the *Webster Correspondence*, the *Jefferson Papers*, and the *Johnson Papers*.

Although reviewers have not given as much attention to such supplementary tools as to editorial annotation, many have addressed the subject intelligently. See especially the reviews and review essays dealing with documentary editions in *American Philosophical Society Memoirs* 35 (1953), *Journal of American History* 68 (September 1981): 366–67, *Mississippi Valley Historical Review* 48 (December 1961): 510–11, *William and Mary Quarterly* 12 (April 1955): 358–60, and 22 (October 1965): 660–63, and *American Historical Review* 68 (April 1963): 762–65 and 77 (June 1972): 831.

CHAPTER 10

The Editor and the Publisher

The documentary transcriptions and notes so lovingly prepared by the editor and his staff must sooner or later be surrendered to a publisher. In years to come, all editorial projects may be able to maintain complete control over the production of their volumes, generating the magnetic tapes or disks that will drive computerized equipment to produce printed pages without the intervention of anyone outside the project's staff, but for most projects that day is still far in the future. Creation of a print edition requires the co-operation of dozens of technicians who know nothing of the rationale for any editorial decisions and who sometimes do not share the editor's passionate concern for every mark of punctuation in the printer's copy. The process of converting documentary transcriptions and notes to printed pages in a bound volume requires the editor's relentless attention to tasks that can be challenging or frustrating, even dull. The editor must, of course, maintain his program of proofreading or collation of copy throughout the book's production cycle to ensure an accurate edition. But he must also prepare or revise the front and back matter (elements that precede or follow the documentary texts) for the finished volume, complete an index, and maintain his own sanity.

I. THE DOCUMENTARY EDITOR AND THE DOCUMENTARY PUBLISHER

The most important factor in making the process as painless as possible is the degree to which the editor and publisher view this as a cooperative venture, not a war between competing factions. The best defense against such friction is an exchange of ideas. Misunderstandings usually arise from mutual ignorance. A press that has survived one documentary series is more likely to be prepared for the special problems presented by a second, while the veteran of one documentary edition is more likely than a novice to understand the limitations and capabilities of modern book design and technology. It is the editor's responsibility to make himself and his edition's needs known to the publisher—and to do so as early as possible. He cannot assume that anyone else will understand the special problems of his texts, notes, and apparatus, and if he fails to explain them to his press, he risks a print edition that will be a source to be avoided rather than one to be consulted eagerly and conveniently. Publishers' editors and book designers who have lived to tell their tales offer three sound rules for the documentary editor in dealing with a press:

1. Confer with the publisher's editors and designers as soon as a press has been chosen.
2. Never be afraid to betray ignorance by asking questions.
3. Never hesitate to volunteer information or ideas to the publishing staff.

The documentary editor who is unfamiliar with the principles of book design should brief himself in this area, formally or informally. By consulting other editions, he will soon learn which methods are visually effective for certain kinds of texts and annotation. Whenever he reaches a tentative decision concerning the design of his own series, he should consult an expert in book production to learn whether his plan is economically practical and technically feasible. Ideally, he will choose his publisher early in his project's career, and he can direct his questions to the designer or production director who will be responsible for his volume. If this is impossible, he must recruit his own advisers.

The editor using computer-assisted equipment should also seek advice from systems experts, who can show him the most efficient and accurate methods of coding the information to be entered on his system months or years before these data will be converted to copy submitted to a compositor or to machine-readable disks or tapes transmitted directly to a computerized typesetting system. Here, too, early consultation with the publisher is mandatory. One word processor's disks, for example, may not be compatible with the system used by the press's compositor, in which case the editor must allow for the costs of converting these disks into a form that can be "read" by the printing system.

An editor's questions cannot stop with broad considerations of design or electronic systems. If copy will be entered on a keyboard by a compositor, the editor must be sure that the printer's copy is marked in a form intelligible to the compositor. Most major university presses and commercial publishers claim to follow the methods described in the *Chicago Manual of Style*, but all have their peculiar house rules for certain matters.

Details that seem obvious to the editor after years of experience with the documentary edition may demand explanation to those who will publish those volumes. The designer cannot project the patterns of the printed book until he knows which elements of the texts or notes require visual emphasis and which can be left to speak for themselves. The editor who submits machine-readable copy that includes his own in-house codes and neglects to give the compositor a key to those codes might as well have submitted photocopies of the source texts themselves.

When the editor does not have the luxury of furnishing his press with machine-readable copy for a computerized system, he must be an especially effective communicator of his own wishes. He will, for instance, learn to place a check mark or an "O.K." above odd usages in the documentary texts so that no publisher's editor will "correct" such authorial errors. He must follow every rule for the considerate author, furnishing his publisher with legible typed copy, double-spaced, with generous margins for questions from the press or for instructions to the compositor.

A. HOT TYPE AND COLD TYPE

Modern technology introduces a new set of questions that every editor must ask of his press. Even the editor whose project does not use computer equipment must now familiarize himself with an important group of electronic systems: those used to produce his books. Many of the practices of proofreading and collation now in use rest on the assumption that printer's copy is still set by a compositor whose work produces metal plates which, in turn, are inked to produce impressions on sheets of paper that will be folded and cut to produce the pages of the published volume.

For practical purposes, the traditions of this *hot-type* process are a thing of the past for most American book publishers. Although some still use linotype or monotype to produce metal plates, these plates are seldom used for *letterpress* printing. Instead of each page's being printed from an inked plate, only one set of pages is printed. This serves as the master image for *photo-offset* production of the multiple copies of each page for the edition. Moreover, even photo offset based on a hot-type *master* is vanishing. An increasing number of documentary editions, like other books, are now produced by *cold-type* process, photocomposition or computer composition that bypasses the stage of inked metal plates. In both systems, a compositor enters the words and phrases of the printer's copy on a keyboard along with symbols for indentation, spacing, and changes of typeface. This, in turn, produces a machine-readable record (a magnetic tape or disk), which is fed into the computer-driven system that converts the machine-readable symbols into the desired typeset characters, arranged as titles, documents, and notes.

In photocomposition, the system employs a series of disks that carry the images of the letters, numerals, and other characters available in a specific typeface. The symbols on the tape or disk signal the system to position the disk so that the appropriate images are recorded photographically in the system's printout.

In computer composition, the system stores sets of images of the letters, numbers, and other symbols used in printing. When a particular letter is called for, that letter is created by projecting a series of dots or lines on photosensitive paper. Because the dots or lines are spaced so closely together, they appear as unbroken letters to the naked eye. Computer composition systems can produce the standard characters of any type font, and the most sophisticated of the systems can create almost any graphic character imaginable. Thus the documentary editor may have more options in reproducing unusual symbols that would otherwise have to be drawn by hand. Both photocomposition and computer composition offer great economies in production costs, but they can create new problems for the documentary editor.

With hot type, the editor could assume that the compositor who reset corrected galleys would reset only those sections where errors had occurred. The galleys of type were then broken into pages, and new proofs were prepared, with running heads and page numbers. The editor or author proofread or collated *page proofs* against corrected *galleys* to ensure that all errors had been eliminated and that no new ones had been introduced in resetting or in creating running heads. Because of the labor costs involved, the compositor seldom reset more material than was absolutely necessary. Some editors confined their collation or proofreading to lines where corrections were demanded and to the lines above and below these passages. Any errors were marked on the page proofs for corrections. After the compositor reset the page plates, the editor again focused his attention on the corrected lines and those immediately around them.

Even with hot type, compositors were known to introduce new and inexplicable errors after page proof had been checked and ap-

proved: a dozen years ago, CEAA editors learned to employ mechanical collators to compare corrected page proofs against pages
pulled from the first print run of their volumes. Cold type can
generate different evolutionary patterns of book composition. For
convenience's sake, publishers still call the printout from the initial
keyboarding of printer's copy galleys. These sheets are given to the
editor-author for proofreading or collation. However, when the
compositor corrects errors in these "galleys," most computer systems generate an entirely new tape or disk instead of entering corrections on the original one. If the computerized system has received
new design instructions in the weeks or months since the creation
of the first tape, these modifications will be reflected in the new
tape, which will be the basis for the printout which is then "pasted
up" for page proofs and photo-offset printing.

Such design modifications are most likely to occur in the spacing
used in the chosen typeface. Thus the line breaks in computer-
generated "page proof" can be entirely different from those in the
"galleys." An editor preparing a record of ambiguous line-end hyphenations in the new edition must wait until page proof is available.
For all editors, the use of cold type means that page proof must be
checked far more scrupulously than formerly. The practice of collating machines to compare cold-type galleys, page proof, and *gatherings* is becoming more widespread. As documentary editors and
their publishers become more familiar with the idiosyncrasies of
cold type, new rules for proofreading and collation will emerge. In
the meantime, the editor must ask as many questions as possible
and leave nothing to chance.

Whether hot type or cold type is to be used in producing his
volume, the editor should demand sample pages from his publisher's
designer. It is the editor's responsibility to submit copy for truly
representative samples of documentary texts, footnotes, textual apparatus, glossaries, and any other special features of the edition that
he has planned. The selection of such samples and preparation of
their typeset pages should begin as soon as the editor and publisher
have signed a contract. Inappropriate design and format can be
corrected easily at this point. But even with cold type, an editor is
ill advised to demand a new typeface for footnotes or a revised
pattern of paragraph indentation after he has received galley proofs.

II. FRONT AND BACK MATTER

Because of the special production problems created by documentary
editions, their publishers prefer to be given copy for the documen-

tary texts and editorial notes as early as possible. Thus, many editors turn to the preparation of front and back matter after these transcriptions and typed notes have gone to the compositor.

In any documentary edition, such prefatory sections and appendixes are far more significant than in conventional books. If readers are to use a documentary volume intelligently, they deserve a full explanation of the project's standards for establishing texts and furnishing annotation, as well as accurate back-of-book textual records and tables that may be necessary to recover details of the original sources.

"Full disclosure" is the motto of any editor as he prepares these sections of his volumes. The user's need to know is paramount. The various files and memoranda compiled during the editing process serve a vital function when the editor prepares the explanatory statements and apparatus that will allow his readers to make use of the printed volumes. Specific groups of documents may require special editorial discussions, but each volume or set of volumes published simultaneously must contain the following elements:

1. A statement of textual method.
2. A statement of editorial standards for nontextual annotation.
3. A list of all textual symbols used in the editorial texts and a list of any abbreviations used to describe such forms of the source text as "ALS," "D," and "Dft."
4. A list of short titles for published works and abbreviated forms designating repositories used in the edition.
5. If the provenance of the source text demands, the editor must inform readers that permission to cite or to quote certain items should come from their private or institutional owners. In some cases, the sources' provenance may also require formal statements that the editor has received permission to reproduce these texts or that he has been granted permission to reprint copywritten material.

Editions that employ clear text often place the first and third of these elements in the back of the book, immediately preceding the record of emendations and inscriptional details. In other editions, all five elements usually precede the first documentary text.

A. THE STATEMENT OF TEXTUAL METHOD

The statement of textual method indicates which of the broad options the editor has chosen for textual treatment of his sources. In an edition employing anything but printed facsimiles or diplomatic transcriptions, the editor must expand on this general statement and elaborate upon his treatment of specific textual problems in the source materials.

Whichever textual method he chooses, the editor should also make clear the implications of his textual method for the documents at hand. Even with back-of-book textual record, the reader deserves fair warning if clear text produces printed versions of letters that are at substantial variance with the texts read by their recipients. Editorial decisions on what is included in inclusive texts may consistently mask categories of details that are significant to a group of readers. Of course, the responsibility of the editor who does not supply such a textual record is even greater in this regard. Should certain items in the edition demand textual treatment different from the norm, the editor should warn the reader of such exceptions. If the textual notes to these exceptional items do not indicate that special liberties have been taken with them, the editorial introduction must list such documents for the reader's guidance.

CSE requirements suggest that the editor also describe the methods followed by his staff in proofreading, collating, and perfecting the editorial texts of documents. Among historical editions, only the *Woodrow Wilson Papers* offer the readers a similar exposition of editorial practices. Ideally, all documentary editions should provide this information.

B. THE STATEMENT OF THE PATTERN OF ANNOTATION

The statement of the pattern of annotation presents the editor's general policies on providing identification or explication of matters mentioned in the documentary texts. It also points out any supplementary devices such as sections of biographical sketches, glossaries, or gazetteers. The editor should never hesitate to be honest about the limitations of his informational annotation. The preface in each of the twenty-six volumes of the *Hamilton Papers* closes with the forthright statement, "Finally, the editors on some occasions were unable to find the desired information, and on other occasions the editors were remiss." Such an admission of human fallibility does not prevent scholars from benefiting from the edition's documentary texts and editorial notes.

C. TEXTUAL SYMBOLS AND FORMS OF SOURCE TEXTS

The editor can never assume that any symbol or abbreviation that he uses for textual details or the forms of source texts will be self-evident in its meaning. No reader can be expected to guess about such matters. Although few editors would be rash enough to omit a list of their textual barbed wire, some have been careless in offering adequate definitions of the meanings they have adopted for the inscriptional forms represented in their editions. Indicating that "L" stands for *letter* is not enough. The editor must indicate whether *letter* means the final version of that source, the recipient's copy. Such definitions may vary according to the peculiarities of the source texts involved, and the reader deserves every clue he can be given.

D. SHORT TITLES AND SYMBOLS FOR REPOSITORIES

Most editors have found it desirable to separate lists of short titles and symbols for repositories from the list that explains alphabetical symbols for the forms of source texts. If a large number of printed sources and repositories have been cited in abbreviated form, it is best to provide a separate list for each category.

The four sections listed above should appear in every volume or unit of a continuing series. Some editors have assumed that they need be discussed fully only in the first volume of such an edition, but this places an unreasonable burden on the reader, for few individuals can afford to purchase every number in a series, and no library can guarantee its patrons that volume 1 in each set will remain on its shelves. Since these sections should be as concise as possible, their repetition in each volume involves the addition of comparatively few pages, and their inclusion makes succeeding volumes much more useful.

E. OPTIONAL FRONT AND BACK MATTER

The editor's design of his volumes may demand special front and back matter. Annotation may be supplemented by glossaries, gazetteers, and discrete sections of biographical sketches. Editors of clear-text editions ordinarily furnish textual records, historical collations, and hyphenation lists. And the special features of some editions may demand still further additions to the list of mandatory editorial explanations. The circumstances that most commonly require such additional explanatory sections arise from the edition's scope (i.e., whether it is a continuing multivolume series) or its organization (i.e., whether it is selective in nature).

Continuing multivolume series may create a need for modified statements of editorial method. First, editorial practices may change over the years in which the volumes are published. Whenever this occurs, the editor is obliged to explain modifications of textual treatment, informational or textual annotation, and format. Next, successive volumes in a chronologically arranged series may take the editor into new categories of documents that require fresh textual or annotational methods. Whenever this occurs, the introduction to the volume in which this problem first occurs must carry an explanation of the problem and of the solution adopted by the editors. Third, succeeding volumes in a series frequently adopt devices that will allow the reader to consult the edition as a whole. The clearest example of such a technique is the Madison editors' use of an index to provide cross references to pertinent annotation in earlier volumes. Whenever the index to a specific volume becomes part of a broader information-retrieval system, the editorial note introducing the index entries must be expanded to explain the method involved.

Any selective edition not supplemented by a comprehensive microform of the large collection from which it is drawn should provide the reader with some sort of calendar or checklist that provides access to the documents that are not part of the printed volumes. And any selective edition—as well as editions organized by topic rather than by chronology—must provide the reader with a table of contents.

III. CSE INSPECTIONS

CSE editors do not have the option of preparing front and back matter after the body of the edition has been sent to the printer. To qualify for the CSE seal, an editor is required to submit to the CSE-appointed inspector not only documentary texts and informational notes but also draft introductory statements and textual apparatus. In the past, these inspections were generally conducted at the project's offices, but budgetary considerations now make it almost impossible to maintain the practice of on-site inspection for all volumes. While the CSE prefers to conduct the inspection of the first volume in a continuing series at the project's offices, the review of later volumes is customarily performed long-distance, with the editor submitting materials to the inspector by mail and answering pertinent questions by letter or by telephone.

For the initial volume in a series, the inspection should be performed when the manuscript for the volume has reached the status of printer's copy. At this point, the initial proofreading and perfection of documentary texts and textual apparatus have been completed, and there are final versions of nontextual annotation ready for review. If the inspector raises points that require clarification or correction of textual method, the editor can make these adjustments in the printer's copy rather than risk the anger of his publisher by requesting extensive alterations in galley proof.

The inspector will read the statements of editorial method carefully and make comparisons of a representative sample of editorial texts and textual apparatus against photocopied source texts provided by the editor or against originals of those sources located at repositories that the inspector can visit conveniently. The editor must be prepared to answer any questions about his project's procedures regarding textual matters, and the inspector may raise issues concerning informational annotation.

Upon completing this review, the inspector submits recommendations to the CSE. Should the report be unfavorable, the CSE will forward it to the editor so that he may reply to the points the inspector has raised. The most common reasons for denying a CSE emblem to documentary editions are:

1. Detection of a significant number of errors in the printer's copy of the source texts or the textual apparatus
2. Imprecise statements of editorial policy in textual matters or failure to follow stated principles
3. Unsatisfactory procedures for proofreading and perfecting the text and its apparatus
4. Indefensible choices of source or copy-texts
5. Badly designed textual apparatus
6. A choice of textual method inappropriate to the sources

If a volume fails to meet CSE approval after its initial inspection, the editor can reapply at any time, even asking for a different inspector for the second review if he wishes. When a volume is recommended by its inspector and approved by the CSE, the editor can immediately submit the copy to his printer, and he can inform his publisher that the verso of the book's title page may bear the emblem "An Approved Text."

IV. FINAL ESTABLISHMENT OF THE DOCUMENTARY TEXT

Even though CSE inspections ordinarily occur before copy is submitted to a compositor, no responsible scholarly editor pretends that responsibility for guarding the integrity of his texts ends at this point. All of the editor's painstaking work can be undone if he does not monitor the progress of the texts through the ensuing stages of production.

CSE guidelines suggest that any editorial text be given five independent proofreadings at the "most appropriate" points in the process of creating printed volumes. At least one (and preferably two) of these proofreadings should precede submission of copy to the printer. And, of course, the corrected textual apparatus must be proofread in conjunction with the perfected transcription before texts and apparatus go to press. At most CSE projects, galley proofs are given two proofreadings against either printer's copy or the source texts or their photocopies. Page proof must be proofread against corrected galleys, and corrected pages must be proofread against the original page proofs. Frequently, these editors perform machine collations of the unbound gatherings ready for the binder to compare them with the corrected page proofs.

Even the editor who does not choose to match these standards should establish his policies for proofreading or collating proofs long before they appear in his office. Publishers do not applaud delays in production schedules caused by an editor's agonizing over the best methods for checking these materials. Whatever combination of proofreading or collation he chooses, the editor must establish a system of clearly assigned responsibility for these tasks. And he must follow his press's instructions explicitly in making corrections upon these proofs.

In addition to such proofreadings and visual collations, editors, like any responsible authors, must read transcriptions, galleys, and page proof of documentary texts for sense. Oral team proofreading can conceal errors of transcription in homophonic words, and human fallibility is always at work. Completely illogical words and inexplicable omissions can survive the most rigorous series of independent proofreading sessions.

A. TEXTUAL NOTES AND APPARATUS

Only with a printed-facsimile edition will proofreading, collation, and perfection of the documentary transcription end with checking the body of that transcript. With all other methods, there will be editorial notes that point to specific details in the source that have been emended or suppressed in the version that the new edition presents.

The completion of review of galley proofs may allow some CSE editions to proceed with the completion of their textual apparatus. If the publisher can assure the editor that line breaks will remain constant in page proofs, the editor whose textual apparatus refers to lines of documents rather than lines of pages (as with the *Howells Letters*) can begin the work of calculating these line numbers. Projects whose editions use justified righthand margins will begin checking galleys for the introduction of new ambiguous line-end hyphenations introduced by the typesetter. However, these lists remain tentative until page proof arrives.

Page proofs must first be proofread or collated to ensure that errors marked in the galleys have been corrected and that no new errors have been introduced. Once this process is complete, the CSE editor can prepare his final version of the back-of-book textual apparatus and hyphenation lists. And the additional series of galleys and page proofs must be proofread once these notes and lists are submitted to the compositor.

Editors who do not employ back-of-book textual records will, of course, confine such reports to notes adjacent to their texts. Such notes must meet the edition's general standards for the accurate rendition of a source text. And these notes should be phrased with a consistency bordering on tedium. The editor must always describe the same detail or form of emendation in the same fashion. These notes are not the place for literary inventiveness or the use of clever synonyms for *deleted, interlined,* or *inserted in margin.*

B. NONTEXTUAL ANNOTATION

Even though published standards for the verification and proof-reading of nontextual annotation do not exist, an editor cannot ignore his responsibility to maintain the integrity of these editorial contributions as well as that of the documentary texts. As noted above, any quotations in such notes deserve the same high standards of proofreading, collation, or perfection as those applied to the documentary transcriptions. And these standards must be maintained when the editor reviews galley proofs, page proofs, and gatherings.

V. PREPARING THE INDEX

Traditionally, the preparation of index slips began only when page proof was available. A senior editor marked the words or phrases in the proof that deserved index entries. The correct versions of subject entries and proper names were scribbled in the margins of each page, and a junior member of the staff then wrote out a slip for each entry. Once slips had been made for the volume or volumes to be covered by the index, they were sorted manually. The editor was able to make some corrections and changes once the slips had been sorted. A typist then transcribed the slips on sheets of paper for the printer. After a final editorial review, the typed index was proofread. Galley proofs and page proofs were proofread as well.

Documentary editors have tried nearly every conceivable device to speed the task of indexing. Some have even prepared a preliminary form of the index slips from printer's copy, entering handwritten page numbers on these slips once page proof became available. However, the most effective aid now available to the indexer is the computer. The human brain and eye remain the best instruments for designing index entries and pinpointing references that the index should carry, but the human hand cannot compete with the computer's speed and accuracy in sorting, arranging, and printing out entries.

Computer recording of index entries has special advantages beyond its speed. The indexer enters the number for each page only once on the computer terminal. This is followed by the subject headings for that page. A quick review of these entries ensures accuracy of page references, and there is no danger that the indexer will err while preparing two dozen separate slips for page 119 or 536. What is even more important, computer indexing can allow the editor to begin indexing as soon as copy is ready for the printer. The CINDEX system, devised by David Chesnutt of the *Laurens Papers*, is now used by several projects, and its programs allow the editor to begin not only the planning but the execution of the index months earlier than would otherwise be possible. Quite simply, the index entries can be made from printer's copy, using the sequential page numbers assigned in that copy. The computer will then sort the entries, and the editor can refine and correct all of his entries, subentries, and sub-subentries at this point. When page proofs are available, the computer can display the corrected entries in their old page order, corresponding to the pages of printer's copy. In a matter of hours, any member of the staff can manually change these page numbers to correspond with the page numbers and page breaks in page proofs.

VI. CONCLUSION

When the last bit of corrected page proof for the index or textual apparatus has been proofread or machine collated, the editor can do little but wait for the reviews of his printed volumes. While some reactions from readers will be fair and helpful, others will be ill informed and illogical. But the editor must consider them all. The elegance of his annotation and the scrupulous accuracy of his texts mean nothing if they have not served his audience's purposes.

Perhaps the most frequent criticism of documentary editions is the complaint that their editors produce these volumes too slowly. More realistically, observers might wonder that any editorial staff survives to produce a single tome, much less to publish ten or twenty. Yet, somehow, dozens of editors have done so, and this guide attempts to share the lessons drawn from both their mistakes and their inspired decisions.

What editors cannot share in this book is the paradoxical satisfaction of documentary editing. If editors do their job well, they will inspire work that will supersede much of their own. The documents that they print will lead other scholars to search for sources that escaped their attention, and their notes should encourage others to dig a bit deeper for the historical truth that evaded them. What seemed comprehensive or definitive in their volumes may later prove to be only a landmark step toward that ultimate goal.

And the honest editor is, if anything, pleased by such results. Documentary editions are properly regarded not as the end of scholarly research but as only its beginning. The scholar who finds documentary editing a congenial discipline must be a pioneer at heart, ready to establish a foundation of evidence upon which others will build.

SUGGESTED READINGS

Perhaps the most useful aid prepared by a publisher for documentary editors whose series it will print is the *Guide for Authors and Editors Compiled by Historical Publications Editors*, published by the Historical Publications Section, Division of Archives and History, Department of Cultural Resources, Raleigh, North Carolina, 1979. Philip Gaskell, *From Writer to Reader: Studies in Editorial Method* (Oxford, 1978), provides useful comparisons of the methods employed by twelve different literary editions in presenting their series. An interesting presentation of comparative design is found in *One Book/Five Ways: The Publishing Procedures of Five University Presses* (Los Altos, Calif., 1978).

The experiences of university presses with scholarly editions are presented in Herbert S. Bailey, Jr., "Thoreau and Us," *Scholarly Publishing* 2 (July 1971): 327–28; Harry Clark, *A Venture in History: The Production, Publication, and Sale of the Works of Hubert Howe Bancroft*, University of California Publications, Librarianship, no. 19 (Los Angeles, 1973); Chester Kerr, "Publishing Historical Sources: A Prejudicial View of the Problem of Finance," *American Philosophical Society Proceedings* 98 (August 1954): 273–78; and Henry H. Wiggins, "Publisher to Alexander Hamilton,

Esqr.," *Scholarly Publishing* 9 (April 1978): 195–206 and (July 1978): 347–60.

Helpful comments on the computer revolution in publishing can be found in Greaser, "Authors, Editors, and Computers," ibid. 12 (January 1981): 123–30; David W. Packard, "Can Scholars Publish Their Own Books?" ibid. 5 (October 1973): 65–74; and S. W. Reid, "Definitive Editions and Photocomposition," *Publications of the Bibliographical Society of America* 72 (1978): 321–26.

Models for elements of front matter can be found in the explanations of symbols for textual sources in the *Franklin Papers* volumes; and models for explanations of changing editorial methods, in the *Wilson Papers*, vol. 3, and the *Madison Papers*, vol. 8.

A good comparative analysis of production procedures and the quality of indexes and other supplementary sections can be found in Haskell Monroe, "Some Thoughts for an Aspiring Historical Editor," *American Archivist* 32 (1969): 147–59.

Practical advice on proofreading galleys, pages, and gatherings can be found in Frederick Anderson, "Team Proofreading: Some Problems," *CEAA Newsletter* no. 2 (July 1969): 15; Michael De Battista, "Tape Proofreading: An Adaptation for Part-Time Staff," *Scholarly Publishing* 7 (January 1975): 147–50; Eleanor Harman, "Hints on Proofreading," ibid., 151–57; and James B. Meriwether, "Some Proofreading Precautions," *CEAA Newsletter*, no. 2 (July 1969): 17–18.

The best exposition of the rules for manual indexing of documentary volumes is the in-house "Directive" on the subject at the Adams Papers project. The only printed exposition of the methods of the CINDEX program documentary volumes is Chesnutt, "Comprehensive Text Processing and the Papers of Henry Laurens." However, that presentation is already out of date, for the CINDEX program now offers provisions for sub-subentries, refinements in "sort first" and "sort last" procedures, programs for single or multivolume indexes, and other refinements not mentioned in Chesnutt's article.

APPENDIX

Form Letters

I. A "BLIND" SEARCH LETTER TO LIBRARIES

These form letters represent the communications that might be issued by the editor of the mythical Margaret DeWitt Papers as he begins his search for DeWitt records. The first is a letter prepared for libraries not known to be repositories of DeWitt manuscripts:

Dear _____:

This project is sponsored by the National Endowment for the Humanities, the National Historical Publications and Records Commission, and the East Utopia University Department of American Studies. We plan to publish an edition of the papers of Margaret DeWitt (1841–1913), and these volumes will be issued by the East Utopia University Press. We wish to obtain photocopies of all surviving letters to and from DeWitt, as well as any other papers written by DeWitt or addressed to her.

If your collections include any such manuscript or printed materials, we wish to order positive photocopies (preferably Xerox or similar paper prints) at this time. Should your institution's policy require advance payment for such photoduplication orders, please advise us, and we shall be happy to oblige. Otherwise, we shall send payment promptly upon receipt of the photocopies.

Thank you for your attention to this request.

II. A LETTER TO LIBRARIES OWNING PERTINENT DOCUMENTS

When the editor of the DeWitt Papers writes to an institution where DeWitt materials are known to exist, the second paragraph of the form letter would be expanded to read as follows:

Listings in *Hamer's Guide* and *American Literary Manuscripts* indicate that your collections include correspondence between DeWitt and Teresa Snyder and Mertie Maria Pedrick. Alfonse Gaston's biography of DeWitt includes a reference to a draft essay by DeWitt of 7 October 1879 in the Aikman collection at your library. We would like photocopies of these items as well as of any other DeWitt material in your collections.

III. Letters to Autograph Dealers and Auctioneers

The DeWitt project's form letter to dealers and auction houses that have listed DeWitt manuscripts for sale should open with the standard paragraph describing the project's scope and sponsorship (see above). It might then continue:

We noted with interest the listing for a DeWitt letter to Susan Aikman of 12 April 1877 in your recent catalog #124. While we realize that you cannot disclose the identity of the purchaser of this item, we ask your cooperation in forwarding the enclosed letter to the client who has made this purchase.

Thank you for your attention to this request. Should any other DeWitt materials come to your attention in the future, we would appreciate advance notice of their sale. If you could furnish our staff with a photocopy or detailed abstract of such manuscripts, we, in turn, could provide you with historical background for the item, as well as comments on its significance for DeWitt's career, which might expedite preparation of your catalog entries. This would only increase the value of the document to its eventual purchaser, and it would ensure a complete record of DeWitt material for our files.

The "to whom it may concern" letter enclosed to dealers and auctioneers for transmittal to the purchaser of a DeWitt letter would be in this style:

Mr. X, the proprietor of X Manuscripts, Inc., has kindly agreed to forward this request to you as the purchaser of the DeWitt letter of 12 April 1877 offered for sale by his firm.

[Here insert the description of the project's scope and sponsorship.]

We would be most grateful if you could furnish our project with a photocopy of this item for our files. No further use of the photocopy will be made without your permission, and, of course, the photocopy will not be made available to scholars outside our staff.

Should the letter be considered for inclusion in our edition, we will honor your wishes in regard to any further publication of the manuscript and to the protection of your privacy as the item's owner.

We hope that you will agree to cooperate in our work. For our part, we will be delighted to inform you of any new light that our research sheds on the DeWitt letter in your collection.

INDEX